Designing the Search Experience

Designing the Search Experience
The Information Architecture
of Discovery

Tony Russell-Rose
Tyler Tate

AMSTERDAM • BOSTON • HEIDELBERG • LONDON
NEW YORK • OXFORD • PARIS • SAN DIEGO
SAN FRANCISCO • SINGAPORE • SYDNEY • TOKYO
Morgan Kaufmann Publishers is an imprint of Elsevier

Acquiring Editor: Meg Dunkerley
Development Editor: Heather Scherer
Project Manager: A. B. McGee
Designer: Joanne Blank

Morgan Kaufmann is an imprint of Elsevier
225 Wyman Street, Waltham, MA 02451, USA

Library of Congress Cataloging-in-Publication Data

Designing the search experience : the information architecture of discovery / [edited by] Tony Russell-Rose, Tyler Tate.
    pages cm
Includes bibliographical references.
ISBN 978-0-12-396981-1 (pbk.)
1. User interfaces (Computer systems) 2. Electronic information resource searching.
I. Russell-Rose, Tony. II. Tate, Tyler.
QA76.9.U83D475 2013
005.4'37--dc23

2012030260

British Library Cataloguing-in-Publication Data
A catalogue record for this book is available from the British Library.

For information on all MK publications visit our website at http://store.elsevier.com

Printed in China
12 13 14 15 16   10 9 8 7 6 5 4 3 2 1

Working together to grow
libraries in developing countries

www.elsevier.com | www.bookaid.org | www.sabre.org

ELSEVIER   BOOK AID International   Sabre Foundation

Dedication

To my sister Nicola: As a student of the written word, I know how much you would have enjoyed seeing this book come to fruition. Wherever you are now, I hope you are smiling.

—Tony

To my wife, Ruth, for her endless love and support.

—Tyler

Contents

Contributors

Ann Blandford is Professor of Human-Computer Interaction at University College London and former Director of UCL Interaction Centre. Her first degree is in Maths (from Cambridge); her PhD is in Artificial Intelligence (from the Open University). She started her career in industry, as a software engineer, but soon moved into academia, where she developed a focus on the use and usability of computer systems. She leads research on how people interact with and make sense of information and how technology can better support people's information needs, with a focus on situated interactions. She has over 200 international, peer-reviewed publications, including a Synthesis Lecture on "Interacting with Information."

Karen Church is a Researcher within the User and Media Intelligence group in Telefonica Research, Barcelona, Spain. She received her PhD in Computer Science from University College Dublin, Ireland in 2008. Her PhD thesis was entitled, "A Study of Mobile Internet Usage and Implications for Mobile Search Interfaces." Karen's research interests include the mobile Web and mobile search space, mobile HCI, social mobile services, mobile user experience, and mobile interfaces. Karen was awarded a Marie Curie Fellowship in 2010. The fellowship involves investigating future mobile information access behaviors and trends. Her current research focus is on social mobile search services.

Rory Hamilton is a freelance service design consultant, and educator in service and interaction design. His main interests are in service design, user-centered design, and user research methodologies. Rory previously worked as head of user insight for a service design company called Livework. He was also Course Leader of Computer Related Design/Interaction Design at the Royal College of Art. Before that, he taught computing and took a thesis group in Virtual Environments at the Bartlett School of Architecture and was a contributor to BBC radio on Internet issues (GLR).

James Kalbach is a Principal UX Strategist with USEEDS°, a leading design and innovation agency in Germany, and is the author of *Designing Web Navigation* (O'Reilly Media, 2007). He blogs at www.experienceinformation.com and can be found on Twitter as @jameskalbach.

Joe Lamantia blends insight and design to improve peoples' experiences with business, technology, brands, products, and services. A natural builder, innovator, and change catalyst, Joe has 14 years of success in user experience, strategy, and technology management. Joe has led the launch of digital experiences ranging from complex business services and enterprise productivity and information management solutions to social media, networked communities, games, mobile, and ecommerce. His clients range from the Global Fortune 100 to start ups and nonprofits, in media and entertainment, financial services, mobile and telecommunications, high technology, health care, insurance, pharmaceuticals, consumer goods, marketing and communications, manufacturing, and business services.

Greg Nudelman has been designing experiences that work for Fortune 500 companies for over 12 years. Greg is the author of *Designing Search: UX Strategies for eCommerce Success* (Wiley, 2011). Greg's second Wiley book on mobile and tablet design is due out in late 2012. He writes about mobile and tablet UX design on designcaffeine.com.

Lou Rosenfeld is an independent information architecture consultant for Fortune 500 corporations and other large organizations, and founder of Rosenfeld Media, a publishing house focused on user experience books. He has been instrumental in helping establish the fields of information architecture and user experience, and in articulating the role and value of librarianship within those fields. Lou is coauthor of *Information Architecture for the World Wide Web* (O'Reilly Media, 3rd edition 2006) and *Search Analytics for Your Site* (Rosenfeld Media, 2011), cofounder of the Information Architecture Institute, and a former columnist for *Internet World*, *CIO*, and *Web Review*. He blogs regularly and tweets (@louisrosenfeld) even more so.

Ian Ruthven is a Professor of Information Seeking and Retrieval in the Department of Computer and Information Sciences at the University of Strathclyde. He graduated from the University of Glasgow with a BSc in Computing Science before completing a Master's in Cognitive Science at the University of Birmingham and a PhD in Interactive Information Retrieval at Glasgow. His research investigates how people use information systems to find information, the design of interactive systems to support online searching, and the social and psychological factors that influence information seeking behavior.

Daniel Tunkelang leads a data science team at LinkedIn, which analyzes terabytes of data to produce products and insights that serve LinkedIn's 150 M+ members. Prior to LinkedIn, Daniel led a local search quality team at Google. Daniel was a founding employee of faceted search pioneer Endeca, where he spent ten years as Chief Scientist. He has authored 14 patents, written a textbook on faceted search, created the annual symposium on human–computer interaction and information retrieval (HCIR), and participates in the premier research conferences on information retrieval, knowledge management, databases, recommender systems, and data mining. Daniel holds a PhD in Computer Science from CMU, as well as BS and MS degrees from MIT.

Martin White is Managing Director of Intranet Focus Ltd. and Visiting Professor, iSchool, University of Sheffield. As well as working with clients on large-scale intranet and information management projects, he has been involved with search-related projects for more than 35 years. In 2011, he undertook a study of the enterprise search market in the EU for the Joint Research Centre, European Commission. He is the Chairman of the Enterprise Search Europe conference; later in 2012, his third book on enterprise search will be published as an ebook by O'Reilly Media.

About the Authors

Tony Russell-Rose is director of UXLabs, a UX research and design consultancy specializing in complex search and information access applications. Before founding UXLabs, he was Manager of User Experience at Endeca and editor of the Endeca UI Design Pattern Library, an online resource dedicated to best practice in the design of search and discovery experiences. Prior to this, he was technical lead at Reuters, specializing in advanced user interfaces for information access and search. And before Reuters, he was R&D manager at Canon Research Centre Europe, where he led a team developing next generation information access products and services. Earlier professional experience includes a Royal Academy of Engineering fellowship at HP Labs working on speech UIs for mobile devices and a Short-Term Research Fellowship at BT Labs working on intelligent agents for information retrieval.

His academic qualifications include a PhD in human–computer interaction, an MSc in cognitive psychology, and a first degree in engineering, majoring in human factors. He also holds the position of Honorary Visiting Fellow at the Centre for Interactive Systems Research, City University, London.

He is currently vice-chair of the BCS Information Retrieval group and chair of the IEHF Human–Computer Interaction group.

Tyler Tate is the cofounder of TwigKit, a London-based software company that provides tools for rapidly building data-driven applications. At TwigKit he has helped numerous government, Fortune 500, and other large organizations achieve superb search experiences. Prior to specializing in search, Tyler lead design at Nutshell CRM, designed an enterprise content management system, ran a small design studio, and taught a university course on web design.

Tyler has written articles for publications such as A List Apart, Boxes & Arrows, UX Magazine, Johnny Holland, UX Matters, and Smashing Magazine. He also organizes the Enterprise Search London meetup, and has created popular CSS frameworks such as the Semantic Grid System. He is @TylerTate on Twitter and blogs at TylerTate.com.

Tyler is an American currently living in Cambridgeshire, England with his wife, Ruth, and their two boys, Galileo and Atticus.

Acknowledgments

This book is the work of many hands. In particular, we'd like to thank Cennydd Bowles, James Kalbach, and Max Wilson for their heroic efforts in reviewing every chapter and providing invaluable feedback all along the way. We are greatly in their debt.

We are also very appreciative to those who contributed essays to the book: Ann Blandford, Karen Church, Rory Hamilton, James Kalbach, Joe Lamantia, Greg Nudelman, Louis Rosenfeld, Ian Ruthven, Daniel Tunkelang, and Martin White. They have all enriched the book with their expertise.

Thank you to Meg Dunkerley, Heather Scherer, Andrea Dierna, Rachel Roumeliotis, and the rest of the Morgan Kaufmann team for their ongoing support. We are proud of what we've achieved together.

Tony would particularly like to thank his wife Carole, for indulging and supporting him in the writing of this book, and for being the calm voice of reason throughout. He'd also like to thank his daughters Lucy, Jessica, and Katie for reminding him that being a good daddy is his real job anyway.

Tyler would like to especially thank Stefan Olafsson—the guy who got me into search in the first place and is the single greatest contributor to my understanding of the field. This book wouldn't have happened without him. The book also owes a great deal to my wife Ruth, whose love and support transcended the early mornings and late nights of writing; to my little boys Galileo and Atticus, for inspiration; and to my parents, for teaching me to learn.

Introduction

In the summer of 1804, Meriwether Lewis and William Clark embarked on an epic journey west. President Thomas Jefferson had commissioned the Corps of Discovery to explore, to chart, and—above all—to search for a navigable water route leading to the Pacific Ocean and, by extension, commerce with Asia.

Their journey led them up the Missouri River, through the Great Plains, over the Rocky Mountains, and eventually to the Pacific Coast. Over the course of 28 months and 8,000 miles, Lewis and Clark accounted for 72 native tribes, drew 140 maps, and documented more than 200 new plants and animals.

In the end, Lewis and Clark failed to find a northwest passage to Asia. Yet their journey was hardly in vain. The expedition contributed a wealth of scientific and geographic knowledge, established diplomatic relations with dozens of indigenous tribes, and explored territory never before seen by Europeans. In other words, the journey itself became more important than the destination.

The same is true when searching for information. On the surface, search may appear to be simply a box and ten blue links—a query and a set of results. It may seem a personal rather than social activity; a brief interaction confined to a single medium. And of course, we assume that we know what we're looking for in the first place.

But on closer examination, these assumptions break down. Sure, there are times when search is simply looking up a fact or finding a particular document. But search is also a journey. It's an ongoing exploration where what we find along the way changes what we seek. It's a journey that can extend beyond a single episode; involve friends, colleagues, and even strangers; and be conducted on all manner of devices.

Our concern is with search in its broadest, most holistic sense. By investigating why and how people engage in information seeking, we learn not just about information retrieval but also about how people navigate and make sense of complex digital information environments. What we learn along the way will prepare us for both the search experiences of today and the cross-channel, information-intense experiences of tomorrow.

This book explores both the art and the science of search in three parts. Part 1 focuses on theory. It sets out a conceptual framework for information seeking, investigating human characteristics, models of information seeking, the role of context, and modes of search and discovery.

Part 2 turns theory into practice. It applies the principles from Part 1 to the art of search user interface design, from entering queries to displaying and manipulating results. It also looks closely at faceted search and the emerging worlds of mobile and collaborative search.

Part 3 looks to the future. It returns to the domain of ideas and reimagines the framework of Part 1 within the context of cross-channel experiences in the era of ubiquitous information.

For Lewis and Clark, and for all of us, the journey is indeed more important than the destination. So let's get ready: it's time to embark on our own journey of search and discovery.

A Framework for Search and Discovery

"This is a huge change to the overall user experience. It transforms the way we think and opens opportunities to use search in a disruptive fashion. I love it!"

"Personally, I think people will get annoyed with it. The interface itself isn't anything new, and it's an outdated concept. When you think about state-of-the-art search, it should be less about searching and more about finding."

"I'm excited to see how this will affect our searching habits. It has proven to be very useful and intuitive in my research work. In fact, it has also opened perspectives that I would otherwise have missed. Fantastic!"

"I can't stand it—it's a hindrance, not an aid. It slows me down. It is an unnecessary feature that has ruined the interface. I am so annoyed that I have to manually turn this nonsense off."

These are a few of the views that were expressed when Google introduced instant search results that dynamically update as the user types into the search box (Figure P1.1). It's a simple concept, but one that polarized opinion—some declared that it would revolutionize the way we search; others saw it as a mere distraction.

The same debate could apply to almost any aspect of the search experience. Different people have different views, so conflict is inevitable. Design is a matter of opinion, and there is no "right answer." Right?

Although it's difficult to rule out subjectivity entirely, there are productive ways we can move such a debate forward. The most fundamental step is to recognize that the opinions are themselves based on a set of *assumptions*—in particular, assumptions about *who* is doing the searching, *what* they are trying to achieve and under *what circumstances*, and *how* they are going about it. Each of these assumptions corresponds to a separate *dimension* by which we can define the search experience.

THE DIMENSIONS OF SEARCH USER EXPERIENCE

The first of these dimensions is the *type of user*, in particular his or her *level of knowledge and expertise*. For example, consider the users of an online retail store: are they knowledgeable enthusiasts or novice shoppers? Likewise, for an electronic component

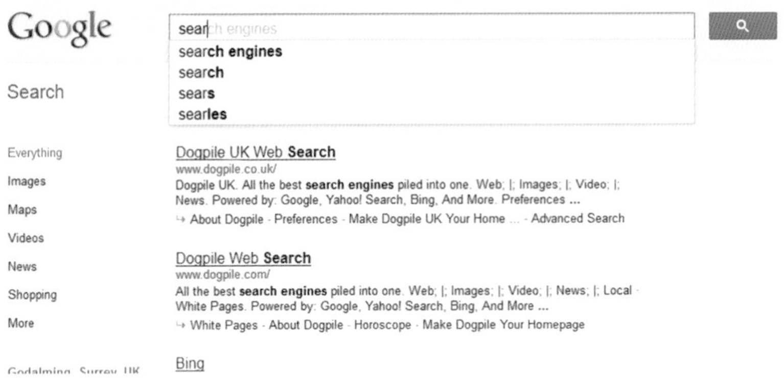

FIGURE P1.1 Instant search results from Google.

supplier: are the users expert engineers or purchasing agents with limited domain knowledge?

Once we understand the user, we can move on to the second dimension: his or her *goal*. This goal can vary from simple fact checking to more complex explorations and analyses. For example, are users searching for a specific item such as the latest Harry Potter book? Or are they looking to choose from a broader range of possibilities, such as finding shoes to match a business suit? Or are they unsure of what they are looking for in the first place, knowing only that they would like to find a suitable gift?

Knowing the users and their goals, we can now consider the third dimension: the *context*. Context includes a range of influences, from the physical to the intangible. For example, is the user at the workplace, where the *task* and the *organizational setting* dominate? Or is the user at home, where *social context* might become more important? Perhaps he or she is using a mobile device while travelling, during which *physical context* shapes the search experience.

Finally, based on our understanding of the users, their task and the wider context, we can consider the fourth dimension: their *search mode*. Search isn't just about finding things—on the contrary, most finding tasks are but a small part of a much larger overall task. Consequently, our focus must be on understanding the complete task life cycle and helping users complete their *overall* information goals. This includes activities such as comparing, exploring, evaluating, analyzing, and much more.

So returning to the opening exchange, we can now see the debate in a different light: to understand those differences in opinion, we need to recognize the underlying assumptions. Likewise, to understand human information seeking behavior, we need a framework by which it can be defined: the users, their goals, the context, and search modes. In the following four chapters, we examine each of these dimensions and explore how to apply them in designing the search experience.

The User

1

"Man is a being in search of meaning."

— *Plato*

We begin where every discussion of design should: with the user. Although the entire book is about crafting user-centered search solutions, Chapter 1 homes in on the human mind itself. We want to know what makes people tick. What are the cognitive processes that govern how information is perceived, stored, and retrieved? What are the individual differences between how people learn, analyze information, and approach problems? By applying insights from cognitive psychology, we'll be able to better understand how users approach the tricky problem that is search.

The rest of Part 1 deals with situated users: their goals (Chapter 2), context (Chapter 3), and modes of interaction (Chapter 4). Here, however, we look at users in isolation and focus on their intrinsic characteristics. We begin by looking at behavioral differences between novices and experts, continue by contrasting cognitive styles, and end by considering modes of learning.

NOVICES AND EXPERTS

Are you more comfortable taking a photograph using your mobile phone, a point-and-shoot camera, or an SLR brimming with buttons and dials? How you answer that question is probably a good indicator of your photographic expertise. If you primarily take quick, off-the-cuff snapshots, your phone or point-and-shoot camera will probably suffice. If you're a professional photographer (or a serious amateur), on the other hand, you probably prefer using an SLR that gives you full control over the focus, aperture, exposure, and other variables of the image. In other words, both novices and experts gravitate toward the tools that best match their abilities.

Expertise plays a significant role in how people seek information. Understanding the differences between novices and experts will enable us to design better search experiences for everyone. But first, it's worth distinguishing between two dimensions of expertise.

Domain expertise versus technical expertise

Expertise is frequently lumped into a single category, but there are in fact two types of expertise that affect information seeking: domain and technical expertise. *Domain* expertise defines one's familiarity with a given subject matter; a professional photographer, for instance, has substantial domain expertise in the field of photography. *Technical* expertise, on the other hand, indicates one's proficiency at using computers, the Internet, search engines, and the like.

Each dimension of expertise is valuable, but users are most likely to succeed when both are present. Jenkins et al. (2003) observed that *domain novices* have difficulty discerning the relevance of information or the reliability of its source, whereas *domain experts* make these judgments much more naturally. They also found that *technical novices* tend to practice a breadth-first strategy to information seeking that helps them avoid the disorientation caused by venturing too far away from the their starting point. *Technical experts*, on the other hand, apply a depth-first approach by following a number of links deeper into the information space. In other words, novices *orienteer* by slowly scouting out the territory (O'Day and Jeffries, 1993), and experts *teleport*, quickly jumping to their destination (Teevan et al., 2004).

In combination, the domain and technical dimensions of expertise describe four types of users (Figure 1.1):

- Double experts
- Domain expert/technical novices
- Domain novice/technical experts
- Double novices

Double novices orienteer

The discipline of *orienteering* originated in the Swedish military in the 1800s and is now a sport practiced throughout Scandinavia. Equipped with a map and compass, participants navigate between control points spread over miles of unfamiliar terrain as they strive to complete the course. But the journey is anything but direct. If an orienteerer loses his bearings along the way, heading back to the previous control point may be the only option to avoid becoming lost in the wilderness.

The information seeking of novices shares similarities with the practice of orienteering. Although both domain and technical novices face resistance along the way, the journey is most treacherous for double novices.

Double novices share three main characteristics (Hölscher and Strube, 2000):

1. **Frequent query reformulation.** Novices perform more queries than experts but look at fewer pages. Although they frequently reformulate their query, double novices often make only small, inconsequential changes to their search phrase.

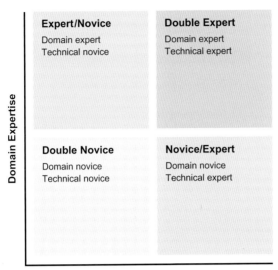

FIGURE 1.1 Two dimensions of expertise: domain and technical.

2. **Going back.** When novices do click on a search result, they are much more likely than experts to then navigate back to the search page. With a fear of venturing too far from safety, double novices practice a hub-and-spoke pattern of information seeking with the search page firmly at the center.

3. **More time spent.** The many queries and frequent backward-oriented behavior of double novices causes them to spend more time on a given search task than would an expert.

The cautious, uncertain orienteering of double novices is fraught with challenges. Search user interfaces designed with double novices in mind should help users reformulate their query, back out of trouble, and—through adequate signposting—avoid disorientation.

Because novices frequently refine their original query but often don't make radical enough changes, showing a list of related searches (as demonstrated by Foodily in Figure 1.2) can help users make more successful query reformulations. In addition, breadcrumbs accomplish the dual purpose of communicating the user's current location, while also providing a path to go back (Figure 1.3).

Double experts teleport

Whereas double novices begin by slowly scouting out the territory, experts often dive straight in. Like being teleported to a precise but distant location, users with high domain and technical expertise often take a depth-first approach and attempt to jump directly to their destination. Double experts are characterized by three tendencies (Hölscher and Strube, 2000):

1. **More pages examined.** Double experts click on more search results than do novices.

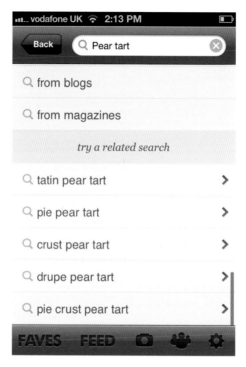

FIGURE 1.2 Foodily's iPhone application places related searches at the bottom of the page, after the search results.

FIGURE 1.3 The breadcrumbs on Zappos.com indicate which filters the user has applied and provide the means to remove them.

2. **Going deeper.** Double novices tend to retreat from the pages they examine; double experts rarely go back. Instead, experts follow links from one page to the next, progressing deeper into the information space with each step.

3. **Less time spent.** Double experts are time-efficient in their search tasks. Not only do they reformulate their queries less often, but they can also determine the relevancy of a given page more rapidly than novices.

In essence, experts are more likely to construct specific queries that quickly and directly teleport them to their destination, often avoiding the chronic, orienteering-like query reformulation practiced by novices.

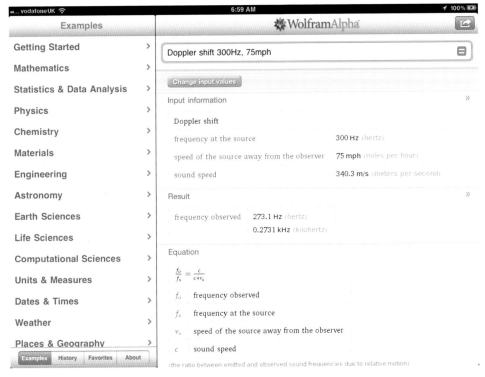

FIGURE 1.4 Wolfram Alpha is designed to return computed answers using advanced syntax and domain-specific terminology.

Expert-friendly search user interfaces should support advanced syntax and filtering to help users quickly narrow their search. Although the Boolean operators AND, OR, and NOT are certainly worth supporting, Wolfram Alpha (shown in Figure 1.4) goes a step further and allows users to input domain-specific terminology and retrieve computed answers. Similarly, a faceted search interface for filtering by format, selecting ranges, or excluding certain categories—such as Getty's Moodstream, shown in Figure 1.5—can help users pinpoint content that's relevant to their information needs.

The in-betweeners

So far we've looked at the characteristics of double novices and double experts. Although these two groups of users provide the starkest contrast, we shouldn't forget about the other two groups: those with high expertise in one dimension but low expertise in the other. Not surprisingly, these hybrid users share some aspects with both double novices and double experts.

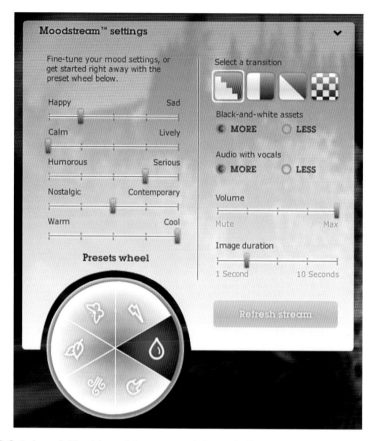

FIGURE 1.5 Getty Image's Moodstream lets users search for stock photos using slider controls.

Domain expert/technical novices, for instance, use their knowledge to enter effective queries and quickly evaluate pages, but they lack the technical confidence to explore unknown territory (Jenkins et al., 2003). Their traits include:

1. **Advanced terminology.** Domain experts are able to rely on their extensive vocabulary to construct more topical queries than are domain novices.

2. **Effective evaluation.** Similarly, high domain knowledge makes the process of evaluating a page more meaningful and timely.

3. **Going back.** A lack of technical expertise, however, contributes to a sense of disorientation, preventing users from venturing too far away from the search page.

Domain novice/technical experts, on the other hand, brim with confidence, but have trouble discerning relevant content (Hölscher and Strube, 2000). They are characterized by:

1. **Advanced formatting.** Technical experts are much more likely to use query formatting techniques—such as double quotes and Boolean operators—than are technical novices.

2. **Confident exploration.** Despite their lack of domain expertise, technical experts exude confidence and never worry about becoming disoriented.

3. **Difficulty with evaluation.** Technical expertise doesn't compensate for a lack of domain knowledge when it comes to evaluating the relevance of a page.

Although novices and experts along both the domain and technical dimensions exhibit unique approaches to information seeking, it's important not to unduly prioritize one group at the expense of another. Understanding the target audience's particular levels of expertise is invaluable; in most scenarios, however, we must design for both novices and experts alike.

Serial and holistic thinkers

Expertise is fickle: experience can turn any novice into an expert over time. There are, however, deeper, more unchanging differences in the way our brains deal with information. Psychologists call these *cognitive styles*—the stable attitudes, preferences, and habits that determine how an individual processes and represents information. We'll begin by looking at the serial-holistic style of information *processing* and then, in the following section, investigate the verbal-visual style of *representing* information (Riding and Cheema, 1991).

The rod-and-frame test

The rod-and-frame test was one of the first exercises developed by Herman Witken and Solomon Asch, pioneers of cognitive style research in the 1950s (Kozhevnikov, 2007). To complete a simplified version of the test for yourself, sketch a slightly askew rectangle on a sheet of paper (or use your imagination and form a mental picture of Figure 1.6). There is only one, very simple instruction involved. Ready? Here it is: draw a *vertical* line inside the rectangle.

Witken and Asch found that not everyone completed this exercise in the same way (Figure 1.7). Some drew a line parallel to the edges of the rectangle; these people Witken and Asch classified as field-dependent, also known as *serialists*. Others, labeled as field-independent or *holists*, drew the line along the north–south axis of the paper rather than the rectangle[1]. Despite this rendition of the rod-and-frame test being more anecdotal

FIGURE 1.6 Complete a simplified version of the rod-and-frame test by drawing a vertical line in the rectangle.

---

[1] The field-dependent vs. field-independent dimensions were originally developed by Witkin in the US, while the serialist vs. holist model was pioneered by Pask in the UK (Ford et al., 2002). However, many recent psychologists (including Riding and Cheema, 1991), have come to the conclusion that the two models are, in fact, one in the same. We have chosen to use the holist and serialist labels here.

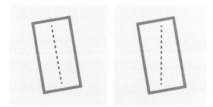

FIGURE 1.7 Serialists complete the rod-and-frame test by drawing the line aligned with the edges of the rectangle (left). Holists, on the other hand, draw the line along the global north–south axis (right).

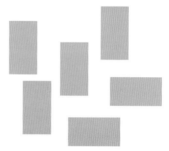

FIGURE 1.8 Serialists concentrate on the individual parts rather than the whole.

than scientific, the serial versus holistic dimension of cognitive style has nevertheless been thoroughly researched over the past several decades. Serialists, it's been found, demonstrate brick-by-brick craftsmanship; holists tend towards divergent, big-picture thinking.

Serialists: brick-by-brick craftsmen

Serialists are characterized by an external frame of reference. They depend on their environment for structure, function best when rules and expectations are clearly communicated, and find their motivation in external sources. Like skilled craftsmen, serialists are highly attuned to the details. When learning, serialists tend to drill down to narrow subtopics and follow a logical progression from one to the next. Despite being skilled at analyzing the component parts (Figure 1.8), serialists have greater difficulty combining the parts into a whole (Kim, 2001).

Holists: big-picture visionaries

Holists are visionaries with a bird's-eye view (Figure 1.9). Operating with an intrinsic motivation that is independent of their surroundings, holists flourish in flexible environments where they are free to pursue their own interests at the pace of their choice. When approaching a topic, they immediately set out to comprehend the big picture, giving holists a more balanced view and helping them put situations into context. However, holists are also prone to oversimplification, sometimes glossing over important details (Ford et al., 2002).

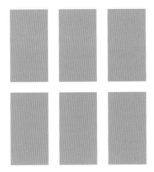

FIGURE 1.9 Holists focus on the cohesive whole rather than on component parts.

The performance gap

These innate differences between serialists and holists are manifest in how people seek information. All else being equal, holists are more efficient at satisfying their information needs. Serialists, by comparison, find it more difficult to discern the relevance of information and consequently spend more time searching for the same answers. A study by Kyung-Sun Kim (2001) found that serialists spend 50 percent more time, visit almost twice as many pages, and are more likely to use the browser's back button or return to the homepage than their holist counterparts.

Fortunately, the story doesn't end there. Kim's study considered not only the cognitive style of users but also their level of expertise. Crucially, she found that although there is a wide gap in performance between serialists and holists who are *technical novices*, the gap all but disappears between the two cognitive styles when technical expertise is high. In other words, user interfaces can become more effective by helping serialist novices—or all novices, for that matter—increase their level of technical expertise.

Designing for learnability

Designing search user interfaces that are easy to learn can help bridge the gap between novice and expert serialists, progressively training them how to use the application (Spool, 2005). Learnability—the ease with which users gain awareness of available software functions and comprehend how to act on them—can be accomplished using contextual instructions, immersive overlays, and subtle visual design.

A simple contextual instruction, for example, can be achieved by adding descriptive placeholder text to the search box (Figure 1.10). The text can inform users about the type of query that the system expects—whether it's the name of a restaurant, an area of a city, or a postal code. This simple indicator can boost the user's confidence in his or her query and increase the likelihood of a successful search.

More overt contextual instructions can be useful in introducing first-time users to an unfamiliar user interface. Contextual popovers, like the ones used by Foodily in Figure 1.11, can augment a well-designed interface and reduce the guesswork required by the user. Immersive, full-screen overlays —such as the welcome screen

FIGURE 1.10 Toptable's iPhone application combines the use of placeholder text and a three-option segmented control to clearly indicate the type of input that the application expects from the user.

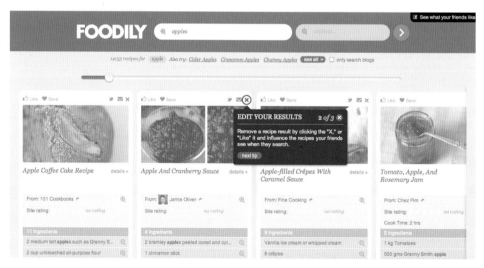

FIGURE 1.11 Foodily, a recipe search site, uses small popovers to introduce first-time users to a few of the features unique to Foodily's website.

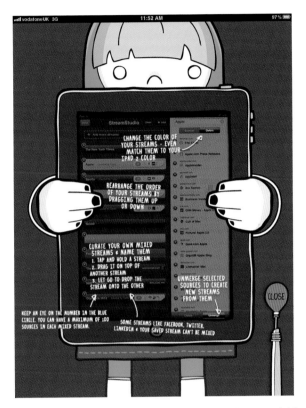

FIGURE 1.12 TapTu, a news-reading application, uses an overlay to provide a tutorial for new users.

to the TapTu iPad app shown in Figure 1.12—can serve a similar purpose. Caution is required in both situations, however; providing tips for new users must be balanced with concern for more experienced users (both Foodily and TapTu, for instance, show the "getting started" advice only on a user's first visit).

A more nuanced method for enhancing learnability is to use subtle animation and tactile textures to suggest gestures, hint at off-screen content, and indicate which elements on the screen are interactive. When a user first views a list of search results using Airbnb's iPhone application (shown in Figure 1.13), for instance, an animation reveals a star behind each result before quickly disappearing, hinting that a swipe from left to right will "favorite" that particular item. Such tactics are especially useful on mobile devices where screen space is scarce.

Brick-by-brick serialists and big-picture holists each process information in their own way. When technical expertise is high, both serialists and holists thrive; when expertise is low, serialists are more prone to struggle. Maximizing learnability can improve the search experience for users in general and serialist novices in particular.

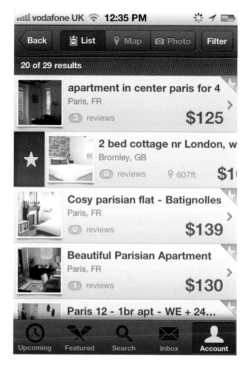

FIGURE 1.13 On the first use, Airbnb's iPhone application reveals a star behind each search result before quickly sliding away, training users to use a left-to-right gesture to "favorite" a result.

VERBAL AND VISUAL LEARNERS

The serial–holistic component of cognitive style that we have just considered deals with how people *process* information; but there is also a second component—the verbal–visual style—that is concerned with how people *represent* concepts when learning (Figure 1.14). It turns out that our senses play a surprisingly large role in the learning process.

From five senses to three modalities

We experience the world through five senses, distilled by psychologists into three "sensory modalities" relevant to learning: verbal, visual, and kinesthetic (Denig, 2004). Though everyone learns through all three modes, we each favor one over the others, resulting in three different styles of learning:

1. **Verbal** learners absorb written and spoken information more readily than visual concepts. Because most learning is either text-based (reading a book, searching online) or auditory (a classroom lecture or personal conversation), verbal learners have ready access to content in their preferred medium.

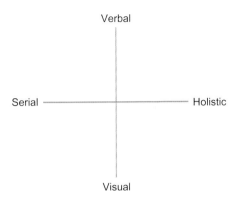

Verbal

Serial ———————————————— Holistic

Visual

FIGURE 1.14 Two dimensions of cognitive style: serial–holistic and verbal–visual.

2. **Visual** learners, on the other hand, digest information from charts, diagrams, timelines, maps, and other concrete images more easily than from the written or spoken word. Visual learners have less access to appropriate content than their verbal counterparts.

3. **Kinesthetic** learners enjoy hands-on activities involving movement, from dancing to woodwork. Although kinesthetic learning is minimally involved in desktop computing, it plays a much more significant role in gestural and touch-based interfaces.

Dual coding theory

Not only do our sensory modalities relay outside stimuli into our brains, they also encode that information into our long-term memory. In the same way that a computer stores text and images in different file types, so our brains use different formats for storing linguistic versus visual information (Mayer and Sims, 1994).

These independent storage schemes mean that translating a linguistic idea into a visual concept is a taxing mental process—albeit one that we must perform all the time. When someone relates driving or walking direction to you, for instance, you probably construct a simple visual map in your mind, converting audio input into a visual form. If you're helping someone assemble a bookshelf using pictogram-based instructions, on the other hand, you must convert the images into a verbal explanation of what to do next.

In the 1970s, psychologist Allan Paivio made an important observation: people learn best when information is presented in two modalities at the same time, which is now known as the Dual-Coding Theory. Paivio believed that providing both verbal and visual information in parallel would enable the mind to encode information in not just one, but both modalities, while also building referential links between the two (Paivio, 1971). Likewise, Mayer and Sims (1994) found a 30 percent rise in effective problem solving when both verbal and visual instructions were presented in conjunction.

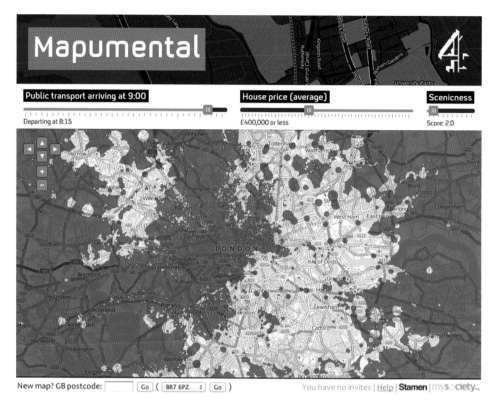

FIGURE 1.15 Mapumental visualizes a synthesis of transit times, house prices, and "scenicness" ratings to help users choose where to live.

Designing with overviews and previews

Although dual coding theory has significant implications for website content, it's also important for the search experience. In particular, visual *overviews* and *previews* can augment text-based lists to both describe the result set as a whole, as well as the individual result itself (Greene et al., 2000).

Just as a map condenses thousands of miles into a few inches, so can visual *overviews* quickly communicate the information landscape to the user (Riding and Sadler-Smith, 1992). When presented as raw data, quantitative information can be difficult to comprehend; when effectively visualized, however, the same information can become easily digestible. Mapumental, for example, distills transit times, house prices, and "scenicness" ratings into a composite map overlay that helps its users choose where to live. Crunching these numbers oneself would be an enormous task, yet the map in Figure 1.15 instantly shows which areas of London are no farther than a 45-minute commute from Waterloo Station, have an average house price of less than £400,000, and score at least 2 out of 10 in scenicness.

Though immersive data visualizations are powerful, there are also humbler, more compact methods for providing visual overviews. Histograms, for instance, concisely communicate statistical distributions and afford a natural partnership with slider controls

FIGURE 1.16 Histograms, such as these from Google Finance's stock screener, instantly convey the distribution of results.

FIGURE 1.17 For many ecommerce websites, such as NorthFace.com, visual thumbnails are more important than textual descriptions.

(Nudelman, 2010). Google Finance's stock screener, for example (shown in Figure 1.16), efficiently combines dual sliders with a histogram to provide contextual feedback for users searching for companies by financial criteria.

While overviews provide a visual depiction of the result set as a whole, *previews* help the user examine an individual result in greater detail—augmenting verbal information with a visual component to help the user make better relevance judgments. In some cases—such as ecommerce—visual thumbnails can even be more important than the text (Figure 1.17).

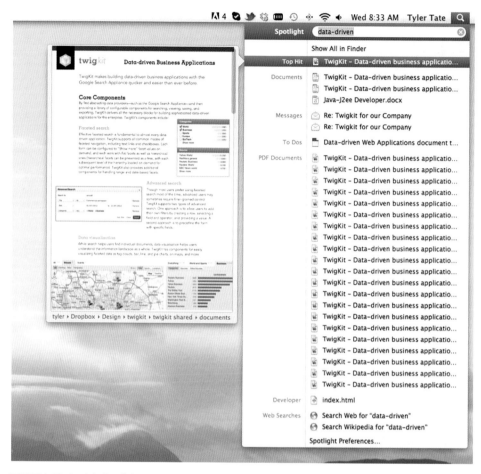

FIGURE 1.18 Apple's Spotlight search shows document previews as the user interacts with the search results.

Larger previews, rather than help the user quickly skim the results, gives the user a chance to verify the relevance of a result before committing to viewing the full item. Apple's Spotlight search, for example (shown in Figure 1.18), previews a document as the user hovers over its title, reducing the inconvenience of opening a new document only to discover that it's irrelevant.

Overviews and previews are two methods for combining verbal and visual information in the search experience, engaging both of the respective sensory modalities and, as a result, enhancing the learning process.

SUMMARY

The domain and technical dimensions of expertise, combined with the serial–holistic and verbal–visual dimensions of cognitive style—though certainly not an exhaustive list of individual differences—do unequivocally demonstrate the true multiplicity of users, even at a purely psychological level. As designers, this rich cognitive diversity reminds us once again that we must go out of our way to identify our users, understand them, and design to meet their needs.

REFERENCES

Denig, S. (2004). Multiple intelligences and learning styles: Two complementary dimensions. *Teachers College Record, 106*(1), 96–111.10.

Ford, N., Wilson, T. D., Foster, A., Ellis, D., & Spink, A. (2002). Information seeking and mediated searching part 4 cognitive styles in information seeking. *Journal of the American Society for Information Science and Technology, 53*(9), 728–735.7.

Greene, S., Marchionini, G., Plaisant, C., & Shneiderman, B. (2000). Previews and overviews in digital libraries: Designing surrogates to support visual information seeking. *Journal of the American Society for Information Science, 51*(4), 380-393.

Hölscher, C., & Strube, G. (2000). Web search behavior of Internet experts and newbies. *Computer Networks, 33*(1), 337.

Jenkins, C., Corritore, C., & Wiedenbeck, S. (2003). Patterns of information seeking on the Web: a qualitative study of domain expertise and Web expertise. *IT&SOCIETY, 1*(3), 64–89.

Kim, K. (2001). Information seeking on the web: Effects of user and task variables. *Library & Information Science Research, 23*, 233–255.6,8.

Kozhevnikov, M. (2007). Cognitive styles in the context of modern psychology: toward an integrated framework of cognitive style. *Psychological Bulletin, 133*(3), 464–481.5.

Mayer, R., & Sims, V. K. (1994). For whom is a picture worth a thousand words? Extensions of a dual-coding theory of multimedia learning. *Journal of Educational Psychology, 86*(3) 389–401.11, 13.

Nudelman, G. (2010). Numeric filters: Issues and best practices. *UX Matters*. Retrieved June 8, 2012 from http://www.uxmatters.com/mt/archives/2010/02/numeric-filters-issues-and-best-practices.php.

O'Day, V., & Jeffries, R. (1993). Orienteering in an information landscape: How information seekers get from here to there. In: *Proceedings of ACM InterCHI '93* (pp. 438–445).

Paivio, A. (1971). *Imagery and verbal processes*. New York: Holt, Rinehart and Winston.

Riding, R., & Cheema, I. (1991). Cognitive styles—An overview and integration. *Educational Psychology, 11*(3), 193–215.

Riding, R., & Sadler-Smith, E. (1992). Type of instructional material, cognitive style and learning performance. *Educational Studies, 18*(3) 323–340.4,15.

Spool, J. (2005). What makes design seem "intuitive"? *User Interface Engineering*. Retrieved June 8, 2012 from http://www.uie.com/articles/design_intuitive/.9.

Teevan, J., Alvarado, C., Ackerman, M., & Karger, D. (2004). The perfect search engine is not enough. Retrieved June 8, 2012 from http://people.csail.mit.edu/teevan/work/publications/papers/chi04.pdf.2.

The Value of Search within the Enterprise
Martin White

Most of the assets of a company can be counted, such as the number of employees, the amount of cash in the bank, and the value of investments. These items all appear on the balance sheet of the company and have to be accurately tabulated. To achieve tabulation, many enterprise systems enable the company to count the records, present the totals, and be compliant with regulations. Historically, this work has been the central focus of IT departments, and over the years they have developed considerable expertise in process analysis and system implementation. In some sectors, such as finance and professional services, it is also a business requirement to manage documents and business records to show that compliance requirements have been met. Here again, IT departments have delivered document and records management applications to be able to find the document related to a specific transaction.

None of these processes help the company gain customers, find new employees, defend a competitive position, develop new products, or solve customer problems, yet these processes are the means by which the company will grow. For such processes, information contained in documents, blogs, wikis, emails, drawings, and videos needs to be found by people other than their original creators. These are the invisible assets that are too numerable to count.

A 2011 survey (MarkLogic, 2011) asked IT managers about the growth of this information in their companies, how important it was, and what level of investment they had made in supporting the process of discovery; 80% of the respondents said that this information will increase over the next three years and 57% said that it was very important to the company. However, 75% said that they felt that their IT infrastructure was inadequate to meet this information discovery requirement. This finding cannot be dismissed as a singular data point. In the 2009 IBM Global CIO Survey, only 50 percent of respondents indicated that they were able to make information available for users who needed it to make business-critical decisions.

Enterprise search has suffered from benign neglect for over a decade. As the levels of information grew, employees found ways to track it down by making phone calls or sending emails. Now companies are beginning to realize that they may be holding terabytes of information that are invisible to employees, representing a total waste of the investment that has been made in the creation of these information assets. I've often asked senior managers to try to find a document of value to the business that they authored six months previously. Even when the company has an enterprise search application, their failure to invest in its ongoing improvement means that the chances of finding the document are slim.

Search is difficult. It deals with fuzziness—which is not a concept that most IT departments feel comfortable with. The development of a good search engine demands a team with skills in computational linguistics, advanced database design, and the mathematics of probability. Making good use of this technology also requires an understanding of how people search and how the system should interact with the user to facilitate the process of search. It also requires knowledge of the business and a grasp of the immense amount of research that has been carried out by the information retrieval community. This is what this book is all about. Informed employees are empowered employees, and the world economy needs the growth that will come from making business decisions based on all the relevant information assets the company possesses.

Martin White is Managing Director of Intranet Focus Ltd. and Visiting Professor, iSchool, University of Sheffield. As well as working with clients on large-scale intranet and information management projects, he has been involved with search-related projects for more than 35 years. In 2011, he undertook a study of the enterprise search market in the EU for the Joint Research Centre, European Commission. He is the Chairman of the Enterprise Search Europe conference; in 2012, his third book on enterprise search will be published as an ebook by O'Reilly Media.

Information Seeking

2

Every one has daily, hourly, and momentary need of ascertaining facts which he
has not directly observed.

— John Stuart Mill

Mankind is an endless pursuer of knowledge. Philosophers and scientists through the
millennia have gathered in libraries and universities to investigate the inner workings of
our world; yet there is also a humbler, more pragmatic form of inquiry at work in every
individual.

Whether planting vegetables, repairing a car, or building software, individuals regularly
need access to information that they don't yet possess. We bridge this knowledge gap by
asking those around us for advice, turning to books and encyclopedias, and, increasingly,
searching the Internet. This journey between need and fulfillment is called *information
seeking*.

We begin the chapter by exploring the evolution of information seeking from that of
a *system*-oriented model at its inception, to today's *user*-centered perspective. We then
examine two forces that mediate the information seeking process—information foraging
and sensemaking—before climbing to higher ground and recasting information seeking as a
long-term, multistage activity.

MODELS OF INFORMATION SEEKING

Designing effective search experiences requires not only an awareness of users' cognitive
characteristics, as we explored in Chapter 1, but also a clear understanding of how users go
about seeking information (Hearst, 2009). Our conception of this process has evolved over
the years from simplistic and static to complex and dynamic. Five models have particularly
shaped our understanding along the way, starting with the classic model.

The classic model

The *classic model* is one of the first models of information retrieval, widely used in information science research for over 30 years (Robertson, 1977). At its core is the action of the search engine, which matches information needs expressed as queries with documents represented by entries in an index (Figure 2.1). Influential though it may have been in its day, this model overlooks the most important element of information seeking: the user. To design effective search experiences, we need models that place the searcher rather than the system at the heart of the process.

The standard model

In contrast with the classic model, the *standard model* places greater emphasis on the user. It portrays information seeking as a type of problem solving (Marchionini, 1995) involving a cycle of four activities (Sutcliffe & Ennis, 1998):

1. Identifying the problem
2. Articulating the information need
3. Formulating the query
4. Evaluating the results

These steps are illustrated in Figure 2.2. Starting with the task at hand, the user articulates an information need that is expressed in verbal form as a query. The query is then matched by the search engine with documents in the collection. This step returns a set of search results that the user then evaluates, refining the query as appropriate. The cycle is repeated until the information need is satisfied.

The cognitive model

Like the standard model, Don Norman's *cognitive model* of task performance (shown in Figure 2.3) also views search as a form of problem solving driven by an explicit user goal (Norman, 1988). But in this case, users apply a *mental model*—an internal representation of the problem situation and its context—to develop a plan of action to achieve that goal. These actions lead to changes in the external world that are evaluated to determine whether the goal has been achieved.

In the context of information seeking, the "execution of actions" corresponds to articulating the query, "changes in the world" to updating the set of matching documents, and the "evaluation" of these changes to reviewing the search results. The gap between the

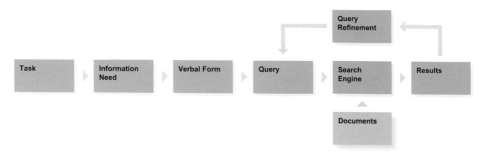

FIGURE 2.2 The standard model of the search process.

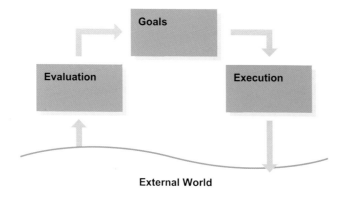

FIGURE 2.3 Don Norman's cognitive model of task performance.

intended result and the actual result is described as the *gulf of execution*; the challenge of determining whether the goal has been achieved is described as the *gulf of evaluation*.

A key insight of Norman's model over the previous two is that it recognizes the importance of domain knowledge (as discussed in Chapter 1): the greater the users' knowledge, the more likely they are to articulate effective queries and accurately determine the relevance of results.

The dynamic model

Both the standard and cognitive models share an underlying assumption that the user's information need remains unchanged throughout a given session. They view the process of information seeking as one of iteratively refining a given query until the ideal set of results is found. However, numerous studies have found that users' information needs evolve as they interact with information and that they formulate new goals as they acquire domain knowledge. Far from being static, search is an interactive, iterative process in which the answer can change the question. As Peter Morville puts it, "what we find changes what we seek" (Morville, 2009).

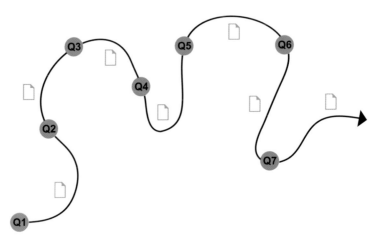

FIGURE 2.4 Marcia Bates' dynamic model.

Consequently, we need a model that accounts for changes in users' information needs as they learn and respond to the information they encounter. The *dynamic model* proposed by Marcia Bates (1989) accomplishes just that (Figure 2.4).

The dynamic model compares the information seeking process with the act of picking berries in the forest. It recognizes that interacting with information can trigger the formation of new, unanticipated goals, which in turn lead to the formulation of new queries and new directions for the search process. It also acknowledges that the user's information need is not satisfied by a single, ideal set of documents, but—like an animal foraging from one berry bush to another—by an aggregation of learning and insight gathered along the way. In this model, search is not a quest for the perfect document but a conversation that helps us understand the right questions to ask.

The information journey model

Others have built upon the insights of the dynamic model. In particular, Ann Blandford and Simon Attfield (2010) have further explored the unfolding journey of information seeking. Like the dynamic model, their *information journey model* (shown in Figure 2.5) has been derived from empirical studies of user behavior. The main activities in their framework are:

1. Recognizing an information need

2. Acquiring information

3. Interpreting and validating the information

4. Using the information

Superficially, these steps may appear similar to those of the standard model. But in spirit, they are closer to the dynamic model and its emphasis on validation, interpretation, and use of information as the key activities shaping the evolution of the information need.

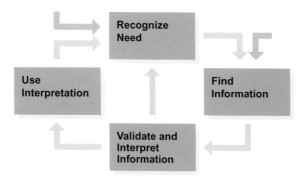

FIGURE 2.5 The information journey model.

This framework also embodies a further key property. In each of the previous models, information seeking is assumed to be an active process, triggered by the conscious recognition of an explicit need. However, there are occasions when information is presented to us without our having actively sought it—the chance encounter, the unexpected insight, the fortunate discovery. These information encounters are what we commonly label *serendipity*. The information journey model, with its multiple entry points, acknowledges serendipity as part of the information seeking experience.

INFORMATION FORAGING

Moving from a static understanding of the user's information need to a dynamic, ever-evolving need highlights the importance of iterative querying and browsing. But if information seeking is a journey, what rules of the road regulate the user's voyage from initiation to completion?

The guiding forces of information seeking are both surprisingly primitive and uniquely human. *Information foraging*, an instinct closely related to that found in animals hunting for food, interacts with *sensemaking*, the cognitive process for deriving meaning from new information. Together, information foraging and sensemaking form a feedback loop (Pirolli & Card, 2005) that underpins the information seeking process.

A biological foundation

Biologists in the 1960s observed that animals often eat a particular type of food in one environment but ignore the same food in other places. Ecologists Robert MacArthur and Eric Pianka set out to discover how animals decide what to eat. Their research, and their accompanying *optimal foraging theory* (MacArthur & Pianka, 1966), provides a foundation for understanding our own behavior when searching for information.

According to optimal foraging theory, animals live in environments consisting of many "patches," each with a unique blend of potential food sources. An Alaskan black bear, for instance, might frequent the prairie for grasses, ants, and small rodents; visit the river for fish and to hunt deer; and enter the forest for berries, leaves, and nuts.

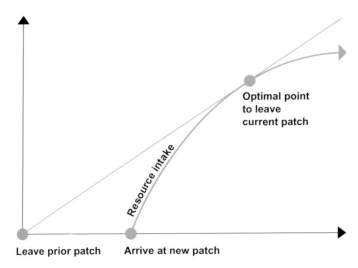

FIGURE 2.6 Charnov's marginal value theorem states that a forager should leave a given patch when the rate of gain within that patch drops below the rate of gain that could be achieved by traveling to a new patch.

When a bear arrives at a new patch, it gravitates toward the most filling food that requires the least amount of effort to consume. Over time, however, the patch dwindles in value as the bear has to work harder for ever-decreasing amounts of food.

This principle of diminishing returns is known in ecology as the *marginal value theorem* (Charnov, 1976). The theory asserts that animals perform a cost/benefit analysis on staying in the current patch versus traveling to a new one—considering both current and potential food supplies as well as the transit time between the two patches (Figure 2.6). Although this occurs at an instinctive rather than cognitive level, studies have confirmed that animals are remarkably accurate judges of when it's best to switch patches (Pyke, Pulliam, & Charnov, 1977).

Man the informavore

Bears aren't the only creatures who are effective foragers; we're pretty good at it ourselves. Unlike animals foraging for nuts and berries, however, we forage for information. George Miller portrayed our species as *informavores*: creatures hungry for information (Miller, 1983). But just like the bear must be selective in its diet (digging all day for a few measly ants would hardly be worthwhile), so must informavores carefully navigate the glut of information in our modern environment. Herbert Simon spoke of this perilous balance in 1971:

What information consumes is rather obvious: it consumes the attention of its recipients. Hence a wealth of information creates a poverty of attention, and a need to allocate that attention efficiently among the over-abundance of information sources that might consume it. (p. 40)

Although information is what we seek, our limited supply of attention forces us to make a tradeoff between comprehensiveness and timeliness. Simon coined the term satisficing—a combination of the words "satisfy" and "suffice"—to describe this pragmatic decision-making strategy that pervades human behavior (Simon, 1956).

Information foraging theory

Peter Pirolli and Stuart Card, researchers at the Palo Alto Research Center (PARC), began applying the principles of optimal foraging theory to information seeking in the early 1990s, establishing a new framework called *information foraging theory* (Pirolli & Card, 1999). Pirolli and Card drew a connection between users moving from one website to the next and animals traveling from patch to patch. They observed that users, in an effort to satisfice, heavily rely on certain cues known as *information scent* to guide them toward their destination.

As users traverse the Web, they encounter information scent when "trigger words"—terms they perceive as meaningful to their task—are used in the text of a hyperlink, as words in a heading, or in a search result's description. The more trigger words that are present, the stronger the information scent (Spool et al., 2004). When information scent grows stronger from page to page, users are confident that they're headed in the right direction. But when it's weak, they may be uncertain about what to do or even give up.

In addition to information scent, Pirolli and Card's research also helps explain *information snacking* (Nielsen, 2003). According to the marginal value theorem, the amount of time a user spends on a given website is proportional to the travel time *between* sites. As between-patch time decreases—thanks to Google and fast Internet connections—users spend less time on any one site. The result is that information seeking has become less of a sit-down banquet and more of an opportunistic buffet.

Designing with information scent

Although the behavioral similarity between omnivorous beasts and man the informavore is striking, information foraging is as practical as it is fascinating. Information scent provides valuable carrots and sticks to guide users through the iterative process of information seeking. Next, we'll look at three basic but important techniques for putting information scent to work in search user interfaces: descriptive titles, hit highlighting, and clear labeling.

Descriptive titles

Before clicking on a search result—or even reading its two-line description—the title must first be deemed relevant. Obvious though it is, the presentation of clear, descriptive titles is the surest method for providing strong information scent when displaying search results. Yet doing so is often more difficult than it sounds; untitled and cryptically named documents abound. Some forgiving search applications make up for human sloppiness by extracting metadata, analyzing the text of the document, and piecing together a title that accurately describes what the document is about.

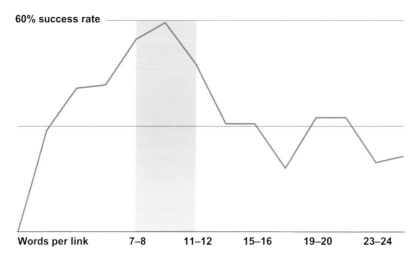

60% success rate

Words per link   7–8   11–12   15–16   19–20   23–24

FIGURE 2.7 Jared Spool found that 7- to 12-word links yield the greatest likelihood of a user finding what he or she is looking for.

Usability advocate Jared Spool found that information scent is strongest when links accurately describe the page they represent, are free from jargon and marketing slogans, and feel clickable (Spool et al., 2004). He also found that reasonably long titles tend to work better than shorter ones, with links of 7 to 12 words being most likely to lead to a successful outcome (Figure 2.7). Although the meaning of the words used is obviously more important than the number, longer titles increase the likelihood of trigger words appearing, thus boosting information scent.

Hit highlighting

If the title of a search result seems promising, the user may then decide to direct his or her attention to the result's description. As with titles, human-provided descriptions are often insufficient. Fortunately, most current search engines dynamically extract an excerpt from what they deem the most relevant portion of the document. Yet *hit highlighting* can increase the information scent of the excerpt further still (White, Jose, & Ruthven, 2003).

When the user performs a query, he or she inputs the most important terms to his or her search—that is, the query's trigger words. Hit highlighting (Figure 2.8) is the technique of emphasizing the words included in the query wherever they appear on the search results page. Using a bold font weight helps to draw the user's eye to the trigger words, increasing information scent.

Clear labeling

There are often just a handful of categories that are significant to the user's current task. When searching through online content, for instance, the user might be looking for business news and wish to skip over sport and entertainment articles (Figure 2.9). Clearly

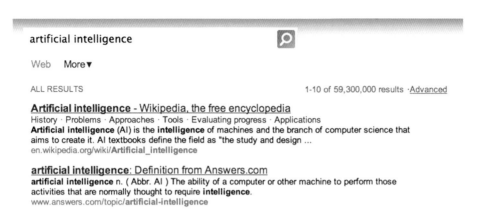

FIGURE 2.8 Bing uses a bold font weight to highlight the user's query terms whenever they appear in the search result list, for both exact phrase matches (e.g., "artificial intelligence") and partial matches (e.g., "intelligence").

FIGURE 2.9 The BBC labels each news story with a category, such as "Europe" or "Business."

identifying which category a given result belongs to can help users ignore unwanted documents and focus on their genre of choice (Drori, 2002).

Like our animal friends, we human foragers follow our noses. Our ingrained instinct to satisfice—to sacrifice the "perfect" for the "good enough" in order to conserve mental resources—has resulted in fast-paced skimming, speed reading, and jumping from one web page to the next as we follow the scent of information. By crafting search user interfaces with optimal levels of information scent, designers can reduce the mental effort users must expend to find what they seek.

SENSEMAKING

Information foraging helps users drown out the noise and tune in the signal. But finding relevant information is only half of the equation; users must also make sense of what they encounter.

Sensemaking—a concept developed in the information science field by Brenda Dervin (1983) and in human–computer interaction by PARC researchers Daniel Russell and colleagues—describes the process through which people assimilate new knowledge into their existing understanding (Russell et al., 1993). Just as the study of information foraging behavior has led to techniques for designing more fluid search experiences, so can an appreciation of how people make sense of information help us design tools that facilitate comprehension, analysis, and insight.

Human memory

Humans are able to remember many different types of information—from how to ride a bicycle (procedural) to the teachings of classical Greek philosophers (semantic) and the fireworks of last New Year's Eve (episodic). Most relevant for our purpose, however, is long-term *semantic* memory, which is responsible for keeping track of our ever-growing conceptual knowledge (Tulving, 1985). Semantic memory organizes knowledge into a schema of interconnected nodes that our minds can manipulate and explore at will (Miller, 1987), a simplistic visualization of which can be represented by mind map diagrams such as the one in Figure 2.10.

This internal semantic schema is constantly in flux. New information may require our semantic memory to add new nodes to the existing schema, reorganize the links between nodes, or discard concepts that are no longer pertinent. This is the realm of sensemaking: growing, rearranging, and pruning the semantic tree of knowledge.

Four stages of the sensemaking process

Sensemaking explains how information seekers go about foraging for information, extracting relevant concepts, and encoding that information into semantic memory while gaining insights along the way (Pirolli and Card, 2005). There are four stages to this process: the first two overlap with information foraging, and the second two are unique to sensemaking. We'll consider the process from the perspective of a patent analyst.

Simon Carter works on a team of patent analysts at a large corporation. When a business unit thinks of a new product, they ask Simon's team to find out whether other companies have similar products and whether the company should seek a patent of their own. His latest assignment is to determine whether the company's new solar cell manufacturing technique could legally justify a patent.

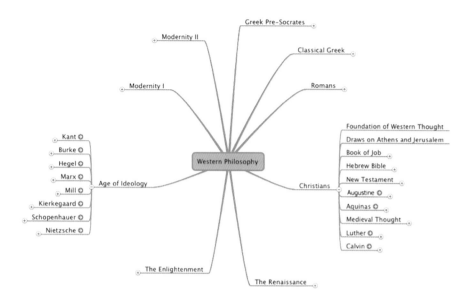

FIGURE 2.10 This mind map created on MindMeister.com visualizes one person's understanding of western philosophy.

1. Search
    The first step toward sensemaking is to locate documents that may be meaningful for the investigation. Simon pulls up his trusted sources—the U.S. Patent Office, specialized patent databases, Google—and casts a wide net for anything and everything that might pertain to solar cell design and manufacturing.

2. Extract
    Once potential documents have been identified, meaningful information must be extracted from them. Simon quickly scans each page and, where there is strong information scent, pauses to inspect the content more closely.

3. Encode
    The extracted ideas must then be integrated into Simon's semantic memory. His schema of the domain is constructed of entities such as products, companies, and manufacturing techniques. The more he researches, the more detail is added to the schema.

4. Analyze
    As knowledge increases, the schema itself can be analyzed to gain insights. These insights prompt Simon to test new hypotheses against his knowledge, potentially reinterpreting the extracted information.

From internal to external schemas

Thus far, we've treated the semantic schema as the internal model of an individual's knowledge. However, the finite capacity of the human mind ensures that one's own understanding is only a subset of reality. In the same way that a map is a compact representation of a much larger landscape, so our internal semantic schema is a simplified sketch of a much broader body of knowledge. Computer scientist Jay Wright Forrester described this discrepancy between the real world and our internal models of it (Forrester, 1971):

The mental image of the world around you... is a model. One does not have a city or a government or a country in his head. He has only selected concepts and relationships which he uses to represent the real system. (p. 54)

Sophisticated information tasks demand that one's *internal* semantic model be disseminated into an *external* schema. External schemas can not only store a greater amount of information than an internal schema, but can also serve as a conduit for collaboration.

Designing for sensemaking

Patent researchers, intelligence analysts, academic researchers, and other knowledge workers must often make sense of in-depth information landscapes for which internal memory will not suffice. Although external memory aids can be as simple as a sketch on the back of a napkin or a wall of sticky notes, digital tools can help users construct and browse external schemas that often lead to insights that might have otherwise been missed.

Pirolli and Card (2005) observed three common practices used by intelligence analysts to conduct large-scale sensemaking, which they term the shoebox, the evidence file, and the schema.

The shoebox

The first step in many investigations is to gather potentially relevant documents into a single collection—what could be coined the *shoebox* (a term that recollects putting something away for later). At this stage, the analyst isn't concerned with a close examination of each document; the top priority is to populate the shoebox as quickly as possible with anything that might be relevant to the investigation. The analyst heavily relies on information scent to make rapid judgments about which documents should and should not be included. To support this behavior, the user interface should enable the analyst to add documents to the shoebox as rapidly as possible. For instance a text link, checkbox, or icon (Figure 2.11) could be provided for quickly saving a given search result.

The evidence file

Once the shoebox has been populated with potentially relevant documents, the analyst often then begins a more thorough examination of the curated collection. This time around, the analyst spends significantly more time scrutinizing the text and images when looking for possible leads. When the analyst spots a striking sentence or meaningful image, he or she extracts that snippet and saves it to a more cogent collection of relevant information: the evidence file.

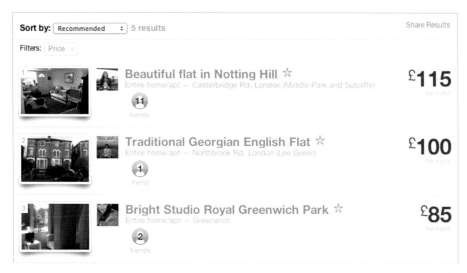

FIGURE 2.11 Airbnb.com places a star icon next to each search result. Clicking on the star saves that result to the user's "favorites list."

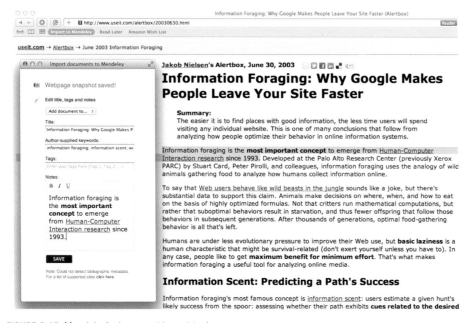

FIGURE 2.12 Mendeley's document import tool.

A simple example of an evidence file is Mendeley, a tool that helps academics manage their research. Mendeley provides a special bookmark that users can add to their web browsers (Figure 2.12). When clicked, a popup window appears and prompts the user to save a title, keywords, tags, and meaningful notes extracted from the current

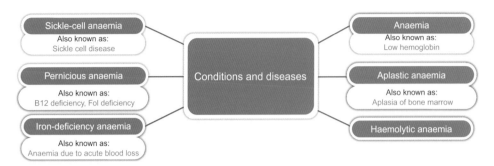

FIGURE 2.13 The "conditions and diseases" node of a much larger external semantic schema on the NHS Evidence website.

page. The shoebox is the outcome of a net widely cast; the evidence file is the product of a fine sieve.

The schema

The external schema provides an even bigger picture of how the extracted evidence fits together. It may be constructed of the people, places, and events surrounding a crime or the causes and symptoms of a disease (Figure 2.13). Also known as an *ontology*—a specification of a shared conceptualization—the external schema enables analysts to continually explore, gain insights from, and test hypotheses against the model as it is constructed.

It's through sensemaking that the information seeker iteratively refines his or her understanding by either updating his or her internal semantic memory or contributing to an external schema. Together, information foraging and sensemaking guide us to and enable us to understand the nuggets of information that satisfy our information need.

STAGES OF INFORMATION SEEKING

As you may recall, the first models of information seeking that we discussed at the beginning of the chapter considered the user's information need to be unchanging, while later models acknowledged its evolving, dynamic nature. Information foraging and sensemaking have also demonstrated that users must sometimes deal with complex tasks that push the limits of human memory. In fact, far from being isolated to a single, self-contained search session, information seeking can be a long-term endeavor made up of not just one, but a multitude of information needs. To understand this macroscopic perspective, we must turn our attention to the stages of information seeking.

The six-stage funnel

Users often engage in episodes of information seeking spread over days, weeks, and even months as they strive to accomplish tasks such as finding a place to live, buying a car, or booking a vacation. But episodes aren't static; in fact, users progress through a series of

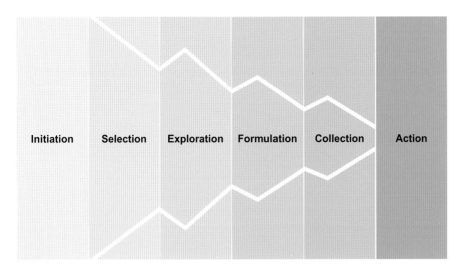

FIGURE 2.14 Kuhlthau's six stages of information seeking can be represented as a funnel that begins open-ended and ends with a resolution.

stages during the lifecycle of a given work task (we'll look at work tasks in more detail in the next chapter). These stages funnel the user's journey from clouded beginnings to a decisive conclusion.

Carol Kuhlthau, a professor at Rutgers University, performed a series of studies during the 1980s to better understand how people seek information to satisfy long-term goals (Kuhlthau, 1991). Her studies included high school and college students who were performing research for a term paper and adults with personal or job-related projects. Kuhlthau identified distinct phases in what she called the *information search process* but is best described as stages of information seeking (Figure 2.14). She observed both the tasks and emotions unique to each of six phases:

1. Initiation
   Initiation is the phase in which one becomes aware of a need for information, an event often accompanied by uncertainty and apprehension. For instance, lets imagine that Fane Tomescu recently decided that he wanted to buy a car, prompting a need to research suitable vehicles.

2. Selection
   The selection phase involves committing to constraints that narrow the information search. Fane quickly eliminated motorcycles, vans, and SUVs, deciding to look only at small family cars. Kuhlthau found that this phase tends to produce a spike in optimism once the user makes the selection.

3. Exploration
   The optimism of selection usually gives way once more to confusion, uncertainty, and doubt as one realizes the many options still left to explore. Even though he had

decided on small family cars, Fane still had to sift through dozens of makes and models, each of which had advantages and disadvantages. In Kuhlthau's study, about half of her students never made it past this stage.

4. Formulation
   Formulation is the crucial turning point at which all the information encountered thus far is formulated into a specific, tangible requirement. Fane's car hunt reached the formulation stage when he decided that a four- to six-year-old VW Golf hatchback with 30,000 to 50,000 miles was the best fit for his needs and budget. The formulation stage is characterized by decreased anxiety and increased confidence.

5. Collection
   Once the problem has been clearly articulated in the formulation phase, the next step is to evaluate the available solutions. Once Fane had a clear idea of the model he wanted, he used automotive websites to search for cars in his area that matched his criteria. Confidence continues to increase throughout the collection process.

6. Action
   The final stage of the process is to act on the newly acquired knowledge. For Kuhlthau's students, this meant writing the term paper. For Fane, it meant going to look at a car, transferring money, and driving the car home.

Designing for the journey

Kuhlthau's study demonstrates that users engage in very different tasks during each stage of the information seeking process. Most search applications, however, invest most of their effort into streamlining only the narrow end of the funnel: the collection and action phases. It's understandable—businesses make money through conversions. However, the company that best supports the user throughout the entire process has the advantage in converting that loyal user into a paying customer or dedicated subscriber. There are a number of methods for assisting the users through this journey, from facilitating exploration and helping organize their findings to enabling them to monitor for changes.

Open-ended exploration

Uncertainty characterizes the initial phases of the information seeking process. Whether the task is looking for a place to live, finding the perfect car, or planning a vacation, it's unlikely that the user knows exactly which house is best, what car is ideal, or precisely where to go on holiday at the outset. Yet these are often the first questions that real estate, automotive, and travel sites ask us (Figure 2.15).

In order to engage users earlier in their journey, we must help them explore (Marchionini, 2006). Flexible filtering controls can facilitate browsing without the need for an initial query, helping the user survey the information landscape and potentially make serendipitous discoveries along the way. Although automotive sites AutoTrader and Motors.co.uk both allow users to choose specific makes and models, the latter (Figure 2.16) also caters to those who haven't yet formulated an exact specification, allowing them to filter by body style, color, number of doors, number of seats, and many other factors.

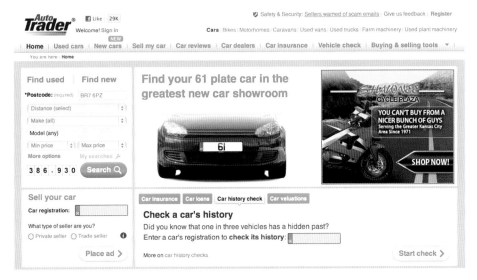

FIGURE 2.15 Autotrader.co.uk asks the user to specify an exact make and model of car up front.

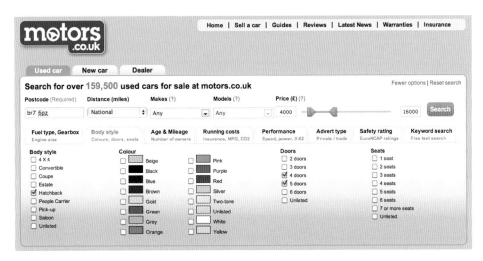

FIGURE 2.16 Motors.co.uk provides flexible filtering options, making it easy for users to look for cars even before deciding on a particular make and model.

Information management

Although users may want to explore early in the process, they must also keep track of what they encounter along the way. As we've seen, the human mind is constantly sensemaking, and we often appreciate tools that augment our memory. Equipping users to bookmark, categorize, and annotate findings can greatly streamline the long-term information seeking process.

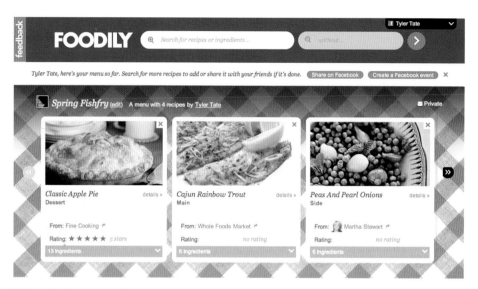

FIGURE 2.17 Foodily, a recipe search engine, allows users to save their favorite recipes and organize them into meal plans.

Bookmarking can help users refind items of interest at a later date. What's more, grouping bookmarks into meaningful sets—like placing recipes into "meal plans" on Foodily (Figure 2.17)—can help users organize large collections of information. Ratings and annotations—such as the personal notes and one- to five-star rankings that can be added to saved properties on Globrix (Figure 2.18)—can further extend the user's memory by making it easier to compare and differentiate saved items.

Monitoring

Toward the end of the information seeking funnel—once the user's exact need has crystallized but before an ideal match has been found—the need to monitor for new opportunities sometimes arises. After searching for VW Golfs in his area, for instance, Fame Tomescu might not have been satisfied with the cars on offer. He may have chosen to patiently repeat the same searches on the same websites day after day, diligently waiting for that perfect deal to show up.

Applications can facilitate monitoring in two ways: on demand or automatically. Enabling the user to save a search query along with any applied filters provides a means for returning to that query *on demand* at a later date. Often, however, users may prefer to be *automatically* notified by email when a new match to their criteria appears, reducing the need to continually check back (eBay, pictured in Figure 2.19, provides both).

Empowering users to freely explore, easily organize their findings, and monitor for new information are just three techniques for assisting the user throughout all the stages of information seeking. The expectations of users are growing, and it's in the best interest of businesses to engage the user at every stage of the process, from initiation to action.

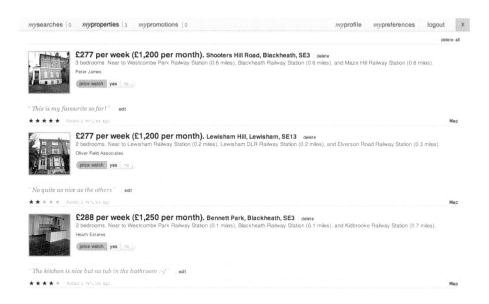

FIGURE 2.18 Property search site Globrix allows users to assign a rating and write notes on each property that they've bookmarked.

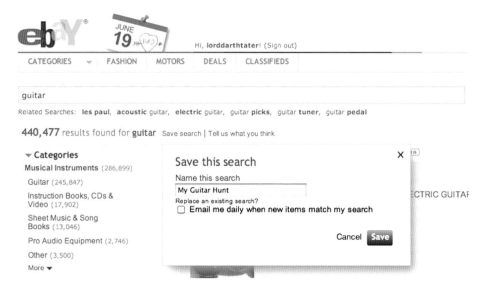

FIGURE 2.19 eBay allows users to save searches and, by checking a box, to be notified by email when new items are added.

SUMMARY

Information seeking is, as we described it at the beginning of the chapter, the journey between the surfacing of an information need and its fulfillment. But it is also an iterative, dynamic activity in which what we find changes what we seek; it is a long-term process spread across distinct stages, each with unique tasks and corresponding emotions. Information foraging keeps the journey moving in the right direction; sensemaking helps us understand what we find along the way.

REFERENCES

Bates, M. J. (1989). The design of browsing and berrypicking techniques for the online search interface. *Online Review*, *13*(5), 407–431.

Blandford, A., & Attfield, S. (2010). *Interacting with Information*. Morgan & Claypool, 29–39.

Charnov, E. L. (1976). Optimal foraging: the marginal value theorem. *Theoretical Population Biology*, *9*, 129–136.

Dervin, B. (1983). An overview of sense-making research: concepts, methods and results. Paper presented at the annual meeting of the International Communication Association. Dallas, TX.

Drori, R. (2002). Using document classification for displaying search results lists. *Journal of Information Science*, *29*(2), 97–106.

Forrester, J. W. (1971). Counterintuitive behavior of social systems. *Technology Review*, *73*(3), 52–68.

Hearst, M. (2009). *Search user interfaces*. Cambridge: Cambridge University Press, 64–90.

Kuhlthau, C. C. (1991). Inside the search process: information seeking from the user's perspective. *Journal of the American Society for Information Science and Technology*, *42*(5), 361–371.

MacArthur, R. H., & Pianka, E. R. (1966). On the optimal use of a patchy environment. *American Naturalist*, *100*(916), 603–609.

Marchionini, G. (2006). Exploratory search: from finding to understanding. *Communications of the ACM*, *49*(4), 41–46.

Marchionini, G. (1995). *Information Seeking in Electronic Environments*. Cambridge: Cambridge University Press, 27–60.

Miller, A. (1987). Cognitive styles: an integrated model. *Educational Psychology*, *7*(4), 251–268.

Miller, G. (1983). Informavores in Machlup, F., & Mansfield, U. (Eds.), *The Study of Information: Interdisciplinary Messages*. New York: Wiley-Interscience.

Morville, P., & Callender, J. (2009). *Search Patterns*. Sebastopol: O'Reilly Media.

Norman, D. A. (1988). *The Psychology of Everyday Things*. New York: Basic Books.

Nielsen, J. (2003). Information foraging: why Google makes people leave your site faster. Useit. com Alertbox. June 30, 2003.

Pirolli, P., & Card, S. (2005). The sensemaking process and leverage points for analyst technology as identified through cognitive task analysis. Proceedings of the 2005 International Conference on Intelligence Analysis. McLean, VA.

Pirolli, P., & Card, S. (1999). Information foraging. *Psychological Review*, *106*(4), 643–675.

Pyke, G. H., Pulliam, H. R., & Charnov, E. L. (1977). Optimal foraging: a selective review of theory and tests. *The Quarterly Review of Biology*, *52*(2), 137–154.

Robertson, S. E. (1977). Theories and models in information retrieval. *Journal of Documentation*, *33*(2), 126–148.

Russell, D. M., Stefik, M. J., Pirolli, P., & Card, S. K. (1993). The cost structure of sensemaking. *Proceedings of the SIGCHI conference on Human factors in computing systems CHI 93*, *93*, 269–276.

Simon, H. (1971). *Computers, Communications and the Public Interest*. The Johns Hopkins Press, 40–41.

Spool, J. M., Perfetti, C., & Brittan, D. (2004). *Designing for the scent of information*. North Andover, MA: User Interface Engineering, 1–26.

Sutcliffe, A. G., & Ennis, M. (1998). Towards a cognitive theory of information retrieval. *Interacting with Computers*, *10*, 321–351.

Tulving, E. (1985). How many memory systems are there? *American Psychologist*, *40*, 385–398.

White, R. W., Jose, J. M., & Ruthven, I. (2003). A task-oriented study on the influencing effects of query-biased summarisation in web searching. *Information Processing and Management (IP&M)*, *39*(5), 707–733.

Information Encountering and Serendipity
Ann Blandford

Most information resources support people searching for information. But people also often encounter information without explicitly looking for it. Information encountering also shifts people's understanding in subtle ways, and these shifts may also be designed. For example, museums and galleries can be designed to support meaning making (Silverman, 1995): through the ways that objects are organized and presented, through the accompanying information, and through the provision of digital tools that allow visitors to negotiate their own understandings of how to interpret artifacts (e.g., Laurillau & Paternò, 2004).

In other contexts, as more information becomes available any time, anywhere, it is harder to design explicitly for particular kinds of information experience. One valued feature of traditional libraries was their support for serendipity: visitors would often come across valuable information that they were not expecting, due to the layout of the collection and the fact that people had to walk past other stacks to reach their intended volume. How to recreate this sense of chance encounters in the digital space, where the quality of search engines is such that people are often taken "straight there" in response to their queries? There has been some work designing technologies (e.g., Toms and McKay-Peet, 2009) to introduce people to new information resources that are relevant to them in their current situation, and there is a growing interest in engineering for serendipity. In our own work, we have gathered lots of serendipity stories. From these, we have developed a framework that starts with events leading up to making a new connection that is unexpected and requires insight (Makri and Blandford, in press). To be recognized as serendipity, the individual has to exploit the unexpected connection and recognize the value of the outcome, which poses a challenge: how do you design for something that depends on chance and insight? We are choosing to focus on nonobvious connections: introducing people to nonobvious literature or to people who have complementary interests, which recognizes the importance of both information resources and other people in the information ecology.

In many situations, people's understanding can evolve in spite of, rather than because of, the ways systems and processes are designed. For example, Brown and Duguid (2000) describe a study of photocopier work, in which the engineers are employed to work individually most of the time but actually meet up regularly (often in their own time) to exchange stories and tips. Brown and Duguid describe the evolving understanding of each engineer as being like the "passage of the sun across the sky" (p. 103): often there are no huge conceptual shifts, but there are imperceptible changes in understanding that become apparent only some time later. Information is encountered through informal chats, to be used when relevant at a later date.

This finding brings into stark relief a challenge that faces all organizations: how to keep people aware of developments and new possibilities. There are of course many facets to this problem, but one is maintaining people's awareness of events and other news in an organization. Adams and colleagues (2005) report on the development of an awareness server that was intended to be used by all groups across an organization (in this case, a hospital). The awareness server was a screensaver that was activated when a computer had been idle for a short period. The initial motivation for developing it had been to ensure that sensitive personal information was hidden from passersby; however, over time, it became valued as an information resource in its own right. Adams and colleagues (2005) identified two key reasons for its success: first, that a participatory design approach had been taken, so that many stakeholders across the organization had input into the design, including the kinds of information that were displayed on the awareness server; and second, that the awareness information was unintrusive but typically available at times when people were working less intensely (e.g., engaged in discussion or having a tea break).

There are many ways of designing resources that allow people to encounter information without actively seeking it, such as designing for meaning making, serendipity, and awareness. Probably the greatest challenge, though, is designing to maximize the value of information encountering while minimizing the sense of information overload.

Ann Blandford is Professor of Human–Computer Interaction at University College London and former Director of UCL Interaction Centre. Her first degree is in Maths (from Cambridge); her PhD is in Artificial Intelligence (from the Open University). She started her career in industry as a software engineer but soon moved into academia, where she developed a focus on the use and usability of computer systems. She leads research on how people interact with and make sense of information and how technology can better support people's information needs, with a focus on situated interactions. She has more than 200 international, peer-reviewed publications, including a Synthesis Lecture on "Interacting with Information."

References

Adams, A., Blandford, A., Budd, D., & Bailey, N. (2005). Organisational communication and awareness: a novel solution. *Health Informatics Journal*, *11*, 163–178.

Brown, J. S., & Duguid, P. (2000). The social life of information: *Cambridge, MA*. Harvard Business School Press.

Laurillau, Y., & Paternò, F. (2004). Supporting museum co-visits using mobile devices. In S. Brewster & M. Dunlop (Eds.), *Mobile Human-Computer Interaction – MobileHCI 2004* (3160, pp. 451–455). Berlin: Springer-Verlag.

Makri, S. & Blandford A. (Forthcoming). Coming across information serendipitously: part 1 – a process model. *Journal of Documentation*.

Silverman, L. (1995). Visitor meaning-making in museums for a new age. *Curator: The Museum Journal*, *38*(3), 161–170.

Toms, E. G., & McCay-Peet, L. (2009). Chance encounters in the digital library. *13th European Conference on Digital Libraries*, *5714*, 192–202.

Context

3

Monday morning, 7:45a.m., Guildford Railway Station. I am standing at the ticket machine cursing the person whose idea it was to place these machines with their reflective glass directly facing the morning sun. Through the glare, I can just about make out the writing on the screen and locate what looks like an option to purchase a return ticket to London's Waterloo Station. I tap the glass, hoping my actions will penetrate the layers of grease and smudges. Eventually, after some whirring and clunking, the machine produces the requested ticket.

I notice someone at the machine next to me peering at the screen with an increasingly furrowed brow. "Does this thing do car park tickets?" she enquires. "Yep," I reply. More peering and brow furrowing ensues. Just as I am walking away, I hear her whisper to herself, "I knew I should have brought my glasses." I turn around and glance over at her screen: "It's the bottom left button." "Thank you so much," she replies.

We take for granted such everyday exchanges, seamlessly communicating ideas and intentions with friends and strangers alike. But how often do we stop to think about what makes such communication possible—about the shared knowledge and assumptions we need to make sense of such exchanges?

I could have perceived her whispered words of frustration as a simple and involuntary observation. Instead, my awareness of the social context suggested it was better understood as a request for help. Likewise, my awareness of the shared physical and task context clarified the meaning of her initial question, without me needing to ask which "thing" she was referring to. Without these shared assumptions, such dialogues would require a never-ending series of clarifications and confirmations.

Search is also a kind of conversation, a dialogue between user and system that can be every bit as rich as the one above. And like human dialogue, it works best when the exchange is based on a shared understanding of the context. This chapter reviews context in its many forms and explores how they guide and shape the search experience. But first we must tackle the most elusive aspect of all: defining context itself.

A FRAMEWORK FOR CONTEXT

Although the notion of context seems intuitively straightforward, applying it in any practical sense is deceptively challenging, and numerous interpretations exist. For example, Schilit and colleagues (1994) define context as "where you are, who you are with, and what resources are nearby" (p. 85). By contrast, Morse, Armstrong, and Dey (2000) define context as "implicit situational information" (p. 371), whereas Dey and colleagues (2001) describe it as "any information that can be used to characterize the situation of an entity" (p. 5). Although the definitions vary, they share the view that context is a user-oriented phenomenon that is focused more on users' immediate surroundings than on their inner state.

Context can also be defined in terms of its constituent parts. Myrhaug and Goker (2003), for instance, propose a framework of five key components:

- **Task.** Any goals, tasks, actions or activities associated with what the user is doing.

- **Spatiotemporal.** Attributes relating to the current time, location, direction, and so on.

- **Personal.** The user's physiological context, mental state, preferences, and so on.

- **Social.** The user's role, status, and relationships with other individuals.

- **Environmental.** Factors including temperature, light, humidity, and, on a slightly different note, the information resources accessed by the user.

Frameworks such as this help us understand the role of context in search and form the basis for a principled approach to design. As Lieberman and Selker (2000) put it:

A considerable portion of what we call…good design in human computer interaction actually amounts to being sensitive to the context in which the artifacts are used. Doing the "right thing" entails that it be right given the user's current context. (p. 617)

To illustrate, consider an analyst in a legal firm who is searching a patent database: in this context, the *task* and the *organizational* setting are a key part of the experience, reflected in the shared workflows and relationships involved in information seeking and analysis. But when that same individual searches the web on a mobile phone while travelling home, the *physical* context becomes a significant influence, informed by geospatial location and immediate environment. And finally, upon arriving home and searching the interactive TV platform for suitable family entertainment, the *social* context becomes central to the experience. In each case, the user's experience of search is shaped by the changing nature of context.

Though some aspects of context may seem abstract, their effects are often quite concrete. Consider a query for the keyword "Java": is this a request for information on the programming language, the Indonesian island, or the type of coffee? Similarly, is a query for the keyword "Olympics" a request for the location of the next host country, the latest results, or the history of the event itself? The ambiguity in the "Java" example is due to multiple senses of the word; with "Olympics," the ambiguity is in the user's intent. Knowing the role, location, or task might provide clues to reduce this ambiguity, but we cannot determine intent from the query alone. Once again, context is the key.

In this chapter, we'll examine a handful of the many ways in which context shapes the search experience. In particular, we'll examine the process of information seeking through the task context, review the role of physical context, and explore environmental context through the lens of the information landscape.

A CONTEXT-BASED MODEL OF SEARCH

In Chapter 2 we reviewed numerous models of information seeking, from an early focus on queries and documents through to a more contemporary notion of search as an information journey driven by dynamic information needs. Continuing this thread of moving from the "micro" to the "macro" level leads us, inevitably, to context.

Four layers of context

The best way to understand how task context influences the search experience is to consider its influence at a number of different levels. Figure 3.1 presents an example of this influence based on the work of Jarvelin and Ingwersen (2004). This model represents the task context as a set of layers that start at the micro level (information retrieval) and extend outward to the macro level (culture).

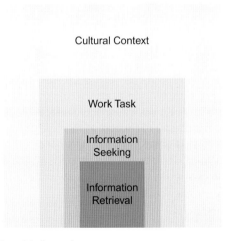

FIGURE 3.1 A context-based model of search.

The information retrieval layer

At the most granular level of the model is *information retrieval*. This layer is typified by simple, focused tasks such as finding a specific document related to a keyword query. Examples include a shopper searching an online bookstore for the latest Harry Potter book and an engineer searching a parts database for a component with a particular serial number. These tasks are often referred to as *known item searches*. They may involve a number of iterations but are usually confined to a single session.

The success of tasks at this level is commonly evaluated using system-oriented metrics such as precision and recall. *Precision* is defined as the proportion of items retrieved that are relevant to the query; *recall* is the proportion of relevant items that are retrieved. In practice, optimizing in favor of one of these metrics often compromises the other.

The information seeking layer

At the next level is *information seeking*. This layer is associated with broader, more complex tasks that attempt to satisfy an information need or problem (Marchionini, 1995). Examples include a shopper trying to find shoes to match an interview suit and an engineer trying to find components that are compatible with a particular product design.

In this context, users need to exercise judgment regarding which strategies to adopt, such as where, how, and when to look for information (Wilson et al., 2010). For example, users may choose to browse, to enter a keyword query, or to apply some combination of the two approaches. Users may find themselves performing a series of information retrieval tasks as part of a broader information seeking session. The success of tasks at this level is usually evaluated by assessing the quality of information acquired relative to the information need.

The work task layer

The information need that precipitates information seeking is itself motivated by a further level: the *work task*. This layer is characterized by higher-level tasks that are created when the user recognizes an information need based on either an organizational need or a personal motive (Marchionini, 1995). An example of an organizational need is an engineer trying to understand product life cycles and manage the risks associated with component obsolescence. An example of a personal motive, on the other hand, is a shopper who wants to understand the available options in selecting an affordable home entertainment system for his or her family.

Work tasks situated in an organizational setting are likely to reflect local resources, constraints, and working practices (Wilson et al., 2010). This list can include which resources are available to satisfy a given information need, such as reference materials, libraries, human experts, and others. Evaluation at this level focuses on assessing performance of the overall task. For the engineer mentioned in the previous example, this could mean developing product designs that use parts from preferred suppliers involving a minimal risk of obsolescence.

The cultural layer

Finally, we have the highest level in the model: the *cultural context*. This level influences not only the overall task requirements but also the collective importance attached to meeting them. For example, the expectations associated with completing a given work task may be perceived differently when considered within the context of a large organization, a small start up business, or a home-based hobby.

Designing across layers

The context-based model provides a useful lens through which to view the layers of the search task. But more important is the framework it provides for identifying the type of design support needed at each layer.

To illustrate, let's return to the example of the shopper who is trying to understand the various options in selecting an affordable home entertainment system. The overall goal is driven by a personal motive at the work task level, but in satisfying this goal, the shopper will need to undertake a number of subtasks across several layers of the task context. We can examine the effect of context at each level and explore what kinds of design support are appropriate. We can also start to think about search as a sequence of subtasks, reflecting the stages in the information seeking process discussed in Chapter 2.

At the outset, the user is likely to be constrained by a lack of domain knowledge (e.g., of the main product types) and may be unsure of what questions to ask or even where to ask them. Perhaps the user starts by searching the website of an electronics retailer such as Comet. Unfortunately, tasks at this level are often poorly supported by online retailers, and a query for "home entertainment" returns an opaque list of product categories that relies on the user understanding the terminology and knowing which category to select (Figure 3.2).

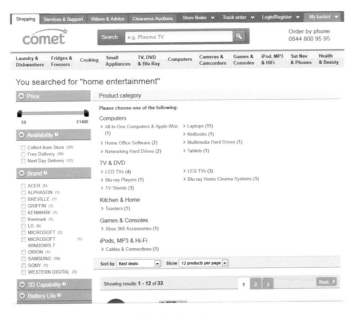

FIGURE 3.2 Limited support for the work task level at Comet.

FIGURE 3.3 Support for the work task level at pluggedin.co.uk.

But behind the tab labeled "Videos and Advice" lies a resource (pluggedin.co.uk) that is much more appropriate for this level of task. Instead of product categories, a query for "home entertainment" here returns content much better suited to the immediate goal (Figure 3.3). This content includes tutorials in the form of buyer's guides and how-to guides alongside product reviews and user-generated content from specialist forums. In contrast to the product category listing seen previously, this material provides far greater support for activities associated with the work task level, such as exploration and learning. In addition, it supports discovery of latent needs through the provision of aspirational articles and expert reviews.

After exploring this material, the user may start to formulate a more specific idea of his or her options and the trade-offs involved in each. In so doing, the focus shifts from the higher-level work task to a set of information seeking subtasks associated with each of those options. As the user's confidence grows, he or she may wish to start collecting a list of ideas or candidates to investigate in greater detail at a later date (echoing the sensemaking process discussed in Chapter 2). Amazon, for example, supports iterative information seeking via a personalized history panel that includes recent searches and recently viewed items (Figure 3.4). This information is augmented by a facility for users to create, organize, and share their own lists.

As the user gets a clearer idea of his or her needs and identifies suitable products, he or she may wish to verify the price and quality of these particular items on independent sites. In this context, the focus shifts from information seeking to a set of specific information retrieval subtasks. This is the level that traditionally has been best supported by online

FIGURE 3.4 Support for the information seeking level at Amazon.

FIGURE 3.5 Support for the information retrieval level at Samsung.com.

retailers. One notable example of design support for information retrieval can be found at Samsung.com (Figure 3.5), which provides a particularly immersive style of instant results and autocomplete. (We'll discuss such design patterns in more detail in Chapter 5.)

This facility helps users to accurately enter valid product names and details and also provides interactive guidance through the product suggestions shown in the dialog overlay.

Search experiences are shaped by the task context: information retrieval, information seeking, work task, and culture. Each of these layers provides a unique lens through which to view the search process and understand the types of design support that are appropriate at each level.

As discussed in Chapter 2, many search applications invest the majority of their effort in the latter stages of the process: the collection and action phases of Kuhlthau's model. However, organizations that support the user throughout the entire process will have the advantage in converting that user into a loyal customer or subscriber. To do so, organizations need to consider the role of context across the layers, from the lowest to the highest.

In the following section, we'll build on your understanding of the task context to explore physical context, examining the fundamental influences that form the mobile search experience.

PHYSICAL CONTEXT

When we look back at the history of search and its theoretical roots in information science, we see that the focus for early pioneers was based on the need to organize paper documents in libraries. Their efforts were later facilitated by the introduction of electronic storage devices and search tools, but the paradigm remained the same: search was a stationary activity in an environment that was relatively unchanging.

Over the last decade, however, a different picture has emerged. Mobile technologies are being adopted at an unprecedented rate, and as of 2012, half of all new Internet connections came from mobile devices. At the same time, smartphone usage is predicted to overtake feature phones, and data usage on phones is poised to exceed voice usage (Osman, 2011).

Much of the growth for this new medium is shared by search, with the number of Google map queries that come from mobile devices having overtaken those made from desktop computers in mid-2011 (Hughes, 2011). This type of interaction reflects a growing demand for services that provide an experience customized to the location of the user. These include searches for local news, weather or sports reports, friend-finder services, entertainment, gaming, "what's around here" services, and more (Mountain, Myrhaug, and Goker, 2009).

Of course, these services are not unique to the mobile platform; many are based on existing counterparts in the world of static or desktop search. But to think of these services as miniaturized versions of the desktop equivalent misses a key point: the physical context of mobile search fundamentally changes the nature of the interaction. We use mobile devices to engage in spontaneous, discretionary usage, often time-slicing our attention between multiple tasks within a dynamic, unpredictable environment. Compared to desktop search, mobile users perform a larger number of shorter sessions, with a focus on completing specific tasks quickly (Mountain and MacFarlane, 2007). This behaviour has significant consequences for the design of the search experience such as limited time and space for examining long lists of search results or manually entering and modifying query strings. This finding suggests that when returning search results to mobile users, it may be prudent to favor precision over recall. (For a more detailed examination of the issues in designing for mobile context, see Chapter 8.)

Here and now

There are many different types of mobile search experience, mediated by myriad different applications and usage scenarios. But one feature they all share is a focus on the physical context, that is, the here and now. Mobile user needs are driven by the spatiotemporal context: they seek results that are not just relevant to their immediate information need (i.e., topically relevant) but also timely and relevant to their physical location (Goker et al.,

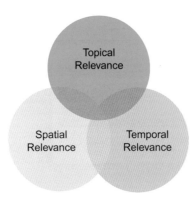

FIGURE 3.6 Topical, spatial, and temporal filters can be combined to increase the relevance of search results.

2004). These influences, coupled with an increased emphasis on precision over recall, suggest an approach in which these factors are combined to deliver the most contextually relevant results (Figure 3.6).

Spatial context

Spatial context can be modeled in a number of ways. One of the simplest approaches is to equate relevance with physical distance; that is, the closer the spatial footprint of a given item, the more relevant it is (Mountain and MacFarlane, 2007). This approach is offered by many directory services such as Yelp (Figure 3.7).

Alternatively, spatial relevance could be based on physical accessibility, that is, the amount of time it takes to reach a particular location. For example, a search for restaurants in central London might favor one that is easy to reach from your current location (e.g., via public transport) over another that may be physically nearer, but less accessible.

Moreover, spatial context of mobile users is rarely static; often the user is in transit during the interaction itself. In this case, it may be more appropriate to consider the user's current trajectory and determine relevance based on the user's predicted location at any point in time.

Temporal filters

Temporal context can be also modeled in a number of ways. One of the most intuitive approaches is to equate relevance with "freshness"; that is, the newer a piece of information, the more relevant it is. This is the strategy adopted by many news services, which continually update their most visible material with the latest content, archiving older material in the process. This approach could be combined with the spatial footprint to provide a feed of breaking news specific to the user's current locality (Figure 3.8).

But temporal relevance isn't just about freshness. Some types of information have a predictable schedule associated with them, such as the timetables for public transport or the opening hours for shops and services. There is little value in finding restaurants that are currently closed or trains that are no longer running. In order to utilize this type of context, it is necessary to filter results according to the time when the user wishes to travel or partake of the particular service. In the case of mobile navigation services, this approach

FIGURE 3.7 Physical distance as a measure of relevance.

FIGURE 3.8 The Associated Press combines temporal relevance with spatial relevance.

can be augmented by the use of traffic information (either real-time or predicted) to avoid congestion and optimize the particular route suggested.

Push versus pull

In the previous, physical context has been used to optimize the relevance of results returned for a particular query. But information doesn't always have to be *pulled* by users in this way. Given knowledge of their preferences, it is possible to *push* information to users whenever it becomes relevant to their physical context. For example, Foursquare, a location-based social network for mobile users, provides real-time push notifications when friends "check in" at various locations (Figure 3.9).

However, push services are by their nature invasive, and the cost of this intrusion must be balanced by the value provided to the user (Goker & Myrhaug, 2008). Location-based

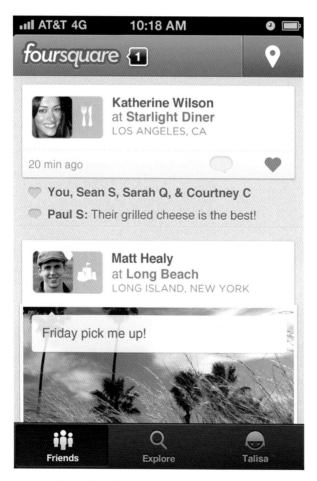

FIGURE 3.9 Foursquare provides push notification of location-based updates.

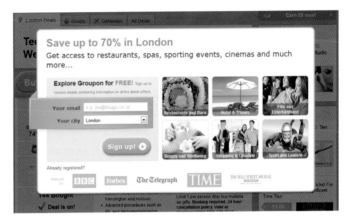

FIGURE 3.10 Location-based promotions employed by Groupon.

advertising is the ultimate example: from a marketing perspective, it offers almost unlimited potential for presenting contextually relevant promotions to consumers based on their current location. However, this type of service will be tolerated only if the relevance and value of the information outweighs the cost of the intrusion and the associated lack of privacy (Figure 3.10).

Mobile technologies are defined by spontaneous, discretionary usage within a dynamic, unpredictable environment. Within this context, search is driven by the here and now: users want information that is not just on topic but also timely and relevant to their location. Whether information is pushed or pulled, physical context is the key to a successful mobile search experience.

THE INFORMATION LANDSCAPE

Thus far we have investigated the task and physical components of context. We now turn our attention to the environmental context of search, focusing specifically on the information environment in which the user operates.

Content frameworks

The design of a search application is clearly influenced by the nature of the content being searched. An application designed for image retrieval, for example, is unlikely to be well suited for retrieving patents or finding contacts in a social network. But to define this influence more formally, we need a way of defining the different content types. Cool and Belkin (2002) suggest an approach in which content is defined by three dimensions:

- **Level:** information, meta-information
- **Medium:** image, written text, speech, and so on
- **Quantity:** one object, set of objects, database of objects

By applying these dimensions, it becomes possible to "classify the whole variety of interactions with information that people engage in during the course of information seeking." (Cool & Belkin, 2002, p1). For example, a set of search results consisting of text documents would be classified as *Level=information*, *Medium=text*, and *Quantity=set of objects*.

Peter Morville (2010) proposes an alternative approach based on four primary content types:

- **Web page:** textual content and metadata in the form of HTML tags, inbound links, and the collective postquery behavior of multiple users

- **Document:** unstructured data in the form of reports, presentations, emails, and so on, usually containing textual content only

- **Book:** textual content and structured metadata, augmented with social and behavioral metadata (e.g., user interaction data collected by online retailers)

- **Object:** defined by structured metadata, often based on product records or derived from user-generated content (e.g., tags and other annotations)

These four types could be seen as instances of Cool and Belkin's (2002) "medium" dimension and provide a way of categorizing the various information objects we've encountered thus far. The web page content type, for example, is featured in many of the examples throughout this chapter. In the rest of this chapter, however, we shift our attention to the specific challenges presented by the second content type: *unstructured data*. We end by exploring search tasks in which the focus is not on locating single information objects but on understanding patterns of distribution at an aggregate level, that is, across a set of objects in the collection.

Unstructured information

It has been estimated that as much as 80 percent of potentially usable business information originates as unstructured data, in the form of text documents, email, social media, and so on. Moreover, search applications that have traditionally focused on highly structured data such as product records are now evolving to accommodate unstructured data. Online retailers, for example, recognize the value of product reviews in influencing consumer buying decisions and are making increasing use of such unstructured content. To fully support the purchasing process, however, this content must become part of an integrated search experience.

At the simplest level, this experience means making the unstructured content searchable alongside the product records they support and presenting the results in a coordinated manner. For example, a search on clothing retailer Moosejaw for men's shirts returns a set of 42 product results displayed in a gallery view (for further details on search result views and layouts, see Chapter 6). By selecting the appropriate tab, the user can pivot to a "Reviews View" that shows those same products displayed in list view with their associated customer reviews and ratings (Figure 3.11).

However, integration can go much further than this. A search for "fridge freezers" on electronics retailer Comet, for instance, returns a set of 273 products with 79 associated reviews. But this time, the user can filter the product results using the review metadata. For example, he or she can choose to see just those products that received five-star reviews from 25- to 34-year-old males in a "small family" (Figure 3.12).

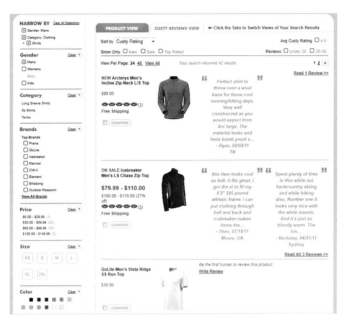

FIGURE 3.11 Moosejaw allows browsing of both product results and reviews.

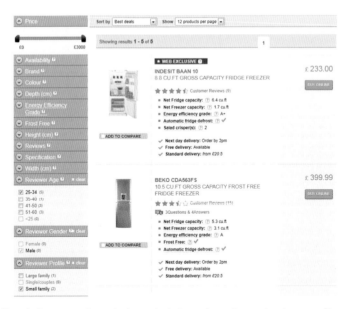

FIGURE 3.12 Comet allows users to navigate products by review rating and reviewer profile.

FIGURE 3.13 Newssift used natural language processing to identify named entities and sentiment.

In the previous illustrations, the review content has been rendered verbatim, as paragraphs of text. But unstructured content can lend itself to a more visual treatment, ranging from simple keyword tag clouds to more sophisticated charts and graphs. News analysis site Newssift (now closed) extracted named entities such as people, places, and organizations (shown in the middle three columns in Figure 3.13) and used various text analysis techniques to measure sentiment of the content, which it rendered using the pie chart on the left.

Another way to improve the experience of searching unstructured content is to organize the results into thematic clusters. For example, the query "genesis" on the Metasearch engine Yippy returns a number of clusters based around themes such as religion, music, cars, and so on (shown in the left-hand panel of Figure 3.14).

Aggregate information

One benefit of the clustering approach is that it communicates the thematic groupings inherent in a collection of search results, facilitating both findability and serendipitous discovery. Indeed, these aggregate patterns often become the focus for the search experience itself. In business intelligence and other analytics applications, for example, the goal is not so much to find individual records but to identify patterns

FIGURE 3.14 Concept clusters for the query "genesis" on Yippy.

of distribution across the collection as a whole. These patterns can be used to answer questions such as:

- "Did we achieve our sales targets for product X last quarter?"
- "Which regions had the best customer satisfaction during the past year?"
- "Which components are most at risk of obsolescence?"

In these and other analytic applications, the focus of the search experience shifts from finding and evaluating individual results to standing back and gaining a more holistic understanding. In this context, we need to extend our design thinking toward the broader fields of information design and visualization (Tufte, 2001).

We can illustrate this concept with an example. Look at the graphic in Figure 3.15 and try to count all the 5s in the image:

Were you able to do it? How long did it take? Now try the same exercise with Figure 3.16.

Why is it so much easier with Figure 3.16? The answer lies in the way the human visual system works (Ware, 2000). Detecting patterns like the one shown previously is something that happens not so much in our eyes, but in our brains. Our visual system is hard-wired to perceive certain visual attributes without any conscious effort. These *preattentive attributes* include shape and color, which is why the 5s in the second example are so much easier to perceive.

We can use this knowledge to our advantage in designing complex search applications, particularly those that involve the display of quantitative information (such as the Newssift example mentioned earlier). If we want to communicate certain patterns visually, or make

5431401720832454226013009072232578748798229487 34
2374548996414732346892084400707781436893 57867827
878465461289543402778783248644684021279487123101
0788967625314678990962645113246691284483211478723

FIGURE 3.15 Example of attentive processing.

54314017208324**5**4226013009072232**5**78748798229487 34
2374**5**48996414732346892084400707781436893**5**7867827
878465**4**61289**5**43402778783248644684021279487123101
0788967625**3**14678990962645113246691284483211478723

FIGURE 3.16 Example of preattentive processing.

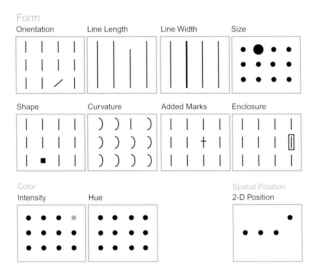

FIGURE 3.17 Preattentive attributes of visual perception.

them stand out from the background, we should use preattentive attributes. Figure 3.17 shows a more comprehensive list of such attributes that can be used in this manner (Few, 2004).

However, not all attributes are created equal: some are more suited to the display of quantitative information than others (Cleveland and McGill, 1984). For example, spatial position and length are both effective indicators of quantitative value, which is why bar charts and line charts are so commonly used for communicating numeric data. Color, on the other hand, is a relatively weak indicator, and is better used to represent categorical

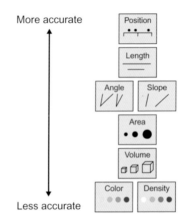

FIGURE 3.18 The accuracy of quantitative perception for various preattentive attributes.

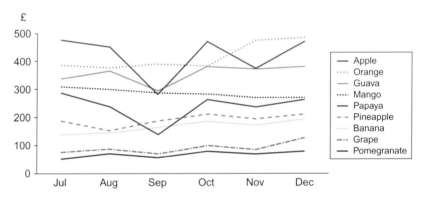

FIGURE 3.19 Using nine variables exceeds the capacity of human short-term memory.

differences (such as identity or status) rather than numeric value. The relative strengths of the various preattentive attributes are indicated in Figure 3.18.

We should also consider the limitations of human short-term memory in designing complex search applications. Short-term memory is where analysis and sensemaking activities take place (we discussed a number of techniques for extending its capacity in Chapter 2). It has long been accepted that human short-term memory is limited to holding a small number of "chunks" of information at any one time (Farrington, 2011). This approach places limits on the number of variables we should represent at any given time, such as the number of lines on a graph (Few, 2004). Figure 3.19 shows one such example: it is difficult to memorize the meaning of the nine different colors used; consequently, the reader is forced to continually switch back and forth between the graph and the legend to correctly interpret the data.

There is a rich and comprehensive literature on the subject of information design and visualization, which we've only just begun to explore here. But it is remarkable how valuable an understanding of the human visual system and the limitations of short-term memory can be in designing complex search and analytics applications.

SUMMARY

Search is a conversation: a dialogue between user and system that can be every bit as rich as human conversation. And like human dialogue, search works best when the exchange is based on a shared understanding of the context.

A key element of that is the task context: information retrieval, information seeking, work task, and culture. Each of these layers provides a unique lens through which to view the search process. Conversely, for mobile search, the physical context is the primary influence: users want information that is not just on topic but also timely and relevant to their location. We've also reviewed the environmental context thru the lens of the information landscape, exploring the challenges involved in dealing with unstructured content and aggregated data.

Search engines may be capable of many things, but they cannot read minds. They cannot determine intent from a query alone. Instead, we must understand the context, for that is the basis of the information seeking dialogue and the foundation of the search experience.

REFERENCES

Cleveland, W. S., & McGill, R. (1984). Graphical perception: theory, experimentation, and application to the development of graphical methods. *Journal of the American Statistical Association*, *79*(387), 531–554.

Cool, C., & Belkin, N. (2002). A classification of interactions with information. In H. Bruce (Ed.), Emerging frameworks and methods: CoLIS4: Proceedings of the fourth international conference on conceptions of library and information science. Seattle, WA. July 21–25.

Dey, A., Kortuem, G., Morse, D., & Schmidt, A. (2001). Special issue on situated interaction and context-aware computing. *Journal of Personal and Ubiquitous Computing*, *5*(1), 1–3.

Farrington, J. (2011). Seven plus or minus two. *Performance Improvement Quarterly*, *23*(4), 113–116.

Few, S. (2004).Tapping the power of visual perception. Perceptual edge. <http://www.perceptualedge.com/articles/ie/visual_perception.pdf>.

Marchionini, G. (1995). *Information seeking in electronic environments*. Cambridge: Cambridge University Press.

Goker, A., & Myrhaug, H. (2008). Evaluation of a mobile information system in context. Special issue on evaluation in interactive information retrieval. *Information Processing and Management*, *44*(1), 39–65.

Goker, A., Myrhaug, H., Yakici, M., & Bierig, R. (2004). A context-sensitive information system for mobile users. 27th Annual international acm sigir conference, workshop on information retrieval in context. July. Sheffield, England.

Hughes, R. (2011). Mobile Google map queries to overtake those from desktop PCs. Clickroutes. Retrieved November 2011 from <http://www.clickroutes.com/2011/05/mobile-google-map-queries-to-overtake-those-from-desktop-pcs/>.

Jarvelin, K., & Ingwersen, P. (2004). Information seeking research needs extension towards tasks and technology. *Information Research*, *10*(1), 212.

Lieberman, H., & Selker, T. (2000). Out of context: computer systems that adapt to, and learn from, context. *IBM Systems Journal*, *39*(3/4), 617–632.

Morse, D. R., Armstrong, S., & Dey, A. K. (2000). The what, who, where, when, why and how of context-awareness. *CHI _00 Extended Abstracts on Human Factors in Computing Systems*, The Hague, The Netherlands, April 1–6. New York: ACM.

Morville, P. (2010). *Search patterns*. Sebastopol, CA: O'Reilly Media.

Mountain, D. M., & MacFarlane, A. (2007). Geographic information retrieval in a mobile environment: evaluating the needs of mobile individuals. *Journal of Information Science*, *33*(4), 515–530.

Mountain, D., Myrhaug, H., & Goker, A. (2009). Mobile Search. In A. Goker, & J. Davies (Eds.), *Information retrieval: searching in the 21st century*. John Wiley and Sons, 103–130.

Myrhaug, H. I., & Goker, A. (2003). AmbieSense—interactive information channels in the surroundings of the mobile user. *Second International Conference on Universal Access in Human–Computer Interaction*. July. Crete: Lawrence Erlbaum Associates.

Osman, H. (2011). CeBIT 2011: Mobile will be bigger than desktop in the next three years, says Google. IDG Communications. Retrieved November 2011 from <http://www.arnnet.com.au/article/388755/cebit_2011_mobile_will_bigger_than_desktop_next_three_years_says_google/>.

Schilit, B., Adams, N. & Want, R. (1994). Context-aware computing applications. In Proceedings of the Workshop on Mobile Computing Systems and Applications, Santa Cruz, C.A. IEEE Computer Society, 85–90.

Tufte, E. (2001). *The visual display of quantitative information*. Cheshire, CT: Graphics Press.

Ware, C. (2000). Information visualization: Perception for design. San Diego, CA: Academic Press.

Wilson, M. L., Kules, B., Schraefel, M. C., & Shneiderman, B. (2010). From keyword search to exploration: designing future search interfaces for the Web. *Foundations and Trends in Web Science*, *2*(1), 1–97.

Five Axes of Contextual Information
Ian Ruthven

Context is a difficult concept to pin down. However, understanding the situational factors that might affect the searcher's decisions can help us design experiences that better meet their needs. In particular, an appropriate understanding of context can lead to better quality of information retrieval, better methods of presenting information, and better ways of interacting with a system. Of course, context is an active condition—one that changes through experience and interaction. Good interaction design not only reacts to a searcher's situation but can also change a searcher's context by helping to place the searcher in a better, more useful context.

Context will remain a difficult concept until we have an appropriate language with which to discuss it. Many pieces of research have suggested variables that may be harnessed to model a searcher's context. However, these variables often have quite different properties, which affect how they may be used in context-aware systems. Here we consider the nature of these variables by presenting five axes along which contextual information may differ.

To begin with, contextual information may be objective or subjective. *Objective* contextual information typically has a commonly agreed-upon standard by which we can measure its value (such as GPS signals to measure position or the Gregorian calendar to measure time). By contrast, *subjective* contextual information requires reasoning, on either the part of the searcher or the system, to gain a value. Such information could include mood, search experience, information literacy, or domain knowledge, which provide valuable contextual information. However, these variables are more difficult to work with, as we currently lack robust methods for obtaining reliable values for them.

Contextual information—and the purpose for which it is used—may also be *individual* or *group based*. Many approaches to utilizing contextual information have been aimed at improving retrieval performance or ease of use for individual searchers. Here contextual information is used for personalizing an individual's experience with a retrieval system using contextual information about that searcher. However, other approaches—such as those based on collaborative filtering—employ group information to support individual searchers' decision making. Even though we usually search as individuals, we may sometimes require information that is relevant for a group of people, such as a family traveling together on holiday, and thus require search results that satisfy the requirements of multiple people.

Thirdly, contextual information may be meaningful or incidental (Bradley & Dunlop, 2005). *Meaningful* context can be defined as contextual information that directly affects how a task is performed or how the task results are interpreted. *Incidental* context is contextual information that is part of a situation but does not significantly affect how a task will be carried out or evaluated. Depending on the situation, a variable can be meaningful or incidental: my physical location is incidental if I am trying to find an online biography of Bill Clinton, and it is meaningful if I am trying to find a restaurant for dinner. Sometimes a lack of domain knowledge will be a meaningful variable; other times it may be my lack of motivation to find a good search result. For humans, distinguishing between meaningful and incidental variables is often easy; for computers, it is decidedly difficult.

Contextual information may also be *extrinsic* or *intrinsic*. That is, contextual information may be a necessary, intrinsic property of the objects we deal with, such as document language or type, or they may be additional, extrinsic factors, such as popularity of documents. Issues similar to the objective/subjective axis also arise here: in particular, the balance between how easy the property is to work with and how powerful it may be as a contextual variable. Many of the most interesting extrinsic properties, such as information quality, have been shown repeatedly to be important in making decisions about which information to use but are difficult to operationalize in search systems.

Last, the effects of contextual information may also be *visible* or *invisible*. Visibility is the degree to which a system captures, uses, and communicates contextual information to the searcher. Hiding the use of contextual information can reduce the cognitive load on searchers, making search decisions simpler and quicker. Query suggestion facilities (Jones et al., 2006), for example, often use geographic context to propose more specific query reformulations. However, making contextual information visible, and allowing users to work with stored contextual information, can make it more precise and accurate. Amazon's collaborative filtering system, for example, allows customers to edit their profiles and rate items they own in order to improve the recommendations provided. Such approaches encourage the user to provide better contextual information to the system.

Differences in what contextual information is captured—and how it is utilized once we have it—offer many possibilities for designing new systems. As Dervin (2003) notes, "context is a necessary source of meaning" (p. 117), and it can be used to understand a searcher's situation and improve the quality of interaction with a system. Simply capturing and using contextual information within a system is not guaranteed to improve the searcher's experience; we need to know what searcher or system decisions are being made, which contextual variables are most important in making these decisions, and how system decisions should be communicated to the searcher. Understanding the nature of the contextual information can help inform useful contextual approaches to system design.

Ian Ruthven is a Professor of Information Seeking and Retrieval in the Department of Computer and Information Sciences at the University of Strathclyde. He graduated from the University of Glasgow with a BSc in Computing Science before completing a Masters in Cognitive Science at the University of Birmingham and a PhD in Interactive Information Retrieval at Glasgow. His research investigates how people use information systems to find information, the design of interactive systems to support online searching, and the social and psychological factors that influence information seeking behavior.

References

Bradley, N. A., & Dunlop, M. D. (2005). Toward a multidisciplinary model of context to support context-aware computing. *Human-Computer Interaction, 20*(4), 403–446.

Dervin, B. (2003). Given a context by any other name: Methodological tools for taming the unruly beast. In B. Dervin, L. Foreman-Wernet, & E. Lauterbach (Eds.), *Sense-making methodology reader: Selected writings of Brenda Dervin (pp. 111–132)*. Cresskill, NJ: Hampton Press.

Jones, R., Rey, B., Madani, O., & Greiner, W. (2006). Generating query substitutions: *Proceedings of the 15th International Conference on World Wide Web (WWW '06)*. New York: ACM. pp. 387–396.

Modes of Search and Discovery

4

Often the search proves more profitable than the goal.

—E. L. Konigsburg

Ask a colleague to define the word "search," and the chances are good that sooner or later he or she will mention words such as "find" or "locate," as if the act of finding were the logical conclusion to the act of searching. Even popular dictionaries would seem to share this view, with definitions such as the following (from dictionary.com):

search

–verb (used with object)

to go or look through (a place, area, etc.) carefully in order to find something missing or lost

But search involves so much more than just finding. Search, in the holistic sense, is a complex cognitive activity involving a broad range of goals and activities. In the task model of Chapter 3, information retrieval was just one of several contextual layers that influence and shape the search experience. From Pirolli and Card's work (1999) on information foraging, we know that searchers exercise judgment and pragmatic decision-making strategies in deciding when to persevere with a given information resource and when to seek another. And from Kuhlthau's investigations (1991) into complex, real-world search tasks, we know that satisfying long-term information goals involves analysis-oriented activities such as exploration, formulation, and collection.

Defining the search problem as one of findability alone is a common misconception. Moreover, it unnecessarily constrains our view and limits opportunities to look beyond information retrieval and on to broader information needs and goals. An online shopper, for example, whose goal is to understand the options available in choosing an affordable

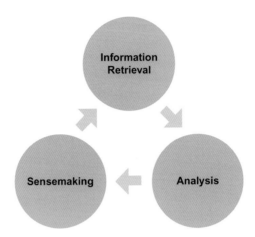

FIGURE 4.1 Search involves the activities of information retrieval, analysis, and sensemaking.

home entertainment system, has needs that go far beyond pure findability. And likewise, an engineer, whose goal is to manage the risks associated with component obsolescence, has needs that go far beyond finding information.

Yet, as shown in Chapter 2, the design of many websites and information systems still focuses on known-item search as the primary means of accomplishing user goals. By contrast, their users' needs would be better served by a framework that defines search in a more holistic manner, integrating findability with broader information activities such as analysis and sensemaking (as illustrated in Figure 4.1).

Framing search as a holistic experience helps us to understand and interpret broader patterns of behavior or *modes of interaction*. These modes, if appropriately defined, can serve a number of purposes. First, they can act as a lens for helping us recognize common patterns of information seeking behavior that are independent of any particular context or user. But more important, they can also serve as a basis for defining the capabilities that a particular information system should offer—for example, supporting an online shopper in understanding the merits of alternative home entertainment systems or helping an engineer make sense of the complex set of parameters that influence component obsolescence.

In the following sections, we examine what such a system of search modes might look like, explore ways in which they can be applied to design, and review their role in the definition of broader search strategies.

SEARCH MODES AND FRAMEWORKS

One of the key insights of Marcia Bates' dynamic model (introduced in Chapter 2) is that information seeking is essentially a nonlinear process in which information needs are not satisfied by a single, ideal set of documents but by an aggregation of learning and insight gathered along the way. However, Bates' work is significant for other reasons. In particular, her 1979 paper explores the techniques that information seekers routinely employ in professional practice, and defines them as a system of search strategies and tactics (Bates, 1979). In subsequent work, Bates extended this framework to accommodate a more sophisticated set of activities, which she referred to as *moves*, *tactics*, *stratagems* and *strategies* (Bates, 1990), defined as follows:

- **Move:** an atomic thought or action, such as entering a particular keyword

- **Tactic:** a collection of moves, such as broadening a search through the use of a more generic keyword

- **Stratagem:** a composite of moves and/or tactics, such as identifying a promising information resource and scanning it for further relevant items

- **Strategy:** a plan for an entire search, consisting of moves, tactics and/or stratagems

Likewise, others have attempted to develop a similar system of search modes. O'Day and Jeffries, for example, examined the information seeking strategies employed by clients of information professionals, and identified three primary categories of search behavior (1993):

1. Monitoring a known topic or set of variables over time

2. Following a specific plan for information gathering

3. Exploring a topic in an undirected fashion

Echoing the phases of information seeking proposed by Kuhlthau (in Chapter 2), O'Day and Jeffries also observed that a given search would often evolve over time into a series of interconnected searches, delimited by triggers and stop conditions that indicate the transitions between specific modes or individual searches within an overall task (1993).

O'Day and Jeffries investigated search as a holistic process, integrating findability with analysis and sensemaking (as illustrated in Figure 4.1). As part of this research, they studied the analysis techniques employed by searchers in interpreting their results and identified six categories:

1. Looking for trends or correlations

2. Making comparisons

3. Experimenting with different aggregations/scaling

4. Identifying critical subsets

5. Making assessments

6. Interpreting data to find meaning

By applying a system of modes such as this, we can start to define the capabilities that a particular information system should offer. For example, an engineer might need to look for trends and correlations (as in item 1 in the previous list) between particular groups of components, or compare obsolete parts with nonobsolete ones (as in item 2), or assess the role of various parameters and interpreting the findings (as in item 5), and so on.

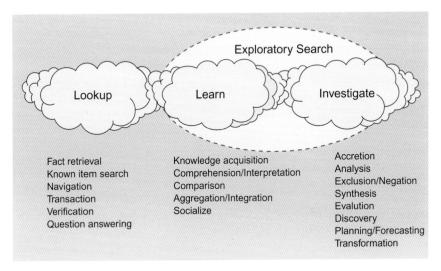

FIGURE 4.2 Marchionini's taxonomy of search activities.

A further influential framework is that proposed by Gary Marchionini (2006), who developed a model consisting of three major categories of search activity: Lookup, Learn, and Investigate (Figure 4.2).

Like the work of O'Day and Jefferies, Marchionini's model reflects the holistic nature of search, subsuming the concepts of findability, analysis, and sensemaking. The three categories are also resonant of the layers in our task model of Chapter 3: information retrieval, information seeking, and work tasks.

Others have attempted to define search modes based on observations of knowledge workers in operational settings. Joe Lamantia, for example, analyzed the behaviors of subscribers to a complex financial information service, and identified four primary modes of interaction (Lamantia, 2006):

- **Seeking information:** conventional keyword search, plus related activities such as faceted navigation

- **Visiting stable destinations:** accessing persistent resources or locations within the information space

- **Monitoring notifications:** maintaining awareness of events, activity, status, and so on

- **Receiving delivered assets:** accepting content via various channels, such as email, RSS, and others

Donna Spencer undertook a similar analysis (Spencer, 2006), inspired by the observation that the traditional information science framing of known item versus exploratory search did not adequately account for the behaviors she was witnessing in her work on designing intranets and complex websites. She observed that in many practical situations, "people didn't necessarily know what they needed to know" and that much of the search behavior she was observing was actually concerned with trying to refind resources that had previously been discovered. From this observation, she proposed the following set of four search modes:

1. **Known item:** in which users know what they want, how to articulate it, and where to look

2. **Exploratory:** in which users have some idea of what they want, but not necessarily how to articulate it or where to look

3. **Don't know what you need to know:** in which users may start with one particular goal in mind, but need to replace it with another if and when they discover some key insight

4. **Refinding:** in which users know what they want when they see it, but not necessarily how to articulate it or where to look

One shortcoming of Spencer's framework is the overlap between items 1 and 4; in that refinding may be considered a special case of known Item searching. But item 3 suggests an intriguing possibility, encapsulating the activities and outcomes associated with the elusive quality we commonly refer to as *serendipity*.

Spencer's work also highlights the qualities by which we might evaluate a given mode framework. Clearly, redundancy in the form of overlap or duplication weakens their expressive power. In addition to this, we might also seek:

• **Consistency:** they present approximately the same level of abstraction

• **Orthogonality:** they are independently applicable

• **Comprehensiveness:** they address a diverse range of search contexts

In our own work as designers and researchers, we've also had firsthand experience observing the search strategies applied by users across a range of work tasks and contexts. In particular, we have studied user scenarios gathered during the development of numerous search and business intelligence applications (Russell-Rose, Lamantia, and Burrell, 2011), and from this derived a set of nine search modes. These modes were developed in recognition of the qualities listed above and the observations made by Marcia Bates (1979) in her original framework:

While our goal over the long term may be a parsimonious few, highly effective tactics, our goal in the short term should be to uncover as many as we can, as being of potential assistance. Then we can test the tactics and select the good ones. If we go for closure too soon, i.e., seek that parsimonious few prematurely, then we may miss some valuable tactics. (p. 208)

These modes are shown in the following list, grouped according to the three top-level categories proposed by Marchionini (2006):

Lookup
1   Locate: To find a specific (possibly known) item
2   Verify: To confirm that an item meets some specific, objective criterion
3   Monitor: To maintain awareness of the status of an item for the purposes of management or control

Learn
4   Compare: To examine two or more items to identify similarities and differences
5   Comprehend: To generate independent insight by interpreting patterns within a data set
6   Explore: To investigate an item or data set for the purpose of knowledge discovery

Investigate
7   Analyze: To examine an item or data set to identify patterns and relationships
8   Evaluate: To use judgement to determine the value of an item with respect to a specific goal
9   Synthesize: To create a novel or composite artefact from diverse inputs

Inevitably, some elements of this taxonomy are open to interpretation. For example, Monitor may be classified as a Lookup activity in the context of an engineer receiving a simple alert message, but it is more of an Investigate activity when viewed in the context of an executive reviewing an organizational dashboard. However, the true value of any mode framework lies not in its conceptual purity or elegance but in its utility as a practical resource. In the next section, we explore some of their implications for design.

DESIGNING FOR SEARCH MODES

Each of the nine modes mentioned in the previous section describes a certain type of behavior that may or may not be well supported in the design of a given information system. For example, an online shopper may be provided with an effective means for locating known items and comparing specific products, but poor support for comprehending the differences between product types and evaluating the tradeoffs between them. Likewise, an engineer may be provided with good support for monitoring and verifying the lifespan of specific component parts, but weak support for analyzing and comprehending the underlying trends and patterns. By understanding the intended user behaviors of a given system, we can optimize our design efforts around the high-priority search modes. Let's look at an example from each of the three levels and explore some of their design implications.

FIGURE 4.3 Google's image results page supports verification of a specific item.

Lookup: verify

In this mode, the user is inspecting a particular item and wishing to confirm that it meets some specific criterion. Google's image results page provides a good example of this mode (Figure 4.3).

On mouse hover, the image is zoomed in to show a magnified version along with key metadata, such as filename, image size, caption, and source, which allows the user to verify the suitability of a specific result and either retrieve it there and then or rapidly switch to alternatives.

A similar example is provided by Netflix (Figure 4.4), which also supports a mouse rollover interaction on its result page. In this case, a dialog overlay is used to verify the film's title and provide further key metadata in the form of a summary, credits, rating, and so on.

Alternatively, there may be cases in which the user needs to verify specific queries rather than search results. With its real-time feedback after every key press, Google Instant provides verification of the interpretation of the current query and the results that will be returned (Figure 4.5). This verification allows users to adapt their query in a highly agile manner: if the interpretation seems unexpected, they can inspect the query for errors or simply back-track and try alternative spellings or keyword combinations.

Learn: explore

In the previous mode (verifying), users' attention was narrowly focused around a specific query or set of search results. By contrast, in the exploring mode, their outlook is broad: they are seeking to explore an information space in an unconstrained manner for the purpose of knowledge acquisition and the prospect of serendipitous discovery.

Serendipity is indeed a property that is as hard to define as it is to capture: its ephemeral nature is such that we often only appreciate its value and significance long after the event that precipitated it. In this respect, designing for serendipity may indeed be the holy grail of the

FIGURE 4.4 Netflix's results page supports verification of specific film choices.

FIGURE 4.5 Google Instant provides support for verification of queries and results.

search experience. That said, Donna Spencer's observations provide us (albeit indirectly) with a foothold on this elusive quality: by recognizing that some types of search may start with one particular goal in mind, but then replace it with another when they discover some key insight, we can start to see ways in which we might provide design support for this type of experience. Spencer's own suggestions (2006) adopt a content-centric approach, emphasizing the value of "related links or contextual links in the body of the content", which act as signposts to guide

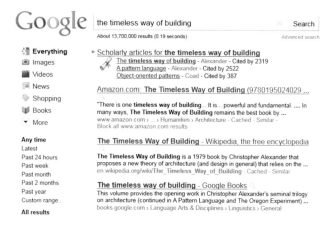

FIGURE 4.6 Differentiating between visited and unvisited links aids exploration.

FIGURE 4.7 Amazon supports exploration by showing recently viewed items.

the user toward sources of related information that may retrospectively fill the gap implied by the "Don't know what you need to know" aspect of exploring.

Moving beyond the level of content, there are a number of other issues we should consider. A key part of exploring is being able to distinguish between *where you are going* and *where you have already been*. In fact, this distinction is so important that it has been woven into the very fabric of the Web itself, with unexplored hyperlinks rendered in blue by default and visited hyperlinks shown in magenta. There are cases in which these colors may be overridden, but the principle of distinguishing between the two cases is almost universally applied. The value of this default behavior becomes particularly apparent on search results pages (Figure 4.6).

Amazon takes support for exploration a step further, through the use of components specifically designed to provide information regarding the user's current location and previous navigational history. These include a Recent History panel, which shows the items recently viewed by the user (Figure 4.7) and a Recent Searches panel, in which the user can view or invoke any the queries previously issued in the current session (Figure 4.8). Along with the wishlist functionality, these components provide support for the "refinding" behavior identified by Donna Spencer. Together, they provide a strong sense of orientation in an otherwise complex information space and encourage further exploration and discovery.

Another simple technique for encouraging exploration is through the use of "see also" panels. Online retailers commonly use these to promote related products such as accessories and other items that complement an intended purchase. But they can be used in a more generic sense to enhance the overall experience of exploring by providing dynamic signposting to content that is directly related to their current task or simply enhances the user's enjoyment of the overall learning and discovery experience. An example of this usage can be seen at Food Network, where a query for "ice cream" returns featured videos and products from the Food Network store alongside the primary search results (Figure 4.9).

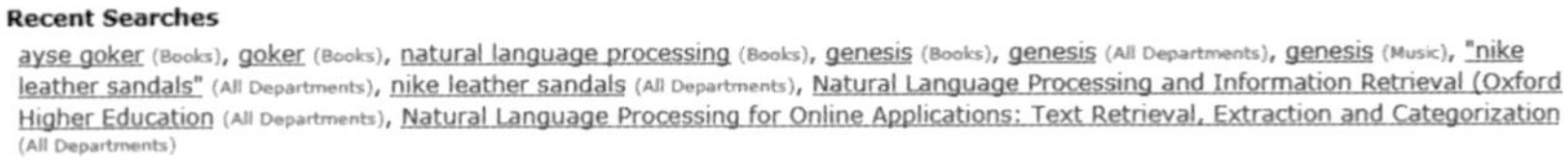

Recent Searches
ayse goker (Books), goker (Books), natural language processing (Books), genesis (Books), genesis (All Departments), genesis (Music), "nike leather sandals" (All Departments), nike leather sandals (All Departments), Natural Language Processing and Information Retrieval (Oxford Higher Education (All Departments), Natural Language Processing for Online Applications: Text Retrieval, Extraction and Categorization (All Departments)

FIGURE 4.8 Amazon supports exploration by showing recent searches.

FIGURE 4.9 "See Also" panels support serendipitous browsing and exploration.

Beyond the page level, there is a further approach we can apply: changing the search paradigm itself. Consider the library site illustrated in Figure 4.10: it uses a *parametric* interface in which users are invited to enter values for each of the attributes in the dropdown menus, then click the search button. If users are lucky, they will get a set of relevant results.

But we all know how this is likely to end. Typically, most users will either under-constrain their search (i.e., specify the parameters too loosely) and get far too many results to manage effectively, or conversely, over-constrain their search and get zero results. Often, users will bounce between the two, iteratively over- then under-constraining, in growing frustration.

But there is an alternative. Consider the library site shown in Figure 4.11. In this instance, they have adopted a *faceted* approach, in which the attributes are not hidden behind dropdown menus but displayed as links in a navigational menu. This approach enables users to intuitively explore by progressively refining their choices in each dimension. Moreover, by displaying only those options that are currently available, the possibility of zero results is avoided and the user need no longer worry about over-constraining or under-constraining queries. In addition, the attributes are shown with record counts (i.e., the number of each option currently available), which provides a strong information scent to guide and support the user's exploration. We'll look more closely at the topic of faceted search in Chapter 7.

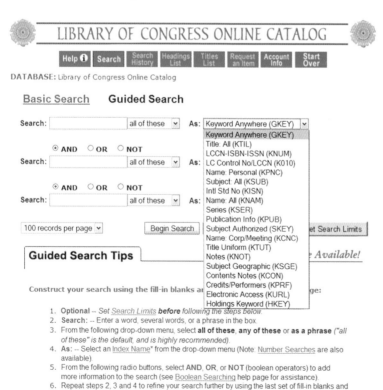

FIGURE 4.10 Parametric search inhibits exploration.

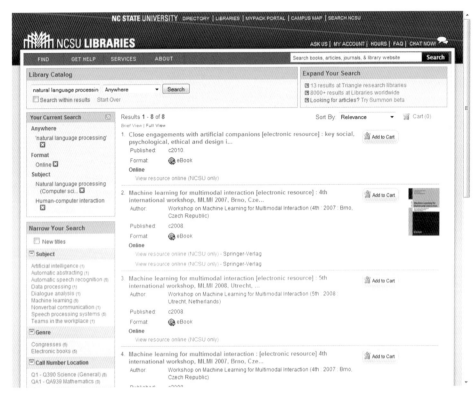

FIGURE 4.11 Faceted search facilitates exploration.

Investigate: analyze

In modes such as exploring, the user's primary concern is to gain a view of the global landscape by understanding the *overall* information space. In so doing, users may discover promising areas that warrant further attention and more detailed analysis. When they find such an area, they may then wish to critically examine the details to identify patterns and relationships.

Analysis, in this sense, goes hand in hand with exploring, as together they present mutually supportive modes that allow search to progress beyond the traditional confines of information retrieval or "findability." Like the foraging and sensemaking behaviors studied in Chapter 2, they form a feedback loop that mediates the information seeking process.

Inevitably, these modes involve complex problem-solving activities, and the interplay between analysis and exploration is such that static, visual illustrations can rarely communicate the full richness and nuanced behavior implicit to these modes. That said, there are some simple examples that can provide an initial insight.

Let's consider again the example of the patent agent, who—having searched for related patents and found an initial set—now needs to extract the relevant information and understand its significance. A simple example of support for this can be found at Google patents (Figures 4.12a and 4.12b). The alternate views (Grid View and List View) allow the

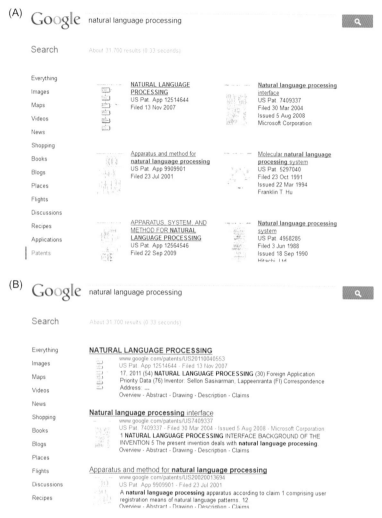

FIGURE 4.12A, B Alternate views at Google Patents support mode switching between exploration and analysis.

user to switch between rapid exploration (scanning titles, browsing thumbnails, looking for information scent) and a more detailed analysis of each record and its metadata.

In the case of Google Patents, the analysis is focused on extracting and encoding *qualitative* information from predominantly textual sources. But there are times when it is necessary to explore *quantitative* data and analyze aggregate patterns across collections of records. In cases such as these, a more sophisticated approach to data display is required, along with a more interactive user experience.

In the course of his initial inquiries, the patent agent may have found a number of related patents. He now wishes to analyze some of the prior art associated with a particular technology and understand how it has been reported in the media. He may turn to a news

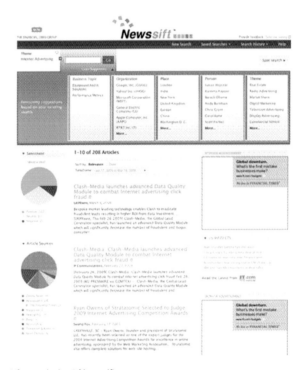

FIGURE 4.13 Support for analysis at Newssift.com.

aggregator site such as the now-defunct Newssift.com (which was in its time a unique resource—see Figure 4.13).

Newssift allows him to locate various documents using keywords and explore using various facets such as topic, organization, place, person, theme, and others. As expected, each of these interactions produces a set of individual results shown in the pane below. But it also produces a set of analytical data visualizations, shown in the graphics on the left. These charts show aggregate patterns that apply to the result set as a whole, rather than just individual records. In this case, they show that the sentiment associated with the topic is largely positive (see the upper pie chart). They also show the distribution of articles across various sources, which in this case is dominated by online news (see the lower pie chart). These visualizations allow our patent agent to analyze a topic at the aggregate level and gain further insight that could not be gained by examining individual records in isolation.

MODE CHAINS AND PATTERNS

Search modes have a value both as a lens for helping us identify common patterns of information seeking behavior and as a basis for defining the capabilities that a particular information system should offer. But they also have a further property that we can exploit. When developing the framework described previously, it became apparent that many of the scenarios we studied involved a number of modes appearing in combination, echoing Belkin (1993):

In the course of information-seeking episodes, people change from one kind of interaction to another, and in the course of problem resolution, people engage in different types of interactions. (p. 59)

This observation suggests that search modes do not occur randomly. Instead, they tend to cluster, forming distinct chains or patterns (Russell-Rose, Lamantia, & Burrell, 2011). In our studies, these sequences sometimes consisted of two or three discrete modes. More often than not, one particular mode played a dominant role in the sequence. This reflects O'Day and Jeffries' observation (1993, p. 438) that a given search will often evolve over time into a "series of interconnected searches", delimited by "triggers and stop conditions" that indicate the transitions between the specific modes.

But the existence of these patterns suggests something even more fundamental: could there be an underlying grammar that defines the particular combinations of modes that are meaningful or productive? We could think of such a grammar in a linguistic sense, as a set of syntactic rules that determine which particular mode sequences are meaningful. Alternatively, we could think of it applying in parallel, defining the combinations of modes that can co-occur harmoniously with one another, analogous to musical notes in a chord progression.

Five example mode chains from the domain of enterprise search are listed here, with an associated example scenario (Russell-Rose, Lamantia, & Burrell, 2011):

1. **Comparison-Driven Search** (Analyze-Compare- Evaluate): "Replace a problematic part with an equivalent or better part without compromising quality and cost"

2. **Exploration-Driven Search** (Explore-Analyze-Evaluate): "Identify opportunities to optimize use of tooling capacity for my commodity/parts"

3. **Strategic Insight** (Analyze-Comprehend-Evaluate): "Understand a lead's underlying positions so that I can assess the quality of the investment opportunity"

4. **Strategic Oversight** (Monitor-Analyze-Evaluate): "Monitor and assess commodity status against strategy/target"

5. **Comparison-Driven Synthesis** (Analyze-Compare-Synthesize): "Analyze and understand market trends to inform brand strategy and communications plan"

We can represent this grammar visually, as in Figure 4.14, which shows how the various sequences combine to form a "mode network." It becomes apparent that some modes (such as Monitor and Explore) appear only as entry nodes at the beginning of a sequence. Conversely, some modes (Synthesize and Evaluate) appear only as exit nodes that terminate a sequence.

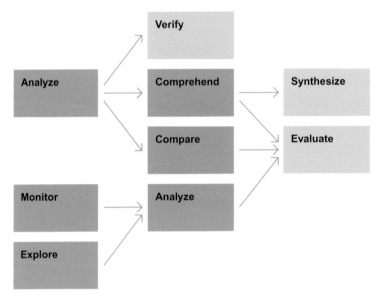

FIGURE 4.14 A network of search modes.

There is also a fractal nature to search modes, in that certain sequences can be found embedded within others. For example, in monitoring an organizational dashboard, an analyst may iterate through the Strategic Oversight sequence while key metrics remain within tolerance. However, as soon as one of these metrics goes beyond its threshold, they switch to a different mode chain. In this case, it might be Strategic Insight to gain an understanding of the nature of the problem, or Comparison-Driven Synthesis to formulate a plan for corrective action.

DESIGNING FOR MODE CHAINS

There is no doubt that search modes can play a vital role in helping us understand the patterns of information seeking we observe in naturalistic settings. But the properties discussed thus far allude to so much more. In particular, could their combinatorial behavior be applied in a generative sense, that is, as a language for the design of search experiences? This notion offers some intriguing possibilities, notably the potential for constructing composite patterns by combining individual modes using operators such as concatenation, iteration, and nesting. A simple example would be the Exploration-Driven Search pattern, which is essentially a concatenation of three individual modes: Explore, Analyze, and Evaluate. A more complex example would be the Strategic Oversight pattern, which iterates over the modes of Monitor, Analyze, and Evaluate until a threshold is exceeded, and then invokes a nested subpattern (such as Strategic Insight: Analyze, Comprehend, and Evaluate).

Our experience suggests both the existence of repeatable patterns in information seeking behavior and the potential to apply these patterns as a framework for the design of search experiences (Russell-Rose, Lamantia, & Burrell, 2011). The implications of such a grammar could be considered at three levels of abstraction:

- A single functional element

- A complete screen composed of multiple functional elements

- An integrated application composed of multiple screens

One of the most common single element patterns is to support the Compare mode by presenting a set of display panes containing individual records or aggregate data elements (such as charts or tables). These are typically shown side by side to highlight similarities and differences. This pattern is generally well supported by online retailers to provide shoppers with a more informed choice between alternative options (see Chapter 6). Another common single element pattern is to support the Verify mode by presenting a foreground view of a specific item surrounded by its contextual "halo," that is, associated metadata in the form of status, origin, relationships to other elements, and annotations. A simple example would be the product detail page for an engineering component, complemented by further information in the form of data sheets, availability, packaging, reviews, and so on.

A common screen-level design pattern for analytics applications is to support the Monitor mode by presenting a dashboard-style view of key metrics and their associated thresholds. A further common screen-level pattern is to support the Explore, Evaluate, and Analyze modes by providing layered views of a single focus area such as a specific process or organizational unit. When switching between the different views, the focus remains the same, but the data and presentation adjust to match the search mode. (For example illustrations of dashboard and analysis screens, see the case study at the end of this chapter.)

An example of an application-level pattern would be a collection of individual screens that address a composite mode sequence, such as 'Strategic Oversight' (Monitor, Analyze and Evaluate). Application-level patterns often address a spectrum of discovery needs for groups of users with differing organizational roles and responsibilities (another issue that is discussed further in the case study).

SUMMARY

Though it's common practice, thinking of search exclusively as information retrieval is an arbitrarily narrow view that unnecessarily constrains our ability to recognize and understand broader patterns of information seeking behavior. Search, in the holistic sense, is a complex cognitive activity that integrates information retrieval with higher-level problem-solving activities such as analysis and sensemaking. Together, these activities form an iterative loop that underpins the information seeking process.

Framing search as a holistic experience helps us understand and interpret broader patterns of behavior and more varied modes of interaction. In defining these modes, we have developed a lens through which we can recognize common types of information seeking behavior that are independent of any particular context or user. And by studying the behaviors associated with individual modes, we learn how to apply them in the design of more effective search experiences.

We have also explored how modes occur in naturalistic settings, observing the formation of distinct patterns and chains. These patterns offer an expressive language for describing information seeking in which individual modes can be combined to form composite elements. This perspective provides a unique insight into information seeking behavior and a framework for the design of more holistic search experiences.

REFERENCES

Bates, M. J. (1979). Information search tactics. *Journal of the American Society for Information Science*, *30*(4), 205–214.

Bates, M. J. (1990). Where should the person stop and the information search interface start? *Information Processing and Management*, *26*(5), 575–591.

Belkin, N. J. (1993). Interaction with texts: information retrieval as information-seeking behavior. *Proceedings of Information Retrieval*, *1993*, 55–66.

Kuhlthau, C. (1991). Inside the search process: Information seeking from the user's perspective. *Journal of the American Society for Information Science*, *42*(5), 361–371.

Lamantia, J. (2006). Goal based information retrieval experiences. JoeLamantia.com. <http://www.joelamantia.com/information-architecture/goal-based-information-retrieval-experiences>.

Marchionini, G. (2006). Exploratory search: from finding to understanding. *Communications of the ACM*, *49*(4), 41–49.

O'Day, V. L., & Jeffries, R. (1993). Orienteering in an information landscape: How information seekers get from here to there: *Proceedings of the INTERCHI Conference on Human Factors in Computing Systems (CHI'93)*. Amsterdam: IOS Press.

Pirolli, P., & Card, S. (1999). Information foraging. *Psychological Review*, *106*(4), 643–675.

Russell-Rose, T., Lamantia, J., & Burrell, M. (2011). A taxonomy of enterprise search and discovery: *Proceedings of HCIR 2011* Mountain View, California.

Spencer, D. (2006). Four modes of seeking information and how to design for them. Boxes and Arrows. <http://www.boxesandarrows.com/view/four_modes_of_seeking_information_and_how_to_design_for_them>.

Designing With and For Mode Chains: A Case Study
Joe Lamantia

At Oracle, our experience of applying search modes within a broad range of product strategy and design activities has demonstrated their effectiveness as a generative language, both individually and in larger composites such as sequences, chains, and groups. The modes have enabled us to address many forward-looking questions about the form, function, value, and experience of our enterprise discovery product over the course of several years.

Customers use our product to build custom discovery and analytical applications. By assembling combinations of configurable components, they are able to work with large amounts of data to answer complex questions. We use the modes to define and design many aspects of the platform, before customers adapt it to their unique needs. For example, the *parti*, or central idea is "*To be a responsive and adaptive workspace for discovery that enables visualization and interaction with diverse information in natural human fashion.*" This means designing components and capabilities that align with users' mental models for discovery, analysis, and sensemaking.

Examples of our use of modes and mode chains include:

- To coordinate the design of product features and functions across channels and form-factors, and evaluate their success in terms of usability, engagement, and value
- To establish a roadmap for the product's evolution
- To shape strategy for our portfolio of products in relation to larger ecosystems and value chains

We also use the modes to guide the creation of specific applications to meet individual customer needs. This includes:

- Identifying information needs that applications must meet by capturing usage scenarios in terms of modes and mode chains
- Defining functional requirements and crafting interaction designs for applications to support these sequences
- Describing patterns and best practices for implementing modes and mode chains

Of course, in articulating good practices for specific customer problems we inevitably come full circle to the definition of the product overall and the mode combinations that it must support. In what follows, we'll explore a template for discovery applications that is structured specifically to support multiple mode chains, exemplifying the role of the modes as a generative grammar or language for search and discovery.

Supply Chain Application Template

Our application templates serve as a starting point for customized discovery and analysis applications. They guide the structure and organization, suggesting which functions and components are needed as well as where and how to present them.

The central focus of a template is the information needs of target users, which we articulate as scenarios and workflows that describe activity in terms of modes. We then synthesize the modes and mode chains in the scenarios, and provide guidance on how to address them using combinations of components in the product and data from customers.

The template we'll explore addresses the needs of supply chain analysts in the consumer packaged goods industry. These Planners must forecast and assess retail demand, inventory levels and supply chain capacity for many products worldwide. Individual Planners in a team are accountable for the quality and accuracy of their forecasts to Planning Managers, who answer to the business units that rely on the forecasts as guidance. Planners and Managers depend completely on the information presented to them, so effective search and analysis capabilities for large amounts of rapidly changing business data – on transactions, inventory, production, trends and causal factors, etc. – are essential.

Search and Discovery Scenarios and Mode Chains

The primary goal for individual Planners and teams is to achieve 100 % forecast accuracy. To achieve this, Planners must understand all the casual, correlative, and other factors that affect the accuracy of forecasts, and adjust their methods, tools, and practices accordingly.

Scenarios illustrating the activities of Planners working to address these goals include:

- Create and update forecasts on a weekly basis
- Improve the accuracy of forecasts and forecasting methods by understanding the nature, degree, and source of forecasting errors
- Analyze and understand changes in the factors affecting forecast accuracy, and enhance forecasting methods to reflect these changes

In addition, Planning Managers need to:

- Monitor and review the accuracy of Planners' forecasts
- Determine the specific metrics and performance measurements used
- Evaluate and improve the effectiveness of forecasting practices and tools used by planning teams

Meeting the layered information needs inherent in these scenarios using a traditional search and retrieval model would be extremely challenging. It is much easier to describe the flows and sequences of search and discovery activity using modes and mode chains.

We begin by seeking out the mode sequences discussed in Chapter 4. For example:

- Planners needing to create new forecasts based on previous ones will follow the *Comparison-driven Synthesis* chain. This involves **analyzing** their previous forecasts and **comparing** them to accuracy baselines, then **creating** (synthesizing) new forecasts that reflect insights from these activities.
- Planners working to improve forecasting accuracy will follow the *Strategic Insight* chain. This involves **analyzing** cumulative accuracy and error rates to **understand** the factors affecting those forecasts, then **evaluating** the relevance of new causal factors.
- Planning Managers assessing the performance of Planners will follow the *Strategic Oversight* chain: **monitoring** the accuracy of forecasts made by individual analysts and the team, **analyzing** forecasts for patterns and trends in variance and accuracy, and **evaluating** the effectiveness of analysts and forecasting methods.

Beyond single chains, the scenarios also imply sequences of multiple mode chains linked together in composite workflows. For example, Planners will follow the *Strategic Oversight* chain for visibility of their final forecasts; but when errors or variances beyond an acceptable threshold emerge, they switch to the *Strategic Insight* chain to understand the new situation. They may then move on to the *Comparison-driven Synthesis* chain to revise their forecasts; and then switch back to *Strategic Oversight* for ongoing awareness.

Similarly, Planning Managers seeking to improve the forecasting practices and methods of their teams may begin with *Exploration-driven Search* to identify exemplars of particularly strong or weak forecasts and forecasting practices. They may then move to *Strategic Insight* to understand why these practices exhibit strength or weakness; use *Comparison-driven Synthesis* to formulate new or improved forecasting practices; and apply *Strategic Oversight* to gauge the effectiveness of new practices.

Let's look at the template to see how it enables these chains and sequences of chains.

Application Structure

The supply chain analysis application includes three types of screens; Dashboard, Analysis, and Trends. The design of each type of screen emphasizes one or more modes or chains. For our discussion, we'll review the Dashboard screen and one instance of an Analysis screen. Figure 4.15 shows the structure of the supply chain application template.

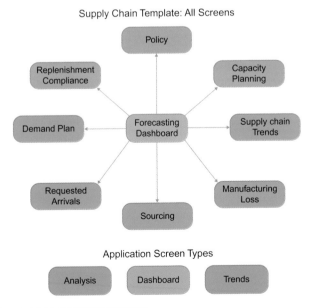

FIGURE 4.15 Supply chain application structure.

Dashboard Screen

The Dashboard screen in Figure 4.16 is designed primarily to enable the *Strategic Oversight* (Monitor-Analyze-Evaluate) chain, by presenting an overview of the major areas of supply chain activity. Individual Planners use the Dashboard to *Monitor* the accuracy of their own forecasts compared with established baselines and targets. Planning Managers use the Dashboard screen to *Monitor* the accuracy of all the forecasts made by the Planning team.

One pane enables *monitoring* of each major area of supply chain activity, providing summaries of the status of KPIs and measurements as well as a chart presenting historical values of these measures for *analysis*.

A list of alerts provides a guide to notable changes across the supply chain, allowing Planners and Managers to *monitor*, *analyze*, and *evaluate* notable events and changes as part of a steady flow of information.

The Dashboard enables Planners and Managers to execute the *Strategic Oversight* chain by following the linked data points in charts, metrics and alerts 'deeper' into the information for *analysis*.

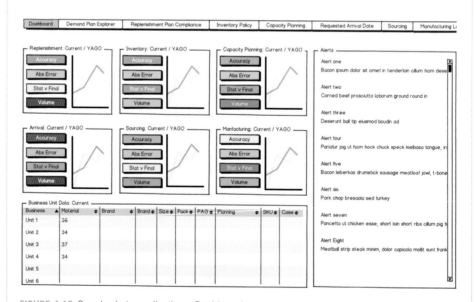

FIGURE 4.16 Supply chain application – Dashboard screen.

Trends Screen

Planning teams use the Trends screen to explore and understand the state of the supply chain, and the accuracy of their forecasts over time. For this purpose, the Trends screen is primarily designed to support the *Exploration-driven Search* (Explore-Analyze-Evaluate) and *Comparison-driven Synthesis* (Analyze-Compare-Synthesize) chains, in which Planners and Managers seek to identify new patterns in time and supply chain activity and suggest potential causal factors. The value of the Trends screen is best understood in the context of sequences of mode chains, such as *Strategic Oversight* in companion with *Comparison-driven Synthesis* or *Exploration Driven Search* in companion with *Strategic Insight*.

Summary and Analysis Screen

The Summary and Analysis screen is designed to support the *Strategic Insight* (Analyze-Comprehend-Evaluate), and *Comparison-driven Synthesis* (Analyze-Compare-Synthesize) mode chains. Each Analysis screen in the template is focused on one sub-function of the supply chain. The Analysis screen in Figure 4.17, for instance, focuses on the forecasts and activity for 'restocking' of products in retail settings and various stages of the supply chain.

On the left side, the Search, Breadcrumb, and Faceted Navigation components allow the user to manage the data that is presented in the tables, charts, and lists to the right, by searching, filtering, and navigating the underlying information space. They also communicate this context to users to keep them oriented.

At the top of the screen is a 'metric summary', which follows on from the performance indicators identified on the Dashboard, providing visibility into the smaller scale measures that determine the status of the supply chain; specifically, the accuracy of forecasts.

Below the summary, a group of components presents a visualization and data grid of a single metric grouped by one or more variables (e.g., quantity by product type). These 'metric breakouts' help Planners and Managers *comprehend* the factors contributing to the status of each metric. This combination facilitates a wider range of sensemaking activities than either presentation method supports alone.

At the bottom of the template is a list of the individual transactions that comprise the summaries presented above. These are useful for error checking and often link to unstructured data such as purchase order delivery notes. This high degree of visibility and interaction is

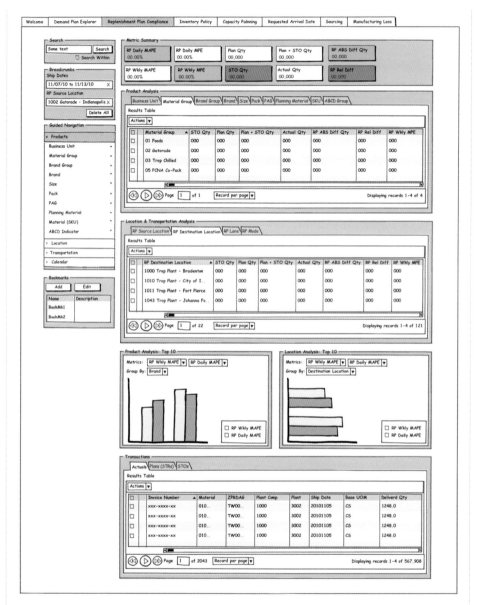

FIGURE 4.17 Supply chain application – Summary & Analysis screen.

necessary for two reasons: first, because planning teams aspire to accuracy rates as close as possible to 100%; and second, because errors of even fractional percentages can equate to significant and costly absolute variances for large supply chains.

Navigation and 'Flow' within Applications

While the three types of screens in the supply chain template support individual modes or mode chains, they also work together holistically as a composite structure. The template is designed to support the natural flow of discovery tasks that users follow during sensemaking activities, by including components that allow users to navigate from screen to screen within the larger application as they switch between modes in a single chain, or follow sequences of mode chains.

To illustrate, Planning Managers may begin a session with the application by working with the Dashboard screen in pursuit of goals that require *Strategic Oversight*, move to the Trends screen seeking metrics or forecast practices to enhance via the *Exploration-driven Search* chain, serially visit several Analysis screens while following the *Strategic Insight* and *Comparison-driven Synthesis* chains with the goal of formulating new or improved forecasting practices, then alternate between the Trends screen and Dashboard on returning to the *Strategic Oversight* chain as a means of gauging the effectiveness of new forecasting practices.

Joe Lamantia is currently the User Experience Lead and Architect for Oracle's Discovery products. He has spent more than 15 years at the forefront of design and technology, working in Europe, the U.S. and Asia as an entrepreneur, management and strategy consultant, and design leader for organizations ranging from Fortune 100 companies to boutique startups. His passion is understanding and bettering how people engage and interact with natural and human-created experiences, systems and services. Joe builds products and services, design and development teams, and research programs that address emerging and rapidly evolving interaction spaces through deep insight and innovation; speaks frequently for the international design and technology community on leading edge practices; publishes extensively in professional design and technology journals; and creates and shares original tools and methods for experience design to enrich the UX and technology communities. He's online as @MoJoe, and at JoeLamantia.com.

PART 2 Design Solutions

In theory, theory and practice are the same. In practice, they are not.

— Albert Einstein (1879–1955)

In Part 1, we reviewed the search process through an analytical lens, exploring the models, frameworks, and principles that underpin human information seeking behavior. In Part 2, we switch our focus from the conceptual to the practical. It's time to apply those concepts in the form of practical design solutions.

We begin where many searches do: with the *query*. Chapter 5 explores the process of query formulation, examining the search box in all its forms, along with three types of as-you-type suggestions: autocomplete, autosuggest, and instant results. We also examine how query corrections, spelling suggestions, and related searches can transform the user's goal from ambiguous to specific.

Chapter 6 considers the *response* to that query in the form of search results. We discuss the various forms that they can take, from generic snippets to precise answers. We also review strategies for managing diversity and clarifying information needs, as well as techniques for manipulating results and mitigating zero-result occurrences.

Moving on, we then turn our attention to *faceted search* in Chapter 7. We begin with design fundamentals such as layout and orientation, display formats, and scale, and then look at advanced topics including interaction models and techniques for wayfinding and navigation.

In Chapter 8, we shift our focus to the unique challenges and opportunities found in *mobile search*. We examine the driving forces behind mobile information seeking, consider design principles for mobile search, and survey mobile-specific design solutions for everything from entering the query and viewing results, to sorting and refining the query.

In the final chapter of Part 2—Chapter 9—we delve into the realm of *social search*. Beginning by quantifying three circles of collaboration—the inner circle, the intermediate social circle, and the outer circle—we then look at how to design for each of the three levels on collaboration, covering principles from shared workspaces, social objects, social networks, and communities of practice to transparent and controllable personalization.

On the surface, it might seem that Part 2 should be somewhat less demanding than Part 1: surely we did all the hard work earlier, and applying it is relatively straightforward? However, user experience design is a little like chess—it takes minutes to absorb the principles but years of practice to apply them effectively. Our aim in what follows is to accelerate that process, bridging the gap between the theoretical and the practical by distilling our own experience into tangible design solutions.

Formulating the Query

5

Asking the right questions takes as much skill as giving the right answers.

—Robert Half

ENTERING THE QUERY

In Chapter 2, we reviewed various models of information seeking, from an early focus on documents and queries through to a more nuanced understanding of search as an information journey driven by dynamic information needs. Although each model emphasizes different aspects of the search process, what they share is the principle that search begins with an *information need* that is articulated in some form of *query*. We begin this chapter therefore by examining the ways in which queries can be expressed, starting with the most ubiquitous of design elements: the search box.

The search box

One of the fundamental concepts in human–computer interaction (HCI) is the notion of *affordance*: the idea that an object's design should suggest the interactions that its function supports. A push plate on a door affords pushing; a handle affords pulling. How many times have you walked up to a door and found it behaved contrary to your expectations? Invariably, this event is caused by a mismatch between affordance and function.

Likewise, the design of the search box should follow its function. If its purpose is to allow the user to enter queries in the form of keywords, then it should look like it will accept textual input and have an associated button that clearly indicates its function, as in Figure 5.1. The examples in Figure 5.2, by contrast, are less functional. The search box should also be wide enough to avoid obscuring parts of the query: Jakob Nielsen suggests that a minimum of 27 characters is required to accommodate 90 percent of

FIGURE 5.1 A match between form and function at eBags.com.

FIGURE 5.2 Less conventional search box designs.

FIGURE 5.3 Minimalist search box design on the Google home page.

queries (Nielsen & Loranger 2006). This approach also encourages users to articulate their information needs in greater detail and obtain more relevant results (Belkin et al., 2002).

The concept of affordance is so fundamental that it should apply universally, across all types of search context and application. However, the major web search engines choose to differentiate themselves through distinct design treatments. Google, for example, uses two buttons on its home page, including the somewhat quirky "I'm Feeling Lucky" option (which takes the user directly to the highest ranked page for the current query). Both of these buttons are centered beneath the text box and given a minimal border that only vaguely suggests their function (Figure 5.3).

However, these design choices are perhaps now so familiar to users that they have become accepted as simply a further expression of the Google brand. Note that the positioning and layout of the search box on the homepage is ephemeral anyway; as soon as the first character is entered, the page layout changes to accommodate the results and the search box relocates to the top left of the page (Figure 5.4). The search button loses its label and gains a looking glass icon, which has become accepted as communicating a search function.

FIGURE 5.4 A more conventional search box design on the Google results page.

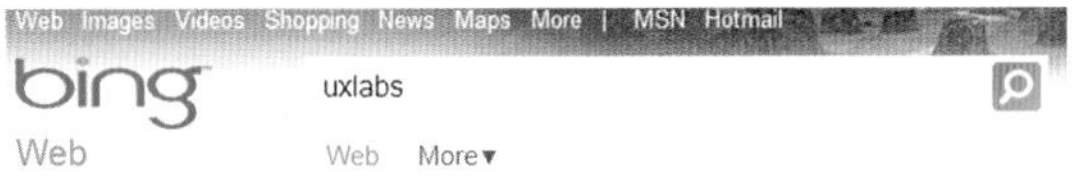

FIGURE 5.5 Search box on the Bing results page.

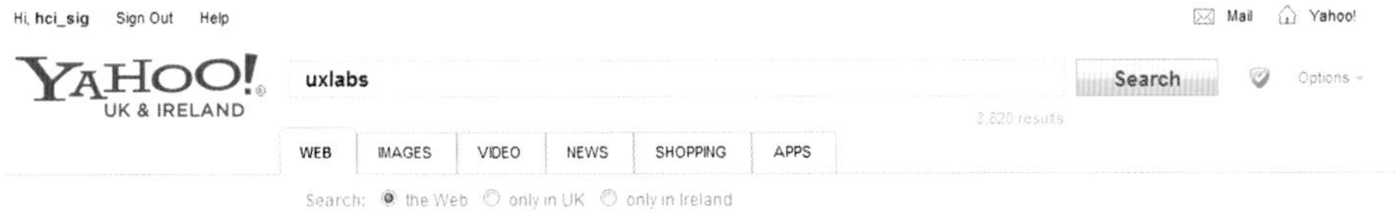

FIGURE 5.6 Search box on the Yahoo results page.

FIGURE 5.7 Pipl search box guides users toward meaningful queries.

Bing offers a search box centered on the home page, which also relocates to top left once the query has been submitted (Figure 5.5).

Yahoo offers perhaps the most conventional treatment, employing a simple layout and button affordance, both of which remain consistent from home page to search results (Figure 5.6).

All three sites assist the user by placing the cursor within the search box upon page load and allowing the user to press the Enter or Return key to submit the query. In addition, they each reserve a consistent location for the search box at the top and bottom of the page.

They also display the query in the search box after submission, which serves as confirmation to the user of what he or she entered. This display may of course differ from how the query is actually interpreted, particularly if an autocorrect or "did-you-mean" is applied (see the section "Keeping on Track" later in this chapter). Retaining the query in the search box also provides a convenient starting point for query reformulation (see the section "Refining the Query" later in this chapter).

On the web, users can search for almost anything, with few constraints over topic or medium. By contrast, in site search (i.e., search of a specific website), the choices are usually much more restricted, which presents an opportunity to provide further support in the form of "placeholder" text and other prompts to help users construct meaningful queries. The site search on Pipl, for example, informs users that they can search for people by name and location, email, username, or phone number (Figure 5.7). Note that this text disappears as soon as the search box receives focus to facilitate keyword entry.

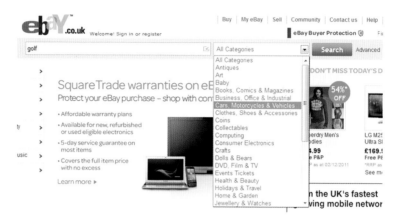

FIGURE 5.8 Search can be restricted to a specific category on eBay.

Scoped search

In some search applications, the content is organized into categories. For example, items available on eBay are categorized according to eBay's content taxonomy, which presents an opportunity to allow searchers to restrict their search scope to a specific category, such as by using a dropdown menu (Figure 5.8).

Inviting users to select a category in advance helps them narrow down their searches more rapidly and enables the refinement options shown with the search results to be tailored specifically to that product category. For example, a query for "golf" in Cars, Motorcycles, and Vehicles would present a very different set of refinement options than the same query in Sporting Goods (see Chapter 7 for further details of faceted search). Users with high *domain expertise* (see Chapter 1) can therefore benefit greatly from scoped search, particularly if they are seeking known items.

Conversely, this approach is less well suited to users with low domain expertise, as they may be unsure which category to select at the outset (unless they take the time to learn and understand the site's category structure). A poor choice can lead to them over-constraining their search, which increases the likelihood of zero results and reduces the potential for serendipitous discovery. Classified advert site Craigslist, for example, offers several category choices (Figure 5.9)—but which one would you choose to find focus group opportunities? (It turns out the correct answer is under "et cetera jobs" or "gigs.") In this case, it would be preferable if scoped search were set to "all categories" by default.

The problem of over-constraining is further compounded if an existing scope restriction is applied by default to a new query. As discussed in Chapter 2, search is a dynamic process in which the results of one query can change the immediate goal (or even the work task itself). In cases such as these, it is prudent to apply a strategy that searches across all categories, particularly if searching within one category produces zero results. For example, a search on business information provider WARC for "text analytics" produces zero results for Charts, but the same query could have been productively applied to "All Categories"

FIGURE 5.9 Scoped search at classified advertisement site Craigslist.

FIGURE 5.10 Scoped search could include a fall-back strategy at WARC.

(Figure 5.10). In all cases (and particularly those for which zero results are returned), it is important to clearly display the scope of the search as part of the results.

Search within

It is common to think of the search box as the "gateway" to the search experience—the most evident way to initiate an information seeking episode. But there are many cases for which keyword search can be productively applied later in the information journey. By allowing users to search within an existing set of results, the query acts as a kind of refinement, narrowing down the results in a manner similar to that of faceted navigation (see Chapter 7).

For this reason, search within is often presented as a dedicated search box within the faceted navigation menu (Figure 5.11). Because there are now two separate search boxes on the page, it is necessary to clearly indicate the function of each through the use of placeholder text and other textual labels. In addition, because the keywords are applied as

FIGURE 5.11 Search within is part of the faceted navigation menu at dabs.com.

FIGURE 5.12 Search within is invoked using a checkbox at bulbs.com.

refinements to the current navigational context, they should also appear as mementos in the breadbox (see Chapter 7 for further details on the breadbox and faceted navigation).

Alternatively, search within can be integrated with the standard search box, using a radio button or checkbox to toggle between the two different types of input (Figure 5.12). In such cases, the toggle control needs to be sensitive to the application context and should therefore be disabled if search within results is not currently possible. In addition, selecting the "search within" checkbox should also remove the current query from the search box as it is redundant within the current result set.

Because search within offers the user the ability to enter ad hoc refinements that may not match the current result set, it is quite possible that zero results may be returned. Although this outcome is generally best avoided, there are various techniques for dealing with it productively such as removing nonmatching search criteria and providing advice and support for query reformulation (see Chapter 6).

FIGURE 5.13 Advanced search is available via a link at WARC.

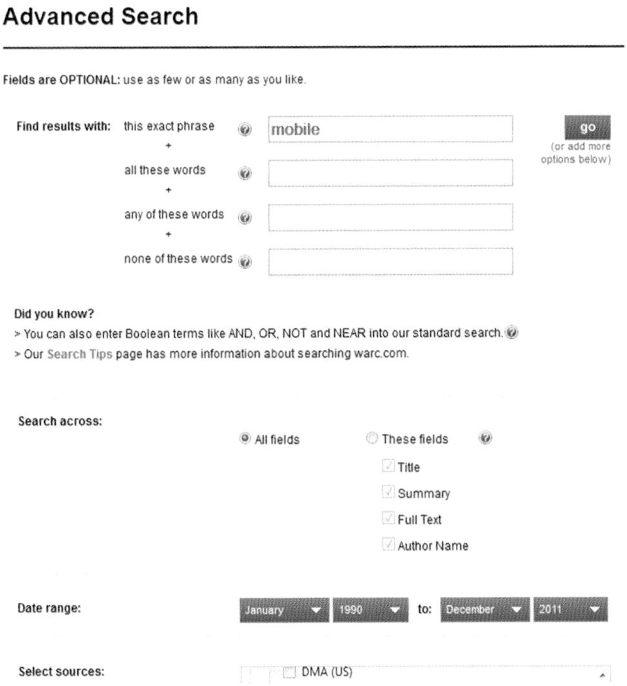

Advanced Search

Fields are OPTIONAL: use as few or as many as you like.

Find results with: this exact phrase ⓥ   mobile   go
                              +   (or add more
                      all these words   ⓥ   _____   options below)
                              +
                      any of these words ⓥ   _____
                              +
                      none of these words ⓥ   _____

Did you know?
> You can also enter Boolean terms like AND, OR, NOT and NEAR into our standard search. ⓥ
> Our Search Tips page has more information about searching warc.com.

Search across:
                          ◉ All fields   ○ These fields   ⓥ
                                                ☑ Title
                                                ☑ Summary
                                                ☑ Full Text
                                                ☑ Author Name

Date range: January ▼ 1990 ▼ to: December ▼ 2011 ▼

Select sources: ☐ DMA (US)   ▲

FIGURE 5.14 Advanced search form at WARC.

Advanced search

In principle, the idea of advanced search is to offer search functionality that goes beyond that implied by the basic search box or the standard search experience. By convention, advanced search is usually invoked through a link adjacent to the regular search box (Figure 5.13).

When parametric search was originally conceived, its interaction was based around the notion of selecting parameters on an extended form. In this context, it may have made sense to withhold some choices from the default view and present them instead as an advanced option (Figure 5.14).

But since then, our understanding of search has evolved, and there seems to be less value in adopting an approach that requires the user to make such a choice in advance. If you were about to initiate a conversation with a stranger, would you ask first that he or she choose a tone of voice (e.g., "casual" or "sophisticated")? A far more productive strategy would be to require no such commitment at the outset but modify the interaction as the discourse unfolds, reacting and responding meaningfully to each exchange.

Of course, there will always be applications for which it makes sense to divide the audience into two or more groups, such as medical information sites that serve both clinical professionals and the general public. But in such cases, a more scalable approach may be to consider how the whole experience (i.e., content, navigation, transactional functionality) could be adapted for each audience, rather than making the search function the only place where special user types get special treatment. An effective search experience puts "advanced" search tools in the hands of all users, as and when the users are able and willing to use them. In practice, many of the instances of advanced search as described previously are either unnecessary or underutilized. We'll return to this theme in Chapter 7, when we review the ways in which faceted search can provide a more elegant and scalable approach to advanced search.

Beyond keywords

So far we've looked at ways of searching using keyword queries, but typing keywords isn't the only way to express a query. In fact, there are many other ways users can articulate an information need, as described in the following subsections.

Natural language

One of the most intuitive is to express the query as you would to another human being, that is, as a natural language question or request. This kind of interaction was popularized by search engines such as Ask (formerly Ask Jeeves), which uses a combination of text analytics and human moderation to produce a question-answering search experience (Figure 5.15).

In fact, natural language has often been portrayed as the "killer app" for search, prompting the creation of numerous start ups over the last decade or more. However, until a few years ago, disappointingly few of these had had a lasting effect on the mainstream search experience, partially due to the inherent challenge of developing robust algorithms for natural language processing (NLP). But it also reflects the dynamics of the search experience itself: to effectively support human information seeking across the widest range

FIGURE 5.15 Natural language question answering at Ask.

of task contexts (see Chapter 3), we need to facilitate an open, scalable, and interactive dialogue. Answering questions may be part of this, but it is not the whole solution. For some types of application, techniques such as faceted search can facilitate the search conversation in a more transparent fashion than an exchange of purely linguistic constructs (see Chapter 7).

But that isn't to say that NLP has no future in search. On the contrary, it just needs to be applied in the right manner. For example, NLP techniques are currently being applied to an ever growing variety of chatbots and interactive agents to provide customer service and other types of automated support across a wide range of industries and domains. And at True Knowledge, NLP is used to provide a question answering service that determines the meaning of questions, which it then matches against discrete facts in its database. Likewise, Wolfram Alpha uses NLP to answer factual queries by computing answers and relevant visualizations from a knowledge base of curated, structured data (Figure 5.16). And Siri takes the interaction even further, using a combination of speech recognition and natural language understanding to provide an automated iPhone personal assistant.

Nontext queries

Information needs don't have to be expressed exclusively in linguistic form. Sometimes a visual medium can be more natural, particularly if an example already exists. Google, for example, allows users to drag and drop an image to use as a search query (Figure 5.17). Similarly, Like.com (now part of Google Product Search) allowed users to use images to describe parts of queries that would have been difficult to describe using keywords alone.

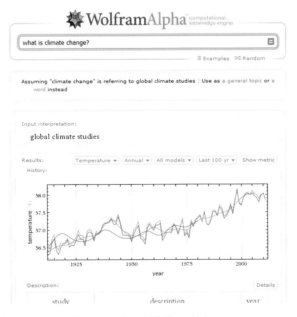

FIGURE 5.16 Natural language question answering at Wolfram Alpha.

FIGURE 5.17 Search by example using images at Google.

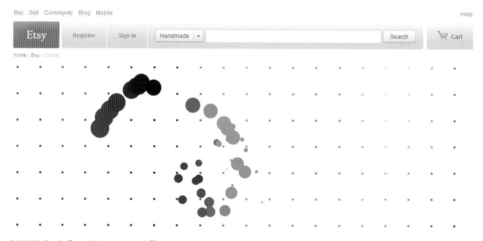

FIGURE 5.18 Search by color at Etsy.

And beyond visual queries, services like Shazam allow users to record music clips that it then identifies by matching them against a database of audio files.

Each of these services represents a type of search known as *query by example*. But queries don't have to be complete samples. Retrievr, for example, allows users to search by sketching a shape or outline. And Etsy allows users to explore by selecting colors from a palette (Figure 5.18).

These alternative forms of input serve to remind us that keywords may be the simplest form of input, but they are not always the most natural. Sometimes our information needs go beyond words. As we saw in Chapter 3, we should choose input methods that match the broader information landscape.

REFINING THE QUERY

Have you ever tried the "I'm Feeling Lucky" button on Google? It's meant to take you directly to the result you want, rather than return a list of results. It's a simple idea, and when it works, it seems like magic.

But most of the time we are not so lucky. Instead, we submit a query and review the results, only to find that they're not quite what we were looking for. Occasionally, we review a further page or two of results, but in most cases it's quicker just to enter a new query and try again. In fact, this pattern of behavior is so common that techniques have been developed specifically to help us along this part of our information journey. In particular, three versions of as-you-type suggestions—autocomplete, autosuggest, and instant results—subtly guide us in creating and reformulating queries.

Autocomplete

One of the key principles in human–computer interaction is *recognition over recall*: the notion that people are better at recognizing things they have previously experienced than they are at recalling them from memory. This concept explains why most of us can find our way around graphical operating systems such as Windows and OS/X, but when faced with a naked command line, we're lost for words.

Autocomplete transforms a recall problem into one of recognition. As you type into the search box, it tries to predict your query based on the characters you have entered. Like a human interpreter mediating between two people speaking different languages, autocomplete facilitates the dialogue between user and search application. The UK's National Rail website in Figure 5.19, for example, recalls the railway stations that match a handful of characters. We must simply recognize the one we want.

Autocomplete does its best to remain unobtrusive: we can still enter a query in full if we choose. But by selecting the completions, we save time and keystrokes. Moreover, they help us avoid spelling mistakes: if we can't recall the exact spelling of "Aberystwyth," no problem—we just need to know it when we see it. This type of interaction is invaluable in mobile contexts, in which accurate typing on small, handheld keyboards is more difficult. On smartphones and tablets, autocomplete is applied to all manner of applications from text messaging to email (Figure 5.20).

Autocomplete makes the most sense when the choices are based on a *controlled vocabulary*—that is, a finite list of items, such as a directory of names, locations, organizations, and so on. But what of situations where the choices are potentially unbounded, or of situations where we're not exactly sure what we're looking for to start with? As we saw in Chapter 2, in exploratory search and other complex information seeking tasks there may be no such thing as a single right answer. In this context, a different approach is needed.

Autosuggest

There's a thin line between autocomplete and autosuggest; both offer varying degrees of support for query creation and reformulation, and the terms are used somewhat interchangeably by many people. But if we were to draw a precise distinction, it could be this: the purpose of autocomplete is to search within a controlled vocabulary for entries matching a partial character string. By contrast, the purpose of autosuggest is to search within a virtually unbounded list for related keywords and phrases (which need not match the exact query string). Autocomplete helps us get an idea out of our head and into the search box; autosuggest actually throws new ideas into the mix. In this respect,

FIGURE 5.19 Autocomplete at the UK National Rail Enquiries website.

FIGURE 5.20 Autocomplete is used for SMS and email on the iPhone.

autosuggest operates at a more conceptual level, offering choices where the relationship to the query may go beyond simple string matching. Both techniques save keystrokes and help us avoid spelling mistakes, but autosuggest can also help us construct a more useful query than we might otherwise have thought of on our own. eBay, for example, provides a variety of different suggestions related to the query "guitar," highlighting the matching terms in blue (Figure 5.21).

Moreover, the same product categories that we showed being used to provide scoped search earlier in this chapter can also be used to drive product suggestions. Home Depot, for example, provides a particularly extensive autosuggest function, consisting of product categories, buying guides, project guides, and more (Figure 5.22). Not only do these suggestions facilitate known-item search, but they also support exploratory search behavior, encouraging the user to discover new product ideas and specialist content. The Home Depot example demonstrates what's possible with autosuggest, but it's worth noting that moving from a single to multiple lists of suggestions demands greater mental effort from users.

FIGURE 5.21 Autosuggest at eBay.

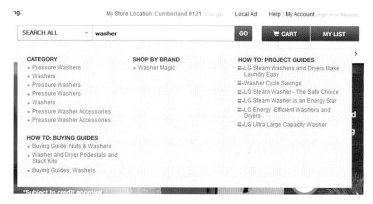

FIGURE 5.22 Autosuggest supports known-item and exploratory search at Home Depot.

One unique asset that the major web search engines have at their disposal is access to vast quantities of user data that they can mine to maximize the value of query suggestions. Google, for example, derives its suggestions both from the user's individual search history and from the collective behavior of many users. Yahoo takes a slightly different approach, using its extensive network of web properties and resources to provide an autosuggest that includes a secondary panel of specific content suggestions. In contrast to eBay, Yahoo emphasizes the ways in which the query may be extended by highlighting the *nonmatching* terms (Figure 5.23).

A further technique to optimize the value of query suggestions is to display them in the context of recent searches. One approach, which Safari utilizes, is to simply present two adjacent groups: one for query suggestions and another for the browser's search history (Figure 5.24).

Instant results

Autocomplete and autosuggest are both valuable techniques to help us conceive and articulate more effective queries. They differ in approach but share the principle that

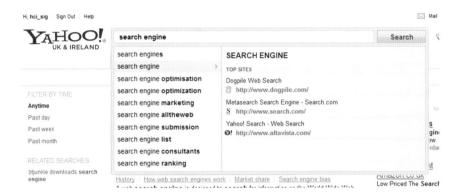

FIGURE 5.23 Autosuggest offers query refinements and content suggestions at Yahoo.

FIGURE 5.24 Query suggestions are presented alongside recent searches in Safari on the iPad.

as-you-type suggestions provide a shortcut from query to search results. But in some cases, it is possible to go even further by offering actual results rather than just query reformulations. For example, if we type the characters "ip" into the search box at Apple. com, six items appear (Figure 5.25). However, if we select one of these, it bypasses the search results page entirely and takes us directly to a product-specific landing page. Rather than suggesting alternative queries, the search box provides "instant results" in the form of a set of matching "best bets" for products and resources.

We can see a similar principle in action in the search function of popular desktop operating systems. In Windows 7, for example, a keyword search invokes a panel of recommended results grouped into popular categories (Figure 5.26). We can either select one directly to open it, or choose the "See more results" option to open a regular search results page.

Of course, in desktop search and online retail the instant results experience can exploit the metadata of a managed collection to optimize the relevance of categories and

FIGURE 5.25 Instant results at Apple.com.

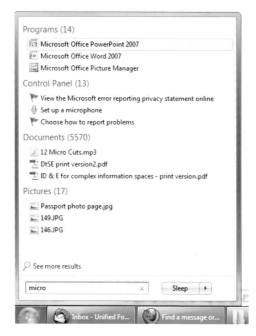

FIGURE 5.26 Instant results in Windows 7 desktop search.

results. On the Web, by contrast, it is somewhat harder to preemptively match queries with results in this way. Nonetheless, Google provides its own type of "instant results," which complement their autosuggest function to provide a highly responsive search experience. Instead of presenting a static page of results after each query, Google Instant updates the search results in real time as each character is entered. If we don't see the results we want, we can just keep typing and watch the results update (Figure 5.27).

Like autocomplete and autosuggest, instant results can save us time and help avoid spelling mistakes. But more important, by providing immediate feedback on our query, instant results can facilitate a more interactive dialogue between user and search engine. Of course, it may not be the complete solution for complex exploratory search tasks, but for known-item search and other simple information retrieval tasks, it provides a clear benefit.

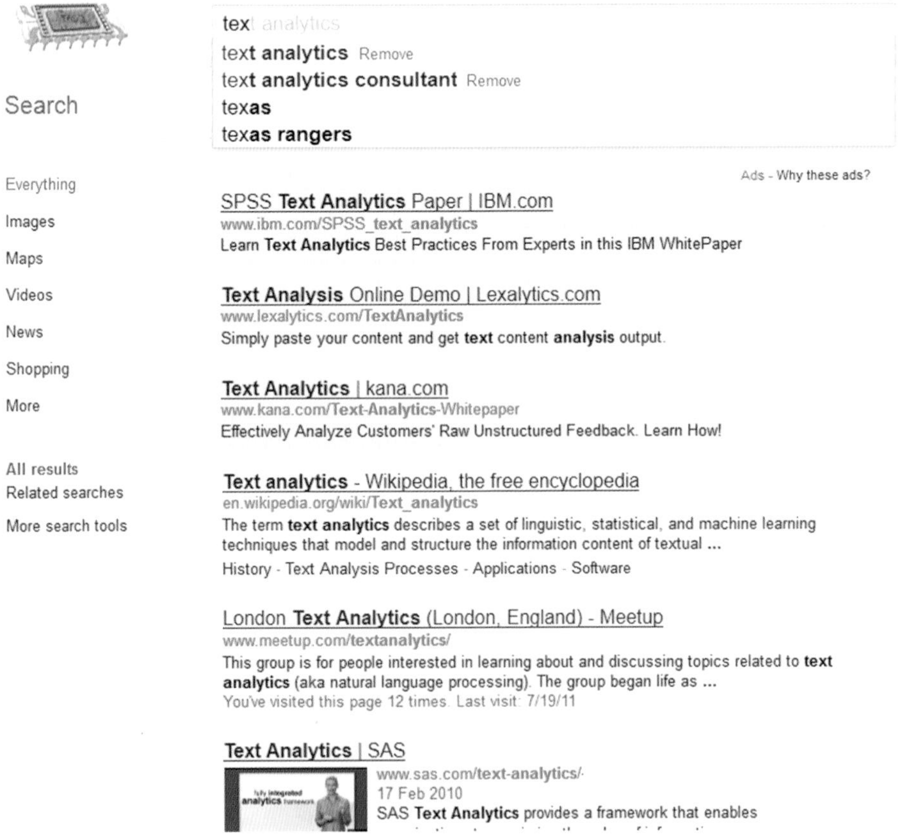

Search

Everything
Images
Maps
Videos
News
Shopping
More

All results
Related searches
More search tools

tex analytics
text **analytics**   Remove
text **analytics** consultant   Remove
tex**as**
tex**as** rangers

Ads - Why these ads?

SPSS **Text Analytics** Paper | IBM.com
www.ibm.com/SPSS_text_analytics
Learn **Text Analytics** Best Practices From Experts in this IBM WhitePaper

Text Analysis Online Demo | Lexalytics.com
www.lexalytics.com/TextAnalytics
Simply paste your content and get **text** content **analysis** output.

Text Analytics | kana.com
www.kana.com/Text-Analytics-Whitepaper
Effectively Analyze Customers' Raw Unstructured Feedback. Learn How!

Text analytics - Wikipedia, the free encyclopedia
en.wikipedia.org/wiki/Text_analytics
The term **text analytics** describes a set of linguistic, statistical, and machine learning techniques that model and structure the information content of textual ...
History - Text Analysis Processes - Applications - Software

London **Text Analytics** (London, England) - Meetup
www.meetup.com/textanalytics/
This group is for people interested in learning about and discussing topics related to **text analytics** (aka natural language processing). The group began life as ...
You've visited this page 12 times. Last visit: 7/19/11

Text Analytics | SAS
 www.sas.com/text-analytics/
17 Feb 2010
SAS **Text Analytics** provides a framework that enables

FIGURE 5.27 Instant results when searching via Google.

KEEPING ON TRACK

In the previous section, we looked at techniques to help us create and articulate more effective queries. From autocomplete for lookup to autosuggest for exploratory search, these simple techniques can often make the difference between success and failure.

But occasionally things do go wrong. The information journey is sometimes more complex than we'd anticipated, and we find ourselves straying off the ideal course. Worse still, in our determination to pursue our initial goal, we may overlook other, more productive directions, leaving us endlessly finessing a flawed strategy. Sometimes we are in too deep to turn around and start again.

Conversely, there are times when we may consciously decide to take a detour and explore the path less trodden. As discussed in Chapter 2, what we find along the way can change what we seek. Sometimes we find the most valuable discoveries in the most unlikely places.

However, there's a fine line between these two scenarios: one person's journey of serendipitous discovery can be another's descent into confusion and disorientation. And there's the challenge: how can we support the former while unobtrusively repairing the latter? In this section, we'll look at four techniques that help us keep to the right path on our information journey.

Did you mean

As shown previously, autocomplete and autosuggest are two of the most effective ways to prevent spelling mistakes and typographic errors (i.e., instances where we know how to spell something but enter it incorrectly). By completing partial queries and suggesting popular alternatives, they avoid the problem at source. But some mistakes will inevitably slip through.

Fortunately, there are a variety of coping strategies. One of the simplest is to use spell checking algorithms to compare queries against common spellings of each word. For example, Figure 5.28 shows the results on Google for the query "expolsion." This isn't necessarily a "failed" search (it does return results), but the more common spelling "explosion" would return a more productive result set. Of course, without knowing our intent, Google can never know for sure whether this spelling was intentional, so it offers the alternative as a "did you mean" suggestion at the top of the search results page. Interestingly, Google repeats the suggestion at the bottom of the page, but with a slightly longer wording: "Did you mean to search for." This is a subtle clarification, redirecting the user's attention back to the original query.

Likewise, most major online retailers apply a similar strategy for dealing with potential spelling mistakes and typographic errors. Amazon and eBay both conservatively apply "did you mean" to queries such as "guitr," faithfully passing on the results for this query but offering the alternative as a highlighted suggestion immediately above the search results (Figures 5.29 and 5.30). And in Amazon's case, the results for the corrected spelling are appended immediately below those of the original query.

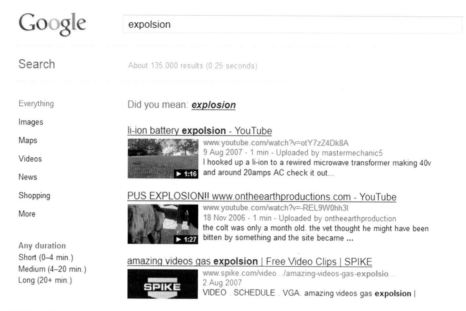

FIGURE 5.28 Potential spelling mistakes are addressed by a "Did you mean" suggestion at Google.

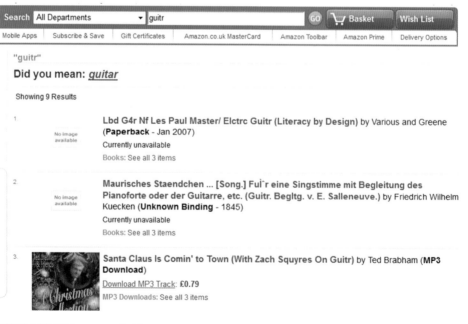

FIGURE 5.29 "Did you mean" at Amazon.

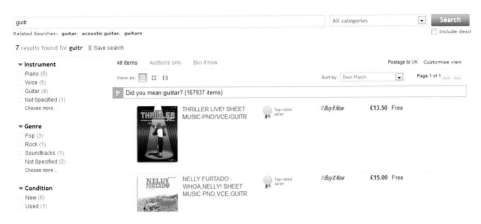

FIGURE 5.30 "Did you mean" at eBay.

Autocorrect

Search engines may be capable of many things, but one thing they cannot do is read minds: they can never know the user's intent. For that reason, when faced with queries like the previous examples, it is wise to keep some distance. Offer a gentle nudge, but leave the choice with the user.

However, there are times when it is possible to be more certain that a spelling mistake has occurred. In these cases, we may not know for sure what the user's intent is, but we can be fairly certain what it *isn't*. In these instances, autocorrection may be the most appropriate response. For example, consider a query for "expolson" on Google: this time, instead of applying a "did you mean," it is autocorrected to "explosion" (Figure 5.31). As before, a message appears above the results ("Showing results for"), but this time the choice has been made for them.

It seems that this time Google is more confident that the query was unintended. Without knowing our intent, how can it determine this? In case you're wondering, it's not simply by looking for relatively low numbers of results: "expolsion" returns approximately 135,000 results, and "exploson" returns approximately 222,000, yet the latter was autocorrected and the former was not. The answer lies in what Google researchers refer to as the "Unreasonable Effectiveness of Data" (Halevy, Norvig, and Pereira, 2009): in this instance, the collective behavior of millions of users. By mining user data for patterns of query reformulation, Google can determine that "exploson" is more likely to be corrected than "expolsion." Knowing this, it applies the correction for us.

In fact, Google applies the same insight to the autosuggest function shown earlier: in addition to completions based on the prefix, it also returns potential spelling corrections (Figure 5.32). This feature is particularly important in a mobile context, as accurate typing on small, handheld keyboards is so much more difficult.

These strategies make a significant difference to the experience of searching the Web. However, for search within a single site (e.g., an online retailer), vast quantities of user data may not be so readily available. In this case, a simple numeric test may suffice: for

FIGURE 5.31 Autocorrect at Google.

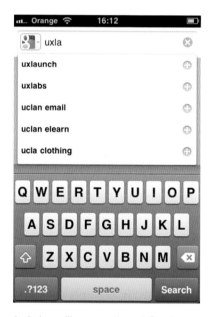

FIGURE 5.32 Query suggestions include spelling corrections at Google.

zero results, look for an autocorrection; for greater than zero but less than some threshold (say, 20 results), offer a "did you mean."

Partial matches

The techniques of autocorrect and "did you mean" are ideal for detecting and repairing simple errors such as spelling mistakes in short queries. But the reality of keyword search

Your search **"fender strat maple 1976 USA"** did not match any products.

"fender strat ~~maple~~ ~~1976~~ ~~USA~~" (See all 364 results)

Fender Strat Wall Clock - Union Jack - G14
Buy new: £10.99
Only 6 left in stock - order soon.
★★★☆☆ (6)

Fender Squier Standard Fat Strat electric guitar by Fender
1 used from £185.00

The Strat Pack: 50th Anniversary Of The Fender Strat [DVD] [2008] (DVD - 2008)
Buy new: £7.99
22 new from £7.80
3 used from £6.55
Get it by **Thursday, Dec 15** if you order in the next 34 minutes and choose express delivery.
★★★★☆ (24)
Eligible for FREE Super Saver Delivery.

"fender strat maple ~~1976~~ ~~USA~~" (See all 7 results)

Maple Strat Guitar Neck: 22 Fret Replacement Stratocaster neck with Rosewood fingerboard by Dr Parts
Buy new: ~~£58.99~~ £52.59
Only 2 left in stock - order soon.
★★★☆☆ (1)

Maple Strat Guitar Neck: 21 Fret Replacement Stratocaster neck with Rosewood fingerboard by Dr Parts
Buy new: ~~£49.99~~ £47.69
Only 3 left in stock - order soon.
★★★☆☆ (1)

Rockburn Vintage ST Style Electric Guitar - Blood Red by Rockburn (Electronics - 7 Oct 2009)
Buy new: ~~£79.99~~ £74.97
Get it by **Friday, Dec 16** if you order in the next 20 hours and choose express delivery.
Only 2 left in stock - order soon.
Eligible for FREE Super Saver Delivery.

FIGURE 5.33 Partial matches at Amazon.

is that many users over-constrain their search by entering too many keywords, rather than too few. This issue is particularly apparent when confronted with a zero results page: for many users, the natural reaction is to add further keywords to their query, thus compounding the problem.

In these cases, it no longer makes sense to replace the entire query in the manner of an autocorrect or "did you mean," particularly if certain sections of it might actually return productive results. Instead, we need a more sophisticated strategy that considers the keywords individually and can determine which particular permutations are likely to produce useful results.

Amazon provides a particularly effective implementation of this strategy. For example, a keyword search for "fender strat maple 1976 USA" finds no matching results. However, rather than returning a zero results page, Amazon returns a number of partial matches based on various keyword permutations (Figure 5.33). Moreover, by communicating the nonmatching elements of the query (using strikethrough text), it gently guides us along the path to more informed query reformulation.

Although conceptually simple, solving the partial match problem is nontrivial: a long query has dozens of permutations, of which only a fraction will return useful results. In addition, out of all those variations, there is only space to present results for a handful, so they need to be chosen to reflect the diversity of the matching products without showing duplicate items. (For further detail on diversity in search results, see Chapter 6.)

A similar strategy can be seen at eBay, which also finds no results for the same query we tried on Amazon. Instead of a zero results page, we see a list of the partial matches with an invitation to select one of them (or to "try the search again with fewer keywords"). These

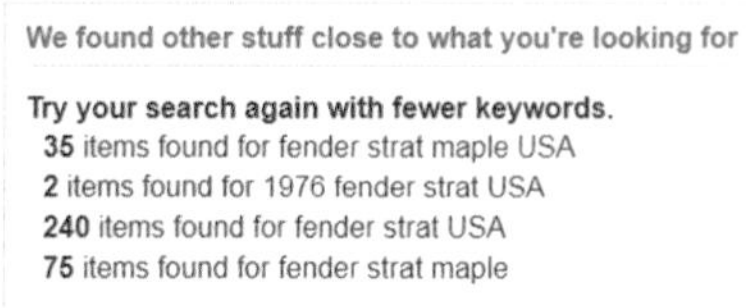

We found other stuff close to what you're looking for

Try your search again with fewer keywords.
35 items found for fender strat maple USA
2 items found for 1976 fender strat USA
240 items found for fender strat USA
75 items found for fender strat maple

FIGURE 5.34 Partial matches using quorum-level ranking at eBay.

FIGURE 5.35 Related searches at Bing.

are ordered using what's known as *quorum-level* ranking (Salton, 1989), which sorts results according to the number of matching keywords (Figure 5.34). Thus products matching four keywords (such as "fender strat maple USA") are ranked above those containing three or fewer (such as "fender strat USA").

Partial matches are a very effective way to facilitate the process of query reformulation, providing us with a clear direction to take along our information journey. Together with autocorrect and "did you mean," they act as signposts that help us decide which of the many paths to take. But sometimes we may see something that motivates us to take a deliberate detour. Like the autosuggest function discussed earlier, *related searches* provides us with the inspiration to embrace new ideas that we might not otherwise have considered.

Related searches

All the major web search engines offer support for related searches. Bing, for example, shows them in a panel to the left of the main results (Figure 5.35).

Google, by contrast, shows them on demand (via a link in the sidebar) as a panel above the main search results (Figure 5.36). Like the Yahoo example seen earlier, they both emphasize extensions to the query by highlighting the nonmatching elements.

Apart from providing inspiration, related searches can be used to help clarify an ambiguous query (see Chapter 7 for the significance of this within faceted search). For example, query on Bing for "apple" returns results associated mainly with the computer manufacturer, but the related searches clearly indicate a number of other interpretations (Figure 5.37).

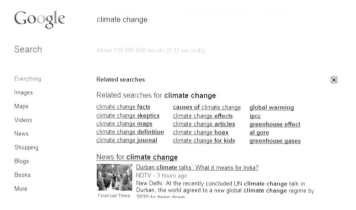

FIGURE 5.36 Related searches at Google.

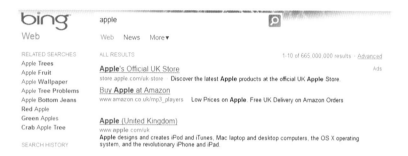

FIGURE 5.37 Query disambiguation via related searches at Bing.

Related searches can also be used to articulate associated concepts in a taxonomy. At eBay, for example, a query for "acoustic guitar" returns a number of related searches at varying levels of specificity. These include subordinate (child) concepts, such as "yamaha acoustic guitar" and "fender acoustic guitar," along with sibling concepts such as "electric guitar," and superordinate (parent) concepts such as "guitar." These taxonomic signposts offer a subtle form of guidance, helping us understand better the conceptual space in which our query belongs (Figure 5.38).

Although related searches offer us a way to open our minds to new directions, they are not the only source of inspiration. Sometimes it is the results themselves that provide the stimulus. When we find a particularly good match for our information need, we try to find more of the same: a process that Peter Morville refers to as "pearl growing" (Morville, 2010). Google's image search, for example, offers us the opportunity to find images similar to a particular result (Figure 5.39).

For image search, the results certainly appear impressive, with a single click returning a remarkably homogenous set of results. But that feature is perhaps also its biggest shortcoming: by hiding the details of the similarity calculation, the user has no control over

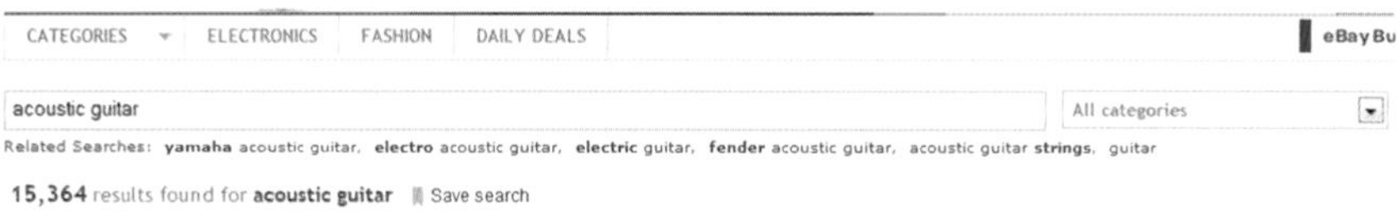

CATEGORIES
ELECTRONICS
FASHION
DAILY DEALS
eBay Bu
acoustic guitar
All categories
Related Searches: yamaha acoustic guitar, electro acoustic guitar, electric guitar, fender acoustic guitar, acoustic guitar strings, guitar
15,364 results found for acoustic guitar
Save search

FIGURE 5.38 Taxonomic signposting via related searches at eBay.

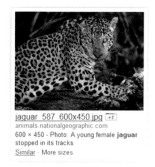

jaguar_587_600x450.jpg
animals.nationalgeographic.com
600 × 450 - Photo: A young female jaguar stopped in its tracks
Similar - More sizes

FIGURE 5.39 Find similar images at Google.

Orange
17:05
Playlists
Genius Playlist
Now Playing
New
Refresh
Save
Andy, You're A Star
Hot Fuss - The Killers
Manhattan
Only by the Night - Kings of Leon
Hysteria
Absolution - Muse
I Predict A Riot
Employment - Kaiser Chiefs
Cemeteries Of London
Viva La Vida Or Death And All His Friends -...
Fluorescent Adolescent
Favourite Worst Nightmare - Arctic Monkeys
Let It Die
Echoes, Silence, Patience & Grace - Foo Fig...
Playlists
Artists
Songs
Videos
More

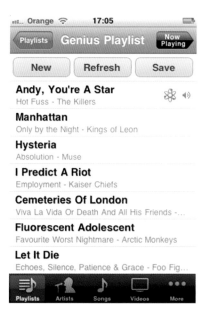

FIGURE 5.40 Genius playlist creates "more like this" from a single item.

what is returned and cannot see why certain items are deemed similar when others are not. For this type of search, a faceted approach may be preferable, in which the user has control over exactly which dimensions are considered as part of the similarity calculation (see Chapter 7).

Google shows how we can actively seek similar results, but sometimes we may prefer to have related content presented to us. Recommender systems such as Last.fm and Netflix rely heavily on attributes, ratings, and collaborative filtering data to suggest content we're likely to enjoy. And from just a single item in our music collection, iTunes Genius can recommend many more for us to listen to as part of a playlist (Figure 5.40).

SUMMARY AND BEST PRACTICES

We began this chapter where so many information journeys begin: in the expression of a query. Through search boxes, scoped search, advanced search and beyond, we've seen the many ways in which an information need can be articulated.

But we've also seen how search tasks of any complexity require an iterative approach, involving the creation and reformulation of queries. In this context, as-you-type suggestions have become invaluable. Autocomplete is best suited to known-item search and simple information retrieval tasks; autosuggest works well for exploratory search and complex information seeking tasks; and instant results provide a direct channel from query to answers.

But there are times when we need more explicit guidance, in the form of spell-checking strategies such as "did you mean" and autocorrect. Likewise, partial matching strategies can provide signposts to guide us toward more productive keyword combinations. And related searches can inspire us to consider new directions and grow our own pearls. Together, these techniques keep us on track throughout our information journey.

The Search Box

- Form should follow function; apply the principles of affordance to interactive design elements.

- Reserve a consistent location for the search box, and make it wide enough to comfortably accommodate the majority of queries.

- Place the cursor within the search box upon page load and allow the user to press the Enter or return key to submit the query.

- Provide direction in the form of placeholder text and other prompts to help users construct meaningful queries (but remove these prompts as soon as the search box receives focus).

- Display the query in the search box after submission.

Scoped Search

- Consider scoped search for applications where users have high domain expertise, but avoid forcing this function on users with low domain expertise. Ensure that it defaults to "all categories."

- Apply a fallback strategy that searches across all categories if searching within one category produces zero results.

- Clearly display the scope of the search as part of the results.

Search Within

- If presented as part of a faceted menu, clearly indicate the function through the use of placeholder text and other textual labels. Ensure that keyword refinements appear as mementos in the breadbox.

- If presented as an option to the global search box, ensure that the toggle control is sensitive to the application context. In addition, selecting the "search within" checkbox should remove the current query from the search box.

Advanced Search

- Review the rationale for advanced search, in particular whether it is better to customize the whole experience (i.e., content, navigation, transactional functionality, etc.) for a specialist audience, rather than assume that search alone deserves special treatment.

Beyond Keywords

Sometimes our information needs go beyond words. Choose input methods that match the medium.

Use autocomplete to:

- Facilitate accurate and efficient data entry.

- Select from a finite list of names or symbols.

Use autosuggest to:

- Facilitate novel query reformulations.

- Select from an open-ended list of terms or phrases.

- Encourage exploratory search (with a degree of complexity and mental effort that is appropriate to the task). Where appropriate, complement search suggestions with recent searches.

Use instant results to:

• Promote specific items or products.

Use "did you mean" when:

• An alternative spelling of a short query would return a more productive result set.

Use autocorrect when:

• An alternative spelling of a short query would avoid a zero result set.

Use partial matches to:

• Find productive permutations of keywords within a longer keyword query.

• Present a subset of those matches to reflect the diversity of the result set.

Use related searches to:

• Provide inspiration and new ideas for extending and refining a query.

• Clarify an ambiguous or generic information need.

• Present associated concepts in a taxonomy.

REFERENCES

Belkin, N. J., Cool, C., Jeng, J., Keller, A., Kelly, D., Kim, J., et al. (2002). Rutgers' TREC 2001 interactive track experience. In E. M. Voorhees, & D. K. Harman (Eds.), *The tenth text retrieval conference (TREC 2001) (pp. 465–472)*. Gaithersburg, MD: U.S. Department of Commerce, NIST.

Halevy, A., Norvig, P., & Pereira, F. (2009). The unreasonable effectiveness of data. *IEEE Intelligent Systems, 24*(2), 8–12.

Morville, P., & Callender, J. (2010). *Search patterns: Design for discovery*. Sebastpol, CA: O'Reilly Media.

Nielsen, J., & Loranger, H. (2006). *Prioritizing web usability*. Berkeley, California: New Riders Press.

Salton, G. (1989). *Automatic text processing: The transformation, analysis and retrieval of information by computer*. Reading, MA: Addison-Wesley.

Q&A with Louis Rosenfeld

Your most recent book, *Search Analytics for Your Site* (Rosenfeld, 2011), is all about "site search analytics" or SSA for short. Many people are already familiar with web analytics—what makes SSA different?

As valuable as other types of analytics are, they tell you precious little about users' intent. But when someone searches your site, they're telling you what they want—in their own words. SSA involves both aggregating those search queries by segments to get a broader sense of intent, as well as sampling individual search sessions to see whether your site is addressing common queries successfully.

What's your advice to people who believe their web analytics package is all they need to deliver a good search experience?

Many analytics packages are starting to provide barebones SSA reporting—specifically, reports that show you the most frequent queries, and reports that show the queries that fail most frequently (as evidenced by quick exits or zero search results).

Those reports are a great start, but they're completely generic. Search is essentially a form of dialogue. You and your users are having a conversation that's unique, and you'll want to employ custom metrics and reports to help you to study and actually learn something from that dialogue. Otherwise it will be difficult to determine what needs to be fixed or improved.

You'll also want to "play" with your query data to unearth patterns and surprises that won't be obvious when the data is bottled up in reports. Metrics-driven analysis is great for helping you better understand how your site is performing in terms of *known* goals, but getting your data into a database or spreadsheet will help you find out what you *don't know* about your users and their needs.

In your book, you talk about the "short head" and "long tail" distribution of search data. How does this distribution pattern affect the amount of analysis it takes to gain insights from SSA?

Search query data, when you sort them by frequency, exhibit an extremely short head—the really, really common queries—before dropping off into an especially long tail of esoteric "singleton" queries. So although your site may have tens of thousands of unique queries during a given time period, a very small number of those queries will account for a huge volume of search activity. For example, your 100 most frequent queries may account for 20 or 30 percent of your entire site's search traffic.

This is a rule for every site. And it's a good thing—it means that if you focus on making your site's most frequent queries work well, you'll get a huge return for your efforts. A little will really go a long way. And you can scale your efforts gracefully: this month, maybe you'll only have time to improve your 20 most common queries. Next month, maybe you'll have built a case to tackle the top 50. And so on.

It seems like there's a lot of statistics involved in analyzing search data. Is this a task that designers have the ability to tackle, or should we leave it to the experts?

Nope, thanks to the short head, you really don't need to be a statistician to analyze and benefit from SSA—you're just not working with huge numbers. My book goes into a bunch of simple, concrete ways you can get useful information and even occasional insights from analyzing your queries, and trust me, I couldn't tell a Chi Square from a T Test.

SSA sounds like a powerful tool for measuring the behavior of users. Is it the only tool needed, or should it be combined with other research methods as well?

All research tools are woefully imperfect and incomplete on their own. As in the fable of the blind men and the elephant, each has a piece of the picture that makes no sense until they're put together.

Many designers rely upon nonquantitative tools, so SSA can be especially useful—it's a great complement to their existing research approaches, especially as it tells so much more than most other quantitative approaches about user intent.

I imagine there are dozens of ways insights from SSA could be used to improve the search experience. What are a few of the most common methods that you've come across?

My book dedicates a chapter to each of these basic analytical approaches: pattern analysis, session analysis, failure analysis, and audience analysis. They're all good for diagnosing problems with your site's content, metadata, navigation, and, of course, its search system.

How did you get into search analytics in the first place?

My friend Rich Wiggins, who started Michigan State University's SSA practice, showed me years ago how powerful it was in driving information architecture design decision making. I'm indebted to him, and hope my work helps others in the same way Rich helped me.

What's your advice for the best way to get started analyzing search data?

Start with those generic reports that show common queries and commonly failing queries. You'll immediately start coming up with follow-up questions—use those questions to shape custom reports for your own SSA practice.

Great, thank you for sharing with us, Lou!

Lou Rosenfeld is an independent information architecture consultant for Fortune 500 corporations and other large organizations, and founder of Rosenfeld Media, a publishing house focused on user experience books. He has been instrumental in helping establish the fields of information architecture and user experience and in articulating the role and value of librarianship within those fields. Lou is coauthor of Information Architecture for the World Wide Web (O'Reilly Media, 3rd edition, 2006) and Search Analytics for Your Site (Rosenfeld Media, 2011), cofounder of the Information Architecture Institute, and a former columnist for Internet World, CIO, and Web Review. He blogs regularly and tweets (@louisrosenfeld) even more so.

References

Rosenfeld, L. (2011). *Search analytics for your site*. New York: Rosenfeld Media.
    <http://rosenfeldmedia.com/books/searchanalytics/>.

Displaying and Manipulating Results

6

However beautiful the strategy, you should occasionally look at the results.

—Sir Winston Churchill

DISPLAYING SEARCH RESULTS

In Chapter 5, we reviewed the various ways in which an information need may be articulated, focusing on its expression via some form of query. In this chapter, we consider ways in which the response can be articulated, focusing on its expression as a set of search results. Together, these two elements lie at the heart of the search experience, defining and shaping much of the information seeking dialogue. We begin this chapter therefore by examining the most universal of elements within that response: the search result.

Basic principles

Search results play a vital role in the search experience: they communicate the richness and diversity of the overall result set, while at the same time conveying the detail of each individual item. Indeed, it is this dual purpose that creates the primary tension in their design: too detailed and they risk wasting valuable screen space; too succinct and vital information may be omitted.

To illustrate, suppose you're looking for a new job role, and you browse to the 40 or so open positions listed on UsabilityNews (Figure 6.1). The results are displayed in concise groups of ten, occupying minimal screen space. But can you tell which particular ones might be worth pursuing? The roles all sound quite similar (and job titles can be misleading anyway). Closing dates seem largely irrelevant, unless we already have a particular position in mind. The end result is a weak information scent (see Chapter 2) that forces us to continually jump back and forth between the individual results and the list to see the information we need. Some degree of movement like this may be inevitable with any design, but when it becomes chronic, it is referred to as *pogosticking* (Spool, 2005).

Lead Visual UI Designer
Deadline: 19 December 2011

Senior / Lead UX Architect - Amsterdam
Deadline: 20 December 2011

Head of User Experience
Deadline: 22 December 2011

Freelance Web Interaction Design - Paris
Deadline: 22 December 2011

Senior User Experience Architect
Deadline: 23 December 2011

User Experience Associate Director
Deadline: 23 December 2011

Mobile User Experience Designer
Deadline: 23 December 2011

Senior User Experience Consultants
Deadline: 23 December 2011

Mid-Weight Mobile UI Designer
Deadline: 25 December 2011

Freelance Senior Mobile Visual Designer
Deadline: 26 December 2011

Previous 1 2 3 4 Next

FIGURE 6.1 Weak information scent in the job listings at UsabilityNews.

What we need instead is information that allows us to make a more informed judgment regarding the suitability of each position: details such as location, remuneration, role description, and so on. A similar search on recruitment agency Reed offers all of these, along with associated tools and controls (Figure 6.2). By presenting supplementary information such as this, the user can more effectively browse the individual results and verify their suitability without leaving the page (Drori & Alon, 2003).

Of course, the corollary is that each item occupies more screen space, and thus fewer results can be shown *above the fold* (i.e., in the area that is visible without scrolling). This setup increases the likelihood that potentially valuable results will be overlooked, particularly if relevance appears to be weaker further down the list. An acute example can be found at electrical retailer Comet, where each individual result extends to over 300 pixels in height (Figure 6.3). Consequently, in many cases it is not possible to view more than two or three results at any one time. In practice, we need a balance that addresses the users' characteristics (Chapter 1), their information seeking behavior (Chapter 2), and the broader search context (see Chapter 3).

The anatomy of a search result

Though the previously defined principles may guide us toward the optimal level of detail for the search results, we still need to structure and display them appropriately. In this respect, the three major web search engines are remarkably consistent (Figure 6.4). By default, each displays the page title, the URL (in abbreviated form), and an informative summary of the content (known as a "snippet"). Moreover, they all apply a similar color scheme to differentiate the information types. Can you tell which is which?

It turns out they are from Google, Bing, and Yahoo respectively. (Of course, Yahoo's results are actually powered by Bing, but that shouldn't constrain their freedom to apply their own design treatment.)

FIGURE 6.2 More informative job listings at Reed.

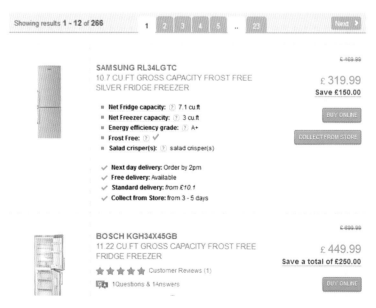

FIGURE 6.3 Highly detailed product listings at Comet.

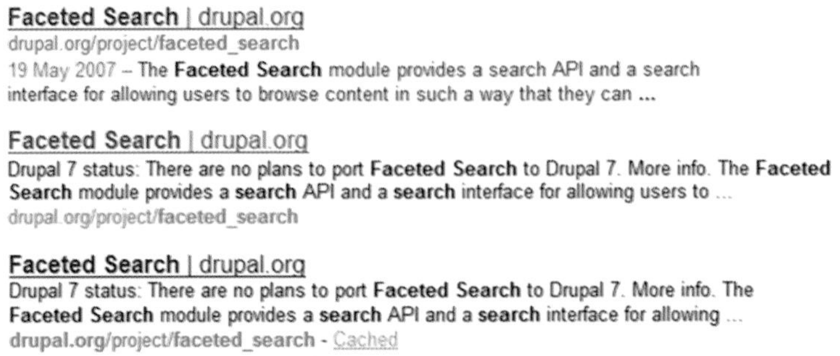

Faceted Search | drupal.org
drupal.org/project/faceted_search
19 May 2007 – The **Faceted Search** module provides a search API and a search
interface for allowing users to browse content in such a way that they can ...

Faceted Search | drupal.org
Drupal 7 status: There are no plans to port **Faceted Search** to Drupal 7. More info. The **Faceted**
Search module provides a **search** API and a **search** interface for allowing users to ...
drupal.org/project/faceted_search

Faceted Search | drupal.org
Drupal 7 status: There are no plans to port **Faceted Search** to Drupal 7. More info. The
Faceted Search module provides a **search** API and a **search** interface for allowing ...
drupal.org/project/faceted_search - Cached

FIGURE 6.4 Commonality of design for the major web search engines.

The order of the components is subtly different: Google displays the URL immediately below the title, perhaps reflecting its value to users in making trust and credibility judgments (Schwarz & Morris, 2011). But one feature they all share is the use of *query-oriented summaries*: snippets that show the query terms in context (Tombros & Sanderson, 1998). In addition, these summaries highlight the matching terms (using boldface), which has the effect of drawing attention to key fragments in the text and communicating how closely the query terms appear to one another (Marchionini, 1995). This is known to be a strong indicator of relevance (Muramatsu & Pratt, 2001).

Of course, one reason these results look similar is that they are all summaries of unstructured documents found on the web. But in a different context, different rules apply. In eCommerce, for example, photos of each product are a vital part of the search results. For news search, publication dates may be essential. And for mobile, almost everything changes. First, it is important to keep the snippets short. But more important, we need results that reflect our spatial location (see Chapter 3). Here, maps become the natural medium for search results, placing each result in its geospatial context (Figure 6.5).

But search results don't have to be text at all. If our goal is to refind a previously known item, it may be quicker for us to view them as a set of thumbnails, flicking through them in sequence (Figure 6.6). When we know exactly what our target looks like, we can rely on recognition rather than recall to find it (see Chapter 5).

Likewise, if we know what type of page we are looking for, we can take other types of shortcut. By offering *deep links* to key pages within popular sites, the major web search engines invite us to skip home pages and navigate direct to content that would otherwise be buried deep within a site's structure (Figure 6.7).

Search result previews

As mentioned earlier, pogosticking occurs when there is insufficient detail for users to make informed judgments about the relevance of individual search results. We can reduce it by adding more information, but at the cost of using more screen space and potentially pushing valuable results out of view. It seems there is no escaping the tension between these opposing forces.

FIGURE 6.5 Search results as map locations in the mobile context.

FIGURE 6.6 Search results displayed as thumbnails on Google mobile web.

FIGURE 6.7 Deep links in search results at Yahoo.

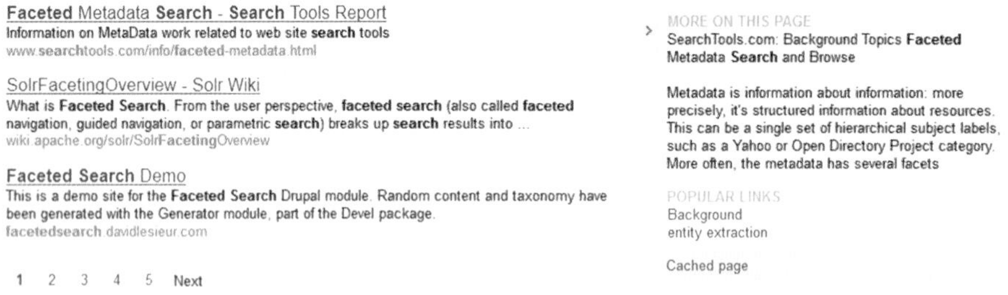

FIGURE 6.8 Search result previews at Bing.

There is, however, an alternative approach. *Previews* allow us to see the detail of an individual item within the context of the search results page. Bing, for example, uses previews to provide further detail in the form of extended snippets, popular links, contact information, and so on (Figure 6.8). Google provides a snapshot of the page with key passages highlighted and displayed in callouts. By being accessible on hover, they provide on-demand access to further detail without interrupting our flow. With previews, we get to see the trees without leaving the wood.

Previews have also been applied to a variety of other contexts, such as for viewing user profiles on social networking sites such as Facebook and LinkedIn. And other organizations (such as Snap Technologies) have extended this approach to the web as a whole, offering on-demand interactive previews for any hyperlinked content. In providing a convenient, lightweight method for *verifying* individual items, previews offer direct support for one of the key search modes discussed in Chapter 3.

Answers and shortcuts

As discussed in Chapter 2, search is a conversation in which we articulate information needs through queries and interpret the responses as matching results. This type of ongoing, iterative dialogue lies at the heart of our information journey. But sometimes our needs can be addressed in a much more direct manner.

Google, for example, allows us to ask direct questions in a variety of forms. When it recognizes the presence of certain trigger words, it responds with weather forecasts, stock quotes, maps, and sports scores (Figure 6.9). We can even track parcels, convert

FIGURE 6.9 Direct answers for focused information needs at Google.

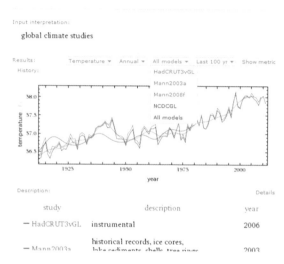

FIGURE 6.10 Beyond traditional search results at Wolfram Alpha.

currencies and ask it to perform all manner of numeric calculations and conversions. In this context, the boundary between search and question answering becomes blurred, with the search box presenting a command-line style of interface to those who can exploit its power and flexibility (Morville, 2010).

Wolfram Alpha extends the concept further still. With graphs, charts, tables, and visualizations all within its repertoire, it chooses the right format for our specific information needs (Figure 6.10). This type of interaction extends the concept of search beyond findability and into a new territory of computational knowledge and inference.

And search results aren't restricted to being passive vessels for communicating information. Quite the contrary: they can become active elements, inviting interaction and direct manipulation. At Google, for example, we can recommend a particular result and share it with colleagues by using the "+1" button (Figure 6.11).

Google Experimental **Search**
www.google.com/experimental/ [·1]
Take **one** for a spin and let us know what you think. Join an experiment and you'll ...
This experiment enables Instant on [Recommend this page] arch results page. ...

FIGURE 6.11 Recommending a search result at Google.

The Masoods headline in Christmas EastEnders

NEW 23 minutes ago
The cast of EastEnders talk about the harrowing
scenes of the **soap's** Christmas episode.

EastEnders previews Christmas twist

Entertainment & Arts / **NEW 47 minutes ago**
... has played Pat Evans - formerly Butcher - since
1986, a year after the BBC One **soap** launched. While
her decision to leave the **soap** was revealed...

Coronation Street stars set for musical stage

21 December 2011
ITV **soap** Coronation Street has been turned into a
stage musical featuring some of the show's best-loved
stars.

FIGURE 6.12 Content can be played directly from the results page at BBC.

Likewise, at major online retailers such as Sainsbury's or Tesco, it is possible to add items to the shopping basket directly from the search results page. And at the BBC, we can play video and audio clips with a single click (Figure 6.12).

Similarly, on iPad and iPhone, we can use Spotlight to search across all our data (Figure 6.13). But the results are more than just placeholders for files: they are actionable objects, offering a direct invitation to play content, make phone calls, or launch applications. In this respect, actionable results provide a bridge to the broader task context of search, helping us progress from finding information to completing goals.

SEARCH RESULTS PAGES

In the previous section, we looked at the ways in which a response to an information need can be articulated, focusing on the various forms that individual search results can take. Each separate result represents a match for our query, and as such, has the potential to fulfill our information needs. But as discussed in Chapter 2, information seeking is a dynamic, iterative activity, for which there is often no single right answer.

A more informed approach therefore is to consider search results not as competing alternatives but as an aggregate response to an information need. In this context, the value lies not so much with the individual results but on the properties and possibilities that emerge when we consider them in their collective form. In this section, we examine the most universal form of aggregation: the search results page.

FIGURE 6.13 Spotlight search provides actionable objects as results.

Basic principles

At its most basic, the role of the search engine results page (SERP) is to present items matching a given query. However, behind this simple brief lies a layer of depth and complexity. First, (as discussed earlier in this chapter), the form of individual search results can vary considerably, from three-line snippets to complex, multifaceted summaries. Second, the structure and organization of the SERPs needs to reflect their context of use, drawing on the dimensions explored in Chapter 3.

Even Google, with its minimalist home page design, manages to pack more than a dozen separate features into its default search results page (Figure 6.14). These can be grouped according their function, such as input, informational, control, or personalization (Wilson, 2011):

1. Input features
   a. Search box including auto-suggest and instant results (on character input)

2. Informational features
   a. Number of results found
   b. Support for query reformulation ("did you mean" and autocorrect)

   c. Individual results consisting of:
      i. Hyperlinked titles with snippets and URLs
      ii. Page preview (available on hover)
      iii. Related metadata, such as previous visits, citations, related articles, and social data (such as page sharing by colleagues)
   d. Related searches
   e. Sponsored links (advertisements)

3. Control features
   a. Faceted navigation menu (for content type, date, etc.)
   b. Search tools menu (sites with images, visited pages, etc.)
   c. Pagination
   d. Options for advanced search and help

4. Personalization features (when logged in)
   a. Profile, settings, notifications, etc.

Despite this apparent complexity, there are some principles that all SERPS should observe. As shown in Chapter 5, query reformulation is a critical step in many information journeys. It is vital therefore that this context is maintained by displaying the current query and allowing it to be edited in place, such as within the search box. Likewise, the SERP

FIGURE 6.14 Minimalist design belies feature-rich complexity in Google's SERPs.

FIGURE 6.15 Smashing Magazine's SERP lacks the context necessary for effective query reformulation.

should also communicate the state of any other navigational context such as current facet selections (see Chapter 7). In fact, this principle is so fundamental that we often take it for granted, and it becomes conspicuous only by its absence: faced with the response shown in Figure 6.15, can you work out what the query was or how best to reformulate it? In this instance, the user is forced to rely on recall rather than recognition, contrary to the principles outlined in Chapter 5. (It was actually a query for the phrase "zero search results," which, ironically for a site with such valuable resources on user experience design, produces zero results.)

A second, related principle is to maintain the context of the current search by displaying the number of matching results. This deceptively simple measure plays a vital role in the information seeking dialogue, as it communicates the magnitude of the current information space and helps the user make more informed query reformulations. For example, can you determine the number of matching iTunes app results shown in Figure 6.16? At first glance (left-hand image), it appears to be absent, but scrolling at the bottom (right hand-image) reveals the value just when we need it most: in the context of a link to show more. Note, however, that the query itself remains absent: perhaps a reflection of the shorter, more focused information needs and reduced query reformulation patterns that characterize mobile search.

Many of the features described above manifest themselves as explicit interface elements. However, there are some features that are implicit to the overall results and become apparent only when we consider the set as a whole. For example, the order in which results are displayed is known to have a profound influence on the search experience, particularly when they are sorted 'best first,' i.e. by topical relevance.

On the web, relevance is calculated using a variety of signals, such as 'on-page' attributes (content and metadata), popularity (inbound links, etc.), behavioral cues (clickstream data) and so on. In fact, the effect of this ordering is so powerful that in

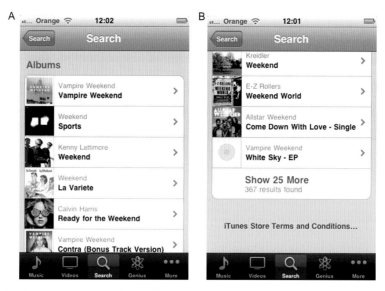

FIGURE 6.16 The iTunes app shows the number of matching results in context.

practice many users go no further than the first page of results, and in many cases scan only the first few items (Joachims et al., 2005). This means that it is important to present an appropriate level of 'diversity' within the first few results. In Figure 6.14 above, for example, we see a diversity represented by a range of different media types and genres (reference works, news items, images, etc.) within the first page of results.

The issue is even more acute for vague or ambiguous queries such as "apple" or "java." Terms like these can have multiple interpretations, and a pure "best first" approach may return an initial page of results biased toward just one of those meanings. A first impression such as this can be misleading, and may undermine the potential for discovery by suggesting to the user that what they are looking for simply isn't there. In this case, 'best first' should ideally provide a little of the best of every interpretation.

Web search engine DuckDuckGo makes a virtue of this: a search for "apple," for example, returns results for all the major senses in the first few results (Figure 6.17). Moreover, it also displays an explicit clarification panel, showing the alternative meanings and offering users the opportunity to clarify their intent. As we will see in Chapter 7, this is a pivotal point in the search experience, when users are invited to explore the subtleties of their information need, and engage in a dialogue that allows them to build their own mental map of the information landscape.

Indeed, the same principle applies within other search contexts. In online retail, for example, it is vital to convey an abundance of product and facilitate serendipitous discovery. Amazon uses this concept to good effect, presenting several alternative interpretations on the first page for an ambiguous query such as "washer" (Figure 6.18).

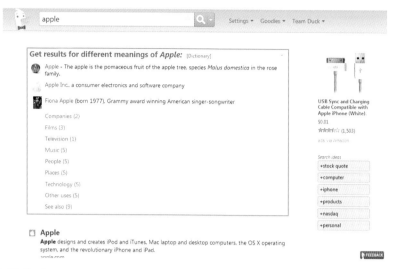

FIGURE 6.17 Clarifying our information need at DuckDuckGo.

FIGURE 6.18 Diversity of search results at Amazon.

Page layouts

In the previous examples, the results are displayed as a list, which is a logical structure for communicating the sort order. But lists don't have to be vertical. In fact, in some environments, it makes more sense to allow users to browse products visually, laying out the results in a two-dimensional grid. This type of "gallery" layout is commonly seen in

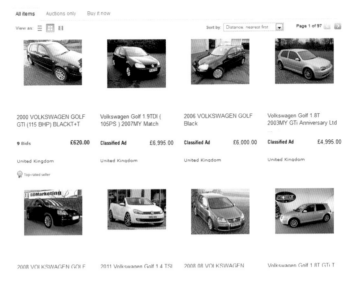

FIGURE 6.19 Gallery view at eBay.

online retail, with each result displayed in a more concise, pictorial form facilitating rapid visual scanning (Figure 6.19). This type of view supports the search modes of exploring and locating that were discussed in Chapter 4.

In a heterogeneous collection, such as a department store, the ideal layout will depend on the particular result set: those items for which appearance is important (e.g., cars, clothing) are naturally suited to a visually oriented layout, whereas others (e.g., computers, electrical goods) may be better suited to a detail-oriented layout. For this reason, it is common to see a control allowing users to switch between views (see top left of Figure 6.19).

Although list and gallery view are popular configurations, they are by no means the only options. Complex products such as electrical components may be more meaningfully viewed using a display that exposes the full detail of their specification, allowing rapid scanning and comparison of their individual attributes (Figure 6.20). This type of view supports key search modes such as analyzing and comparing (see Chapter 4).

In some search contexts, the results may have a geospatial element to them. In this case, the most natural layout is to present them as a two-dimensional map. This approach is particularly appropriate for mobile search results (see Chapter 3), where the spatiotemporal context plays a fundamental role in the relevance of results returned (Figure 6.21).

But maps don't have to be exclusively geographical. In fact, there are other layouts we can use if the landscape we wish to convey is more conceptual in nature. As mentioned in Chapter 3, Web search engine Yippy analyzes the content of search results and presents the output as a set of topical clusters. Carrot2 takes the concept further still, offering a choice of visualizations (Figure 6.22). This approach allows users to gain an impression of the overall themes within the results and explore similar results together within a single group. Like the diversity approaches we discussed earlier, this is another solution for

Viewing 1 - 5 of 3309 products				1 2 3 4 5 Next»
Display			Sort by	Relevancy ▼

	688-9503	255-8450	826-818	466-3891	739-3554
Brand	OSRAM Opto Semiconductors	Avago Technologies	Avago Technologies	Kingbright	New Lumileds Lighting
Manu Part No	LCW W5PM-JZKY-5L7N	HLMP-C315	HLMP-D105	KP-3216SEC	LXM2-PL01-0000
Datasheet					
Mounting	Surface Mount	Through Hole	Through Hole	Surface Mount	Surface Mount
Colour	White	Yellow	Red	Orange	Amber
Intensity	-	147mcd	240mcd	200mcd	-
Peak Wavelength	-	583nm	645nm	610nm	-
Colour Temperature	4000K	-	-	-	-
High Brightness	Yes	-	-	-	Yes
Viewing Angle	120/70°	15°	24°	120°	160°
Luminous Flux	97lm	-	-	-	70lm
Maximum Forward Voltage per Colour	3.7V	2.6V	2.2V	2.5V	3.99V
Maximum Forward Current	1000mA	20mA	30mA	30mA	700mA
Lens Shape Type	Rectangular	Circular	Circular	Rectangular	Circular

FIGURE 6.20 Parametric view at RS Components.

FIGURE 6.21 Search results are shown in map view on Google mobile.

dealing with vague or ambiguous queries, inviting users to explore and comprehend the subtleties of their particular information need.

In the previous example, the clusters are generated dynamically from a particular results set. But it's also possible to generate conceptual maps using static or "curated" metadata. A wine catalog, for example, might have metadata for color, varietal, vintage, region, and so on. These can all be presented as separate dimensions or *facets* by which users can explore and refine a particular result set. This approach, known as *faceted*

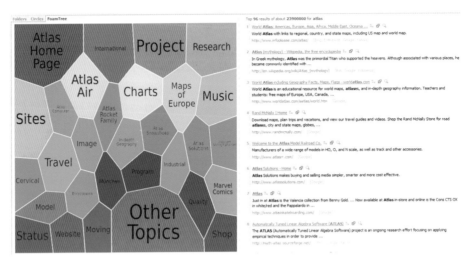

FIGURE 6.22 Search results are clustered by topic at Carrot2.

search, has become the foundation of online retail and many other commercial search and discovery applications. We'll look at faceted search in more detail in Chapter 7.

Blended results

As discussed earlier, one of the challenges of displaying content from a heterogeneous collection is that different types of results require different layouts—some may require a detail oriented view, others visually oriented, and so on. One solution is to invite users to clarify their intent (e.g., by selecting a product category) so that their results converge on a reasonably homogeneous set. Then, as in the eBay example, they can simply select whichever view is most appropriate for their results.

But it isn't always appropriate or desirable to persuade users to narrow their results down to a particular category so early in the dialogue. Sometimes, supporting a multiplicity of formats on the search results page can be a virtue in itself. This approach is particularly appropriate for information- or content-oriented sites, where the goal is not so much to guide users down a specific "funnel" (e.g., to the shopping basket or checkout pages) but to encourage them to engage in further exploration and discovery. The *Guardian* newspaper, for example, shows results laid out in vertical list (Figure 6.23) but grouped according to category (editor's picks, tags, most recent articles, etc.).

A similar approach is applied by web search engines in response to vague or ambiguous queries. Just like the topical diversity we considered earlier, a diversity of formats or media can also facilitate exploration and discovery. A query for "jets" on Google, for example, returns sports scores, news items, web pages and more. However, unlike the previous example, these are displayed in an undifferentiated vertical list (Figure 6.24).

By contrast, business information provider Reuters groups search results according to medium (news, blogs, video, or pictures), which it displays in separate panels

FIGURE 6.23 Search results are grouped vertically by type at the *Guardian*.

FIGURE 6.24 Blended search results and media types at Google.

(Figure 6.25). News items take precedence as the default shown in the main panel, but this display can be replaced by another content type by selecting the appropriate tab.

Apple's iTunes store (Figure 6.26) takes the structured approach a step further, displaying a variety of content types on the SERP as actionable objects (see "Displaying

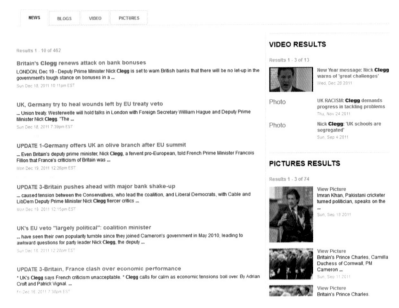

FIGURE 6.25 Search results are grouped by medium at Reuters.

FIGURE 6.26 Varied content types displayed in individual panels with custom controls at the iTunes Store.

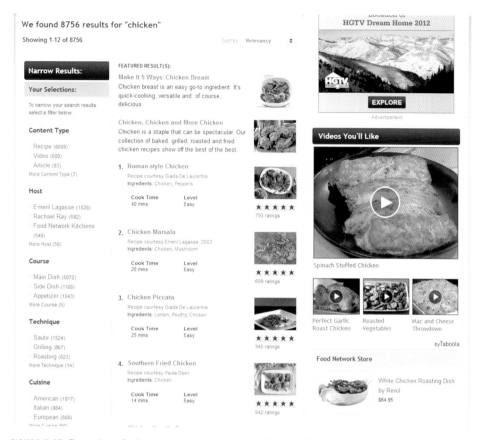

FIGURE 6.27 Promotion of related content and products at the Food Network.

Search Results" earlier in this chapter) in individual panels with custom controls (see "Manipulating Search Results" later in this chapter).

The layout of the SERP can also provide opportunities for promoting particular content items or products. At the Food Network, for example, the primary content consists of recipes, but the SERP also promotes related content in the form of videos and products from the Food Network store, using a sidebar on the right-hand side (Figure 6.27). Like many other online retailers, this site also employs the concept of "featured results," that is, items that would have appeared within the regular search results for a given query, but for commercial reasons (e.g., sponsorship) are prioritized in some way, usually using layout (e.g., by displaying them above the regular search results) or highlighting them visually (e.g., by applying a different design treatment), and so on.

Featured results are typically generated automatically, that is, from the result set returned for a given query. But they don't have to be derived algorithmically: sometimes it makes more sense to exercise some editorial control. At the *Guardian*, for example

(Figure 6.23), we see "Editors' picks" at the top of the SERP. These are commonly known as "best bets," that is, items that are known to be good matches for popular queries. As with many natural language phenomena, keyword queries obey a power law (Zipf, 1949). There are thus a small number of very common terms but a large number of very rare terms, producing a "long tail" distribution. Preselecting good matches for each of the small number of items in the "short head" can deliver a substantial return on investment.

Zero results pages

As seen in Chapter 5, there are many techniques we can apply to facilitate the process of query formulation, such as guidance in the form of as-you-type suggestions and support in the form of "did you mean" and autocorrections. We've also discussed how partial match strategies can deal with esoteric query term combinations that would otherwise produce zero results. And we've discussed how scoped search can benefit from a fall-back strategy that searches across all categories when searching within one produces zero results.

These techniques all help to minimize the likelihood of failed searches by avoiding the problem at the source. But inevitably, some queries just don't return any meaningful results. Sometimes this may be due to an error of some sort; in other cases, the user may be looking for something that simply can't be found. (As shown in Chapter 5, this problem is particularly acute for "search within.") Either way, if we can't prevent a zero results outcome, we must deal with it effectively.

As mentioned earlier, one of the most basic principles of SERP design is to maintain the context of the search by clearly displaying the number of results found. However, there are still many sites and applications that fail to follow this guideline and then compound the problem by failing to provide an explicit message when zero results are returned (Nudelman, 2011).

But the issue isn't just about communication: in addition to ensuring that users understand the outcome, we should also help them to rectify it. In this respect, the zero results page is an opportunity to provide support in the form of advice and tools for query reformulation. Sadly, the zero results page at Smashing Magazine (seen earlier in Figure 6.15) provides neither of these. Slightly more helpful is the Apple Store, which provides basic advice but misses the opportunity to provide direct support (Figure 6.28).

Classified ad site Carzone, by contrast, gives clear messaging and useful advice and also provides the means to address the issue by removing the nonmatching search criteria (Figure 6.29).

In the absence of any of these strategies, it is still possible to facilitate productive interaction with a zero results page. The absence of results creates an opportunity to promote exploration and discovery through a range of other navigation options such as top searches, featured products, popular items, and so on. There seems to be little virtue in presenting a blank screen for a zero SERP when all the other pages work so hard to make every pixel count.

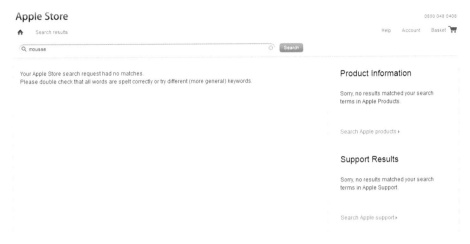

FIGURE 6.28 Limited support for query reformulation on the Apple Store zero results page.

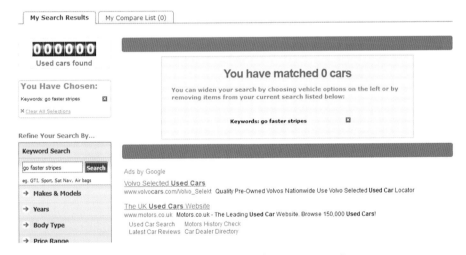

FIGURE 6.29 Direct support for query reformulation on the Carzone zero results page.

MANIPULATING SEARCH RESULTS

One of the key insights to emerge from Part 1 is that search is more than just finding: in fact, search tasks of any complexity involve iteration across a number of levels of task context. From information retrieval at the lowest level to work task at the highest, searchers engage in a whole host of activities in the pursuit of their goals.

Of course, locating (known) items may be the stereotypical search task with which we are all familiar, but it is far from being the only one. Instead, for many search tasks we

FIGURE 6.30 Varying implementations of pagination at Google, Bing, and Yahoo (desktop).

need to analyze, compare, verify, evaluate, synthesize; in short, we need to manipulate and *interact* with the results. The previous section focused on informational features; our concern here is with interactivity. In this section, we consider techniques for managing and manipulating search results.

Pagination

One of the fundamental principles we explored previously was the trade-off between detail and screen space in displaying search results: too detailed and they risk wasting valuable screen space; too succinct and vital information may be omitted. But no matter how compact we make them, at some point there will inevitably be too many results to display on a single screen. When this occurs, the common solution is to apply some form of pagination.

Pagination confers several benefits: it limits load time (by dividing the results into manageable 'chunks'); it provides a measure of how far through the set the user has progressed; and it shows how much further they can go. Implementations vary considerably, with Google, Bing, and Yahoo all offering their own distinctive interpretations (Figure 6.30). What they have in common is a list of numbered pages (with a highlight on the current page) surrounded by links to "previous" and "next." But they differ in that Google uses the opportunity to further reinforce its branding and idiosyncratic use of the Google logo, whereas Bing and Yahoo deliver a more immediately usable design through the use of larger, clearer targets with a visible rollover behavior.

These implementations differ further when applied to the mobile context (Figure 6.31). Google, for example, maintains consistency with the desktop by using a control that differs little in behavior; loading a further ten results each time. Bing, by contrast, offers a link to "more results," which returns a further page of results that load on demand. This design means that the user can simply scroll to the bottom and the next set of results will be appended, without reloading the page. A similar approach is seen at Yahoo, in which ten additional results are appended to the current set on each invocation of the "Show more web results …" button. Interestingly, these approaches are now migrating to the desktop, with Google Images and Twitter both offering "infinite scroll" search results rather than discrete pagination.

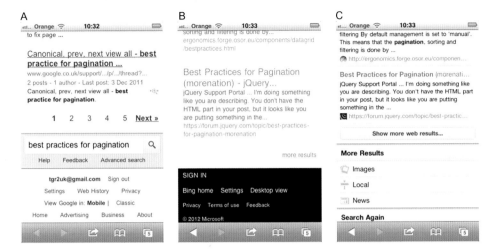

FIGURE 6.31 Varying implementations of pagination at Google, Bing, and Yahoo (mobile).

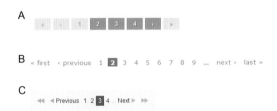

FIGURE 6.32A, B, AND C Augmented pagination controls at Design Snack, Drupal.org, and Programmable Web.

Although infinite scroll offers a more seamless experience (minimizing disruptive page reloads) and forms a natural expression of the fluid interactivity of smartphones and tablet displays, it does have a number of drawbacks. First, it is much harder for users to determine precisely where they are in the result set or to navigate to a particular section. Second, it is no longer possible to bookmark an individual page of results.

Note that in the previous examples, there is no control to navigate directly to the first or last pages because on the Web it may not be practicable to calculate the exact number of results for a given query or indeed be worthwhile offering access to the last page in the list (especially if they are sorted by relevance). Google, for example, does not serve more than 1,000 results for any query. By contrast, for more modest collections such as online discussion forums and other community sites, it may be possible to allow direct access to the complete result set. In such cases, the pagination controls may be augmented with options to navigate directly to the first or last item (Figure 6.32).

Sorting and filtering

In web search, it is common for results to be ordered by relevance to the query. But in other environments, such as online retail, a variety of other sort orders may be possible. These may vary from universal attributes such as price, customer rating or delivery date, to category-specific attributes such as release date for audio content, or publication date for books, and so on. Sort options such as these are commonly implemented using a dropdown control, which allows the user to apply different sort keys (Figure 6.33).

For some types of highly attributed content, it is possible to present the results in a manner that renders the sorting options even more apparent and invites greater interaction. At automotive classified site Carzone, for example, search results can be sorted by year, mileage, engine (size), price, and other factors (Figure 6.34). This is achieved using a tabular panel, in which the column headers can be selected to choose a sort key and toggle the direction (ascending or descending). Likewise, searching the iTunes desktop app produces a heterogeneous, blended results page (see the earlier section "Search Results Pages"), but songs are rendered in their own tabular panel to allow sorting along the dimensions of album, artist, time, popularity, and so on (Figure 6.35).

However, sorting using column headers has a number of shortcomings. For example, the sort direction is not always immediately apparent and may not always default to the most common use case. In addition, sorting by attributes that are not displayed becomes

A	B	C
Sort by Best Match ▾	Sort by Relevance ▾	Sort by: Most Relevant ▾
Price: Low to High	Relevance	Lowest Weekly Price
vious 1 Price: High to Low	Popularity	Most Relevant
New	Price: Low to High	Brand Alphabetical
• 97¢ Best Sellers	Price: High to Low	Best Sellers
• Fre Customer Rating: High to Low	Avg. Customer Review	New In
Title: A-Z	Publication Date	Highest Rated
Title: Z-A		Price High to Low
		Price Low to High

FIGURE 6.33A, B, AND C Drop down controls for sorting at Walmart, Amazon, and Littlewoods.

FIGURE 6.34 Column headers for sorting at Carzone.

impossible, and common retail use cases such as sorting by popularity or bestselling become problematic because the corresponding column would be unlikely to contain anything particularly useful in each of the table cells (Nudelman, 2011).

Note also that not all attributes are equally meaningful as sort keys. For example, the sequence generated when sorting by a nominal attribute such as name or description is not inherently meaningful in the same way as sorting by a quantitative attribute such as mileage or price (Hearst, 2009). However, the alphabetical ordering does support other common use cases, such as scanning the list to find a particular model name.

In addition to sorting, most online retailers also offer options for *filtering* results. In principle, sorting and filtering are quite different operations, in the sense that sorting changes the display order of the results, whereas filtering actually removes items from that set. But in practice, to many users—particularly those with low technical expertise (see Chapter 1)—they are practically indistinguishable, partially due to use of an inappropriate mental model, but this is also an emergent property of the interaction: because many users do not explore beyond the first page of results, sorting controls act like a de facto filter, in the sense that they remove items from the immediate view.

A kind of hybrid example of sorting and filtering (and pagination) can be seen at the iPhone App Store (Figure 6.36). Here, content is grouped into various default categories to facilitate browsing along various popular dimensions (such as Top Paid, Top Free, etc.). Selecting the appropriate category presents the results filtered by that category (e.g., Top Paid filters out any free apps) but also presents them with an associated sort order. However, in some cases the sort key is an independent attribute (e.g., Top Paid filters by category but sorts by popularity), whereas in some cases the category serves both functions (Top Grossing both filters and sorts by revenue).

A more mainstream use of filtering is to allow users to refine their results by one or more independent dimensions or *facets*. This approach, known as *faceted search*, has become the dominant paradigm among online retail and many other commercial search applications. We'll look at faceted search in more detail in Chapter 7, exploring fundamentals such as layout and display along with more advanced topics such as wayfinding techniques and interaction models.

Songs   1-50   See All >

#	Name	Album	Artist	Time	Popularity	Price
1	Last	Last	The Unthanks	7:09		£0.99 BUY ▾
2	Last	Broken - EP	Nine Inch Nails	4:44		£0.79 BUY ▾
3	Last Friday Night (T.G.I.F.)	Teenage Dream	Katy Perry	3:50		£0.99 BUY ▾
4	Last Request (New Version)	Last Request - Single	Paolo Nutini	3:42		£0.99 BUY ▾
5	Last Friday Night (T.G.I.F.)	Last Friday Night (T.g.i.f.) - Single	Last Friday Night	3:50		£0.79 BUY ▾
6	Queen of Hearts	Last	The Unthanks	4:32		£0.59 BUY ▾
7	Last Rhythm	Back to the Old Skool	Last Rhythm	6:29		£0.99 BUY ▾
8	Last	The Ink Victory - EP	The Spin Cycle	4:24		£0.79 BUY ▾
9	The Age of the Understatement	The Age of the Understatement	The Last Shadow Puppets	3:09		£0.99 BUY ▾
10	Best for Last	19	ADELE	4:18		£0.99 BUY ▾

FIGURE 6.35 Column headers for sorting at iTunes.

FIGURE 6.36 Button controls for sorting on the iPhone App Store.

Query clarification

Earlier in this chapter we looked at search result diversity and explored the ways in which this concept can be used to communicate the alternative meanings for vague and ambiguous queries. A query such as "apple," for example, might return results relevant to the company or the fruit. By including these alternative meanings as part of the first results page, we invite users to explore the subtleties of their information need and help them to build their own mental map of the information landscape.

But sometimes it is appropriate to resolve the ambiguity in a more direct manner. In online retail, for example, it is in everybody's interest to help users define their query more precisely, so that products offered more closely match their needs and intentions. A query for "MP3" might return results for players, accessories, or indeed content, but until their real intention is established, the dialogue remains something of a guessing game. Instead, we should first invite users to clarify their intent (Tunkelang, 2009).

There are a number of approaches to query clarification. One of the most common is to display the alternative interpretations in the form of matching categories and invite users to choose a more precise category for their information need. Amazon, for example, does this is in a subtle manner. A query here for "mp3" returns several million results, including players, accessories, and content on the first page (along with best bets such as a promotion for the Amazon MP3 store and featured results for the Electronics Store). However, the primary navigation option in the left hand menu is a category selector (Figure 6.37). In addition, the user is invited to choose a department (i.e., category) to enable sorting. Once a category is selected, facets specific to that category can then be

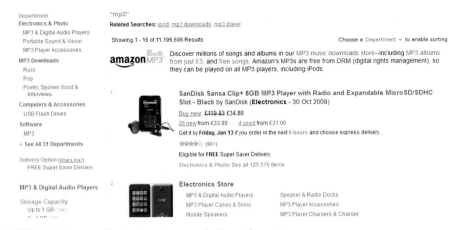

FIGURE 6.37 Query clarification by category selection at Amazon.

FIGURE 6.38 Prominent category selection at Amazon.

offered in the left-hand menu, such as storage capacity and features for an MP3 player, genre for a music download, and so on.

A more conspicuous variant can be seen at electrical retailer Comet. As expected, an ambiguous query here such as "washer" returns a mixed set of results. However, this time the category selector is displayed much more prominently, directly above the search results (Figure 6.38). A more direct approach such as this is more likely to solicit an early clarification, but at the expense of pushing actual product results further down the page. Clearly, there is a balance to be found: even an innocuous query such as "fridge" can

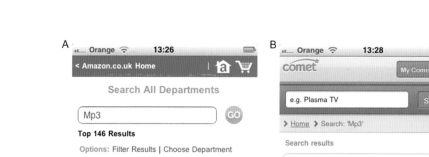

FIGURE 6.39A AND B Contrasting approaches to query clarification at Amazon and Comet.

generate a category selector that extends over 20 lines in height, occupying almost all the visible screen space.

Indeed, the difference in approach is also reflected in their respective mobile sites: Amazon focuses on the search results, with a relatively unobtrusive invitation to select a category from the departments listed at the foot of the page, whereas Comet focuses on category selection (Figure 6.39). Both show the number of results returned, but Comet fails to display the current query in editable form (compromising the principle we discussed previously).

A more immersive approach can be seen at online retailer Littlewoods. Here, the category selector occupies the whole result page, showing examples from each category as separate groups (Figure 6.40). These groups include an invitation to view the complete set, as in, "View all 69 results in Electricals." The selector is also supported by a faceted menu on the left that displays the category headings as menu items.

But presenting a category selector isn't the only way to support query clarification. For certain popular queries, it may be possible to adopt a "best bets" approach that defaults instead to the most likely category. For example, a query for "washer" at online retailer Debenhams returns a custom landing page specifically for kitchen appliances (Figure 6.41). Although the precise query context is missing from this page, further clarification is still possible by selecting a subcategory from the faceted menu on the left.

Of course, all of these approaches are ways of encouraging users to clarify their intent *after* the query has been entered. But we shouldn't forget techniques we can apply *before* we even get to that point. As discussed in Chapter 5, as-you-type suggestions can make a

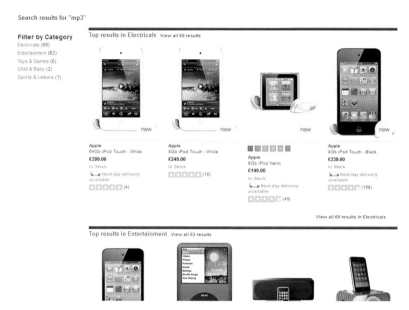

FIGURE 6.40 Full-page query clarification at Littlewoods.

FIGURE 6.41 A "best bets" approach to query clarification at Debenhams.

profound difference to the process of query reformulation, correcting spelling mistakes and offering suggestions that the user might not have otherwise considered.

And once the query has been entered, related searches provide an additional indication of diversity, offering a starting point for further query clarification (such as "mp3 downloads" versus "mp3 player" in Figure 6.37). And of course the facets themselves represent a conceptual map of the information landscape, showing areas of abundance and inviting further productive exploration and discovery. Each of these plays a part in the information journey, facilitating the users' progress from a vague or ambiguous query to the satisfaction of their information need.

Comparing

As mentioned earlier, there is a tension in the design of search result snippets: too detailed and they waste screen space; too brief and they induce pogosticking. But the optimal level of detail is not a static concept. Instead, it depends on the context; in particular, the user's search mode.

In the early stages of the information journey, the user's primary concern is on formulating effective queries and developing an initial overview of the results. This stage is characterized by search modes such as *locating* and *exploring*, in which snippets play a vital role in helping the user identify promising items worthy of further examination. But once those candidates have been identified a different pattern of behavior may emerge, where the focus is less on exploring, and more on *analyzing* and *comparing* individual items. These search modes are fundamental to online retail, where users need to identify the best option from those available. In this context, a different type of view is needed.

A common approach is to provide access to what is popularly known as a comparison view. Computing equipment retailer Dabs, for example, provides a column of checkboxes next to each search result, which marks items for comparison (Figure 6.42).

Selecting a "Compare" button at the head of the column opens a separate view that shows the full detail of each item in a separate column, enabling easy comparison of the individual product attributes (Figure 6.43).

However, in this instance, the user has inadvertently exceeded the maximum number of items that can be shown. A better approach is to avoid that possibility at the outset. Online retailer Best Buy, for example, shows both the size limit and the current state of the comparison view using a dynamically updating preview (Figure 6.44).

The goal of the comparison page is, of course, to support *analyzing* and *comparing* individual products. Best Buy offers further support for these search modes by organizing

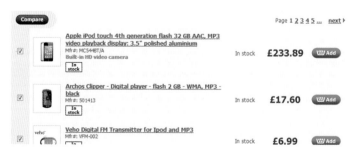

FIGURE 6.42 Selecting items for comparison at Dabs.

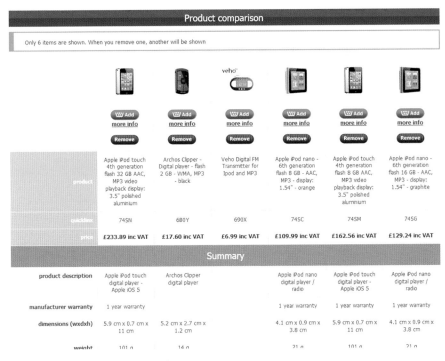

FIGURE 6.43 Product comparison at Dabs.

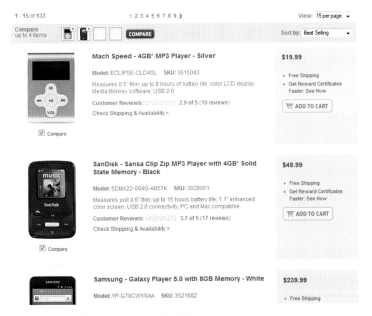

FIGURE 6.44 Selecting items for comparison at Best Buy.

the attributes into logical groups and providing an option to automatically highlight the differences between products (Figure 6.45).

Electrical retailer Comet also provides a comparison preview function using a popup "item tray" attached to the foot of the page (Figure 6.46). However, their comparison page opens as a dialog overlay within the context of the search results page, eliminating the

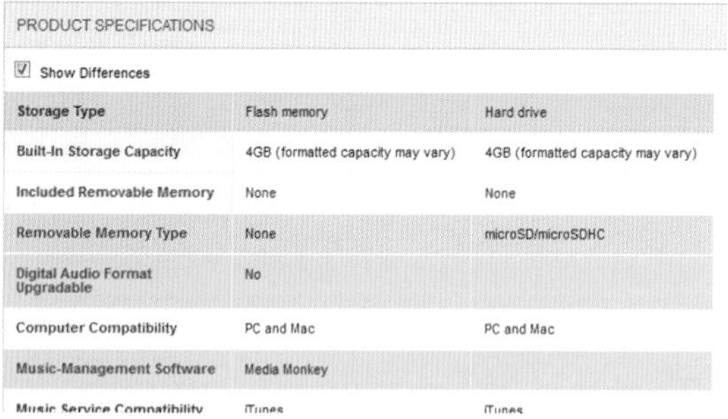

FIGURE 6.45 Highlighting differences between products at Best Buy.

FIGURE 6.46 Product comparison at Comet.

disruptive effect of a page reload and observing the design principle to "stay on the page" (Scott and Neill (2009)). Comet, with its strong emphasis on category selection (see "Search Results Pages"), also maintains independent comparison lists for each of its major product categories. This approach prevents the somewhat nonsensical scenario of a user inadvertently trying to compare completely unrelated items (such as a toaster with a television).

SUMMARY AND BEST PRACTICES

Results pages play a crucial role in the search experience, conveying to users a response to their information needs and engaging them in a dialogue that guides them along their information journey. By drawing on a broad repertoire of layouts, views, and configurations, results pages can support a variety of search modes and contexts. And even when there are no results to return, these pages can still be used to facilitate productive exploration and discovery.

Search results pages should also guide users in clarifying their query and broader information needs. Pagination, sorting, and filtering can then provide the means to explore the results and find promising directions. And in subsequent stages, comparison views can support the detailed analysis of individual items. In the next chapter, we'll add a further layer of depth and refinement, exploring the types of dialogue that can be facilitated by faceted search.

Displaying search results

- Find a balance between richness and diversity: too detailed and screen space is wasted; too succinct and vital information may be omitted
  - Look out for pogosticking and other symptoms of weak information scent
  - Consider the users' characteristics, their tasks and the broader context
- Use query-oriented summaries that show the keywords in context; highlight matching terms
- Adopt a consistent approach that clearly indicates the composition of each search result; Customize the presentation according to the search context
- Use previews to provide access to further detail

Search results pages

- Consider search results not as competing alternatives, but as an aggregate response to an information need
- Maintain context by displaying:
  - The current query (and allow it to be edited in place)
  - The state of any other navigational context such as current facet selections
  - The number of matching results

- Present an appropriate level of diversity, particularly for vague or ambiguous queries

- Apply a layout that matches the result set:
  - Gallery view for items whose appearance is important
  - List or detail view for complex or highly attributed items
  - Map view for geospatial data

- Allow the user to switch between layouts

Blended results

- Use sidebars or complementary panels to promote related items

- Distinguish featured results using layout and/or visual highlighting

- Use best bets to provide effective matches for popular queries

Zero results pages

- Provide an explicit message when zero results are returned

- Provide support in the form of advice and tools for query reformulation

- Display other navigation options such as top searches, featured products, popular items, and so on

Pagination

- Display the page range using large target areas and a hover effect where appropriate

- Identify the current page, and provide Previous and Next options

- Consider an infinite scroll approach where contextually appropriate, such as in mobile contexts

- For limited collections, provide options to navigate directly to the first and last pages

- Allow users to change the default pagination setting (number of results)

Sorting and filtering

- Provide sort options that are specific to the category of results

- Offer a tabular style where sorting is a key user need (e.g., for highly attributed data)

- Be aware that sorting and filtering are often misunderstood by users

Query clarification

- Provide support to clarify vague or ambiguous queries, such as through an explicit category selector; Choose a location and configuration that is consistent with the users, their tasks and the broader search context

- Consider a "best bets" approach for popular queries

Comparing

- Communicate the maximum size of the comparison view; Provide a dynamic preview where possible

- Allow users to highlight the differences between individual results

- Maintain independent comparison lists for different result categories

REFERENCES

Drori, O., & Alon, N. (2003). Using document classification for displaying search results lists. *Journal of Information Science, 29*(2), 97–106.

Hearst, M. (2009). *Search user interfaces*. Cambridge: Cambridge University Press.

Joachims, T., Granka, L., Pan, B., Hembrooke, H., & Gay, G. (2005). Accurately interpreting clickthrough data as implicit feedback. Proceedings of the 28th Annual International ACM SIGIR Conference on Research and Development in Information Retrieval (SIGIR'05), Salvador, Brazil, pp. 154–161.

Marchionini, G. (1995). *Information seeking in electronic environments*. Cambridge: Cambridge University Press.

Morville, P. (2010). *Search patterns*. Sebastopol, CA: O'Reilly Media.

Muramatsu, J., & Pratt, W. (2001). Transparent queries: Investigation users' mental models of search engines. Proceedings of the 24th Annual International ACM SIGIR Conference on Research and Development in Information Retrieval (SIGIR'01), pp. 217–224.

Nudelman, G. (2011). *Designing search: UX strategies for ecommerce success*. Hoboken, NJ: Wiley.

Schwarz, J., & Morris, M. (2011). Augmenting web pages and search results to support credibility assessment. Proceedings of the 2011 Annual Conference on Human Factors in Computing Systems (ACM), pp. 1245–1254. Vancouver, BC.

Scott, B., & Neil, T. (2009). *Designing web interfaces: Principles and patterns for rich interactions*. Sebastopol, CA: O'Reilly Media.

Spool, J. (2005). Galleries: the hardest working page on your site. User Interface Engineering. Retrieved January 13, 2012, from http://www.uie.com/articles/galleries/.

Tombros, A., & Sanderson, M. (1998). Advantages of query biased summaries in information retrieval. Proceedings of the 21st Annual International ACM SIGIR Conference on Research and Development in Information Retrieval (SIGIR'98), pp. 2–10.

Tunkelang, D. (2009). *Faceted search*. San Rafael: Morgan Claypool.

Wilson, M. L. (2011). Search user interface design. In G. Marchionini (Ed.), *Synthesis Lectures on Information Concepts, Retrieval, and Services*. San Rafael: Morgan & Claypool.

Zipf, G. K. (1949). *Human behavior and the principle of least effort*. Cambridge, Massachusetts: Addison-Wesley.

The Element of Surprise
Daniel Tunkelang

Surprise is not a word that user interface designers typically like to hear. Indeed, the principle of least surprise is that systems should always strive to act in a way that least surprises the user—that the user experience should match the user's expectations and mental models (Saltzer and Kaashoek, 2009).

Like many interface design principles, the principle of least surprise assumes that software applications exist to be useful. In utility-oriented applications, surprise causes distraction and delay—negatives that good designers work to avoid. Indeed, surprise requires the user to learn and adjust his or her mental model, thus introducing friction into the goal-seeking process.

But we are seeing a growth of applications whose main value to the user is not utility, but entertainment. Indeed, a recent Nielsen report claims that the top two online activities for Americans are social networks and games (Nielsen, 2010). People increasingly expect the Internet to be at least as fun as it is useful.

Even search, which would seem to be the poster child for the utility of online services, is being pressed into the service of entertainment—particularly in the context of "casual leisure searching" (Wilson & Elsweiler, 2010). There are a variety of scenarios in which search isn't about the use of finding something but rather about enjoying the experience. Indeed, casual leisure searching creates the anomalous situation of information-seeking behavior without the user having an information need.

Surely the primary job of a search engine is to deliver utility to users. Users already have lots of ways to waste time; a search engine aims to make their productivity-oriented time more effective and efficient. But fun and utility are not mutually exclusive. For example, news serves the utilitarian ideal of informing the citizenry, but many people read news as a pleasant way to pass the time. Social networks are another example serving a similar function, perhaps with a balance more toward the entertainment of the spectrum but still providing genuine social utility.

A common feature of both of these examples is that users regularly return to the same site expecting the unexpected. The transient nature of news and social news feeds promises an endless supply of fresh content, produced more quickly than users can consume it. This situation is in stark contrast to those of typical web search queries, for which the results are expected to be largely static. Indeed, people may set up alerts to inform them of novel search results, but they are unlikely to regularly visit a bookmarked search results page the way they regularly visit a news or social network site.

Is novelty the only source of surprise? Novelty certainly helps, but it is not a necessity. An alternative source is randomness—even something as simple as Wikipedia's "random article" feature. But a more plausible place to introduce randomness is in recommendations, whether for products or content. Because recommendations are good guesses at best, a bit of randomness can help ensure that the guesses are interesting. Indeed, people prefer the use of randomness to induce diversity in recommendations, if only to avoid being recommended the same things over and over again (Lathia et al., 2010).

For utility-oriented information needs, it is important to provide users with accurate, predictable, and efficient tools. But we cannot dismiss the value of making the experience enjoyable and even surprising. Sometimes we just need to offer our users a little bit of surprise to keep it interesting. Or, as Mary Poppins tells us, "In every job that must be done, there is an element of fun. You find the fun, and—SNAP—the job's a game!"

Daniel Tunkelang leads a data science team at LinkedIn that analyzes terabytes of data to produce products and insights that serve LinkedIn's more than 150 million members. Prior to LinkedIn, Daniel led a local search quality team at Google. Daniel was a founding employee of faceted search pioneer Endeca, where he spent ten years as Chief Scientist. He has authored 14 patents, written a textbook on faceted search, created the annual symposium on human–computer interaction and information retrieval (HCIR), and participates in the premier research conferences on information retrieval, knowledge management, databases, recommender systems, and data mining. Daniel holds a PhD in Computer Science from CMU, as well as BS and MS degrees from MIT.

References

Lathia, N., Hailes, S., Capra, L., & Amatriain, X. (2010). Temporal diversity in recommender systems. Proceeding of the 33rd International ACM SIGIR Conference on Research and Development in Information Retrieval. Geneva, Switzerland.

Nielsen. (2010). "What Americans do online: social media and games dominate activity. http://blog.nielsen.com/nielsenwire/online_mobile/what-americans-do-online-social-media-and-games-dominate-activity/.

Saltzer, J. H., & Kaashoek, F. (2009). Principles of computer system design: An introduction. Burlington, MA: Morgan Kaufmann.

Wilson, M. L., & Elsweiler, D. (2010). Casual-leisure searching: The exploratory search scenarios that break our current models. 4th International Workshop on Human-Computer Interaction and Information Retrieval, pp. 28–31. New Brunswick, NJ.

Faceted Search

7

You ask what is the use of classification, arrangement, systemization? I answer
you: order and simplification are the first steps toward the mastery of a subject—
the actual enemy is the unknown.

—*Thomas Mann*

In Chapter 5, we reviewed the various ways in which an information need can be
articulated, focusing on its expression via some form of query. And in Chapter 6, we
considered ways in which the response can be articulated, focusing on its expression
as a set of search results. Together, these two elements lie at the heart of the search
experience, defining and shaping the information seeking dialogue. In this chapter,
we take that dialogue to a further level of sophistication, in the form of faceted search.

Faceted search offers a unique potential to transform the search experience.
It provides a flexible framework that enables users to satisfy a wide variety of information
needs, ranging from simple fact retrieval to complex exploratory search and discovery-
oriented problem solving. When combined with keyword search, the approach becomes
incredibly powerful—so much so that faceted search is now the dominant interaction
paradigm for many information access applications, particularly ecommerce and site
search (Tunkelang, 2009).

Moreover, researchers such as Marti Hearst have demonstrated that faceted search
provides more effective information-seeking support to users than conventional keyword
search (Hearst, 2006b). In this chapter, we build on that foundation, reviewing the key
principles and patterns for designing effective faceted search experiences, including layout,
default state, display format, showing additional values, communicating navigational state,
and interaction patterns.

DEFINITIONS

Before we go any further, we should establish some basic terminology. *Facets* are essentially independent properties or *dimensions* by which we can classify an object. For instance, a book might be classified using an Author facet, a Subject facet, and a Date facet. *Faceted navigation* enables users to explore information spaces by progressively refining their choices in each dimension. For example, we could explore a collection of books by selecting a specific author, subject, or date range. Selections are made by applying facet values, which determine the current results set. The set of selections active at any given time is known as the *navigational context*, which corresponds to the user's current location in the information space. *Faceted search* is then the combination of faceted navigation with other forms of search (such as those discussed in Chapter 5).

A key principle of faceted search is to minimize the likelihood of zero results by guiding users toward productive navigational choices. In practice, this means displaying only currently available facet values (i.e., those that apply to the current navigational context), and eliminating those that would lead to dead ends. (However, there are exceptions to this such as the use of *smart dead ends*, which we'll discuss later in the chapter.)

Facet semantics

Facets can be either *single-select* or *multi-select*. In the former case, the facet values are mutually exclusive: only one may be applied at any given time. For example, a particular copy of book may be assumed to have only one location: if it is in Library X, then by definition it cannot be simultaneously in Libraries Y or Z. This facet is therefore single-select. Conversely, some facets represent values that are not mutually exclusive—in other words, more than one may apply at any given time. For example, a given book may have more than one Author: if it is coedited by Professor X, then it could also be simultaneously coedited by Professors Y and Z. This facet is therefore multi-select.

Multi-select facets can either be *multi-select OR* or *multi-select AND*. In the first case, OR, we assume that the values are combined *disjunctively*; for example, a given book may have been published in either 2001, 2002, OR 2003. In the second case, AND, we assume that the values are combined *conjunctively*; for example, a given book may have been coauthored by Tony Russell-Rose AND Tyler Tate. Multi-select AND, which implies that the facet values must be applied in their totality, tends to be somewhat rare in faceted search. One legitimate example could be purchasing a car: if the user specifies that he or she is looking for features *air con*, *sat nav*, and *sunroof*, the assumption is that he or she wants ALL of these features to be present, rather than just a subset of them (e.g., air con OR sat nav OR sunroof). As an aside, if we adopt the definition of facets as representing only mutually exclusive attributes, then a multi-select AND facet is actually a collection of Boolean facets that are grouped together for convenience.

Facet states and behaviors

By convention, values applied *across* different facets are normally applied conjunctively (e.g., Author = Russell-Rose AND Subject = Search AND Date = 2012) whereas values applied *within* a given facet are normally applied disjunctively (e.g., Date = 2010 OR Date = 2011 OR Date = 2012).

Facet states should reflect the current navigational context. For example, if the user selects a particular Location, then any other values for Location are no longer applicable to the current result set (because this facet is single-select). In some faceted search applications, this facet would then be removed from display because there are no further choices available. (Of course, if the user deselects the Location, the facet should reappear.)

Facets can also enter a kind of passive state indirectly. For example, the values applied in Facet A may result in the available values in Facet B being reduced to a singleton. In our library example, if we select books authored by Tyler Tate, we may discover that the only applicable Date is 2012. In some faceted search applications, facets in this state are also removed from display.

LAYOUT

One of the first issues in designing faceted search is deciding where to place the faceted navigation menu. (Note that we use the term *faceted search* here to describe the overall user experience, in contrast to *faceted navigation menu*, which describes the component that displays the currently available facets.) There are three main choices of layout: vertical, horizontal, and hybrid. Let's examine each in turn.

Vertical layout

Vertical layout is by far the most common. This configuration scales well to variations in the number of facets displayed, and the common orientation with the search results (which are also listed vertically by convention) provides a visual coherence that helps reinforce the relationship between the selections made in one component and the results returned in the other. An example of this configuration (from eBay) is shown in Figure 7.1.

Figure 7.1 shows the facets placed on the left, which is a common convention for navigation menus (at least for cultures where the reading direction is left to right). It also helps maintain visibility if the browser is resized. Kalbach (2010a) also argues in favor of location on the left-hand side. However, a number of sites have chosen to locate the facets on the right, including Edinburgh University's library catalogue (Figure 7.2), although the motivation for placing the facets on the right in this case may simply be to direct attention to the "concept browser" control on the left.

Horizontal layout

An alternative to vertical layout is to arrange the facets horizontally, usually across the top of the page as shown at Yelp in Figure 7.3.

In this example configuration, the facets occupy a much more dominant position on the page and present a more visible invitation for interaction. However, this configuration does not scale well beyond a small number of facets, as the maximum that can be simultaneously displayed is normally bounded by the width of the page (in this case, six).

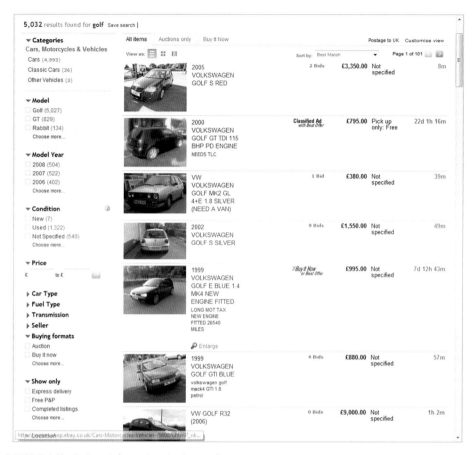

FIGURE 7.1 Vertical stack faceted navigation at eBay.

In addition, the facet menu will no longer be visible if the user scrolls down the results, thus compromising the visibility of the relationship between selections made and results returned.

There are a number of variations on the basic horizontal configuration. An example can be seen at Amphenol, which adopts the principle that *all* relevant facets should be displayed for any given result set and that these should wrap across the screen as necessary. Figure 7.4 shows a search for "connectors" that returns 25 facets displayed in alphabetically ordered, scrollable containers (with the results pushed below the fold).

In contrast with the Yelp example, there is no limit on the number of facets that can be simultaneously displayed. However, the effect on the overall user experience can be quite disorienting due to the sheer number of facets displayed with little sense of priority. A further discontinuity is created by continual changes in the location and order of the facets as progressive refinements are applied. (Of course, this issue can apply equally to vertical

FIGURE 7.2 Facets on the right at Edinburgh University Library.

configurations, but the extended horizontal configuration shown here makes the effect so much more visible on each refinement action.)

Hybrid layout

Most implementations of faceted search follow either the vertical or horizontal configurations outlined thus far. A few, however, adopt a hybrid approach, such as TravelMatch (Figure 7.5).

A vertical layout is used for the majority of facets that are displayed on the left-hand side. However, in this example, the designer has chosen to display three particular facets in a horizontal configuration across the top of the page. These three may have been selected because they manipulate quantitative data and thus are well suited to a slider control (for a broader discussion on the choice of display media, see the following sections). Conversely,

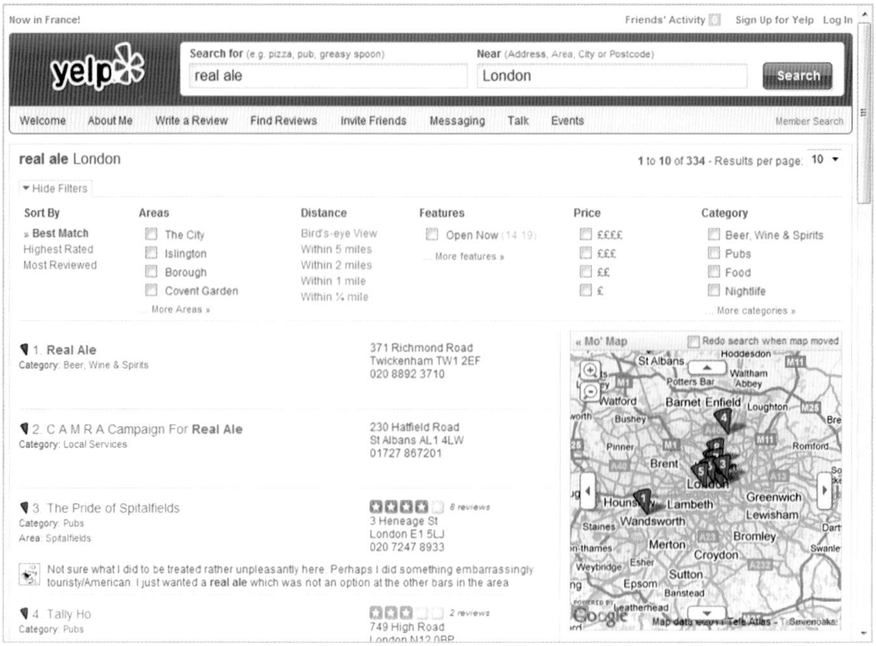

FIGURE 7.3 Horizontal facets at Yelp.

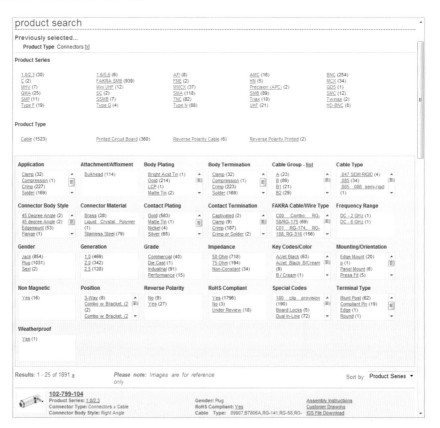

FIGURE 7.4 Facets wrap across the page at Amphenol.

they may have been selected to represent the site's unique feature, that is, the freedom for users to initiate a search using whatever criteria they deem most important. By contrast, the fields used to initiate a search on most online travel sites (number of passengers, date, etc.) are quite possibly the least immediately visible of all those shown on this page.

DEFAULT STATE

Closely coupled with the issue of layout is the choice of default state for each of the facets (Hearst, 2006a). Here, we have three broad choices: closed by default, open by default, or a combination of the two.

Closed by default

The first option is to display all facets as closed by default, which is the approach adopted by TravelMatch in the left-hand menu in Figure 7.5. The advantage is that it uses minimal screen space, and for sites with a large number of facets (such as this), the visibility of

FIGURE 7.5 Hybrid layout at TravelMatch.

that breadth of choice is maximized. (Note that it wouldn't make sense to hide the three horizontal sliders in this case, as little space would be saved and it would compromise the unique feature discussed previously.) The disadvantage is that the information scent offered by each facet is weaker than if they were shown in their open state, with sample facet values clearly visible. As a result, adoption and usage of the facets may be compromised. To mitigate this, the invitation or control to open (and close) each of the facets should be clearly visible and unambiguous.

Open by default

The second option is to display all facets in their open state by default, which maximizes the information scent by exposing example values for each of the facets and helps encourage adoption and usage of the faceted menu. An example of this approach can be seen at the job site Monster (Figure 7.6).

This approach usually limits the number of facet values displayed by default to a handful, which are typically sorted by frequency or some other measure of priority.

FIGURE 7.6 Facets open by default at Monster.

A suitable call to action is then required to invite the user to see further values (e.g., the use of "More Job Types" in the Monster example).

This example also shows the use of "smart dead ends" to indicate facet values that don't apply to the current result set but might otherwise, were some refinement to be removed. These are shown in gray with disabled checkboxes. What this tells the user is that although Monster has jobs that are part-time/per day/temporary in its collection, none of these apply to the query "natural language processing." Smart dead ends can provide a very effective means to help users understand the range of possibilities open to them beyond their current query and thus encourage further serendipitous exploration and discovery.

Open/closed hybrid

The third option for default state is a combination of open and closed. This option is becoming increasingly popular, as it makes efficient use of screen space and provides a stronger information scent for the first few facets (which should ideally be sorted by priority). An example of this can be seen below at NCSU Libraries (Figure 7.7).

FIGURE 7.7 Open and closed facets at NCSU Libraries.

In this example, the primary facets (*Subject*, *Genre*, *Format*, *Call Number Location*, and *Library*) are shown in their open state, and the secondary facets (*Language*, *Region*, *Time Period*, and *Author*) are shown closed. One assumes that this choice reflects the dominant search strategies and mental models employed by the library's users in searching the catalog.

There is also a further variation on this theme. In the NCSU Libraries example, the choice of default state (open or closed) is applied at the outset but is thereafter entirely driven by user behavior. In other words, if the user opens a facet it stays open, and if the user closes a facet it stays closed. Thus the initiative for changing those states lies with the user as he or she progresses through a given search scenario. But for more complex search scenarios, a mixed initiative approach may be adopted. For example, a search on eBay using the query "golf" returns a *query clarification dialogue* (see Chapter 6), as shown in Figure 7.8.

Notice how all the facets are open by default. This design is particularly significant, as the primary role for the query clarification facets (e.g., "Sporting Goods," "Cars,

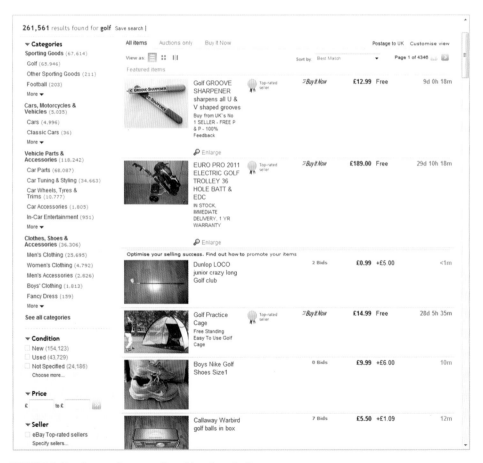

FIGURE 7.8 Facets open for query disambiguation at eBay.

Motorcycles & Vehicles," and "Clothes, Shoes & Accessories") is to guide the users in making an appropriate selection to disambiguate their query. A strong information scent (provided by the example values) is thus vital.

But once a selection has been made, a different approach is adopted. For example, if we select *Category="Cars, Motorcycles & Vehicles"*, we are presented with a refined set of results and further facets, as shown in Figure 7.9.

But on this occasion, the default state is a combination of open and closed. Like NCSU libraries, they have ordered the facets by priority to reflect the dominant search strategies and mental models employed by their users. This means showing the primary facets of *Model*, *Model Year*, *Condition*, and *Price* in their open state, and the secondary facets (*Car Type*, *Fuel Type*, *Transmission*, and *Seller*) in their closed state: a subtle but effective strategy for optimizing screen space, information scent, and query disambiguation.

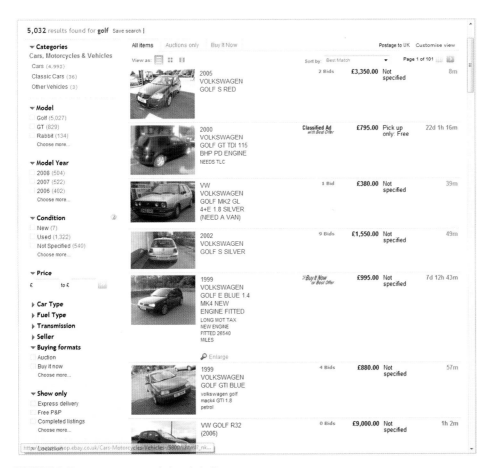

FIGURE 7.9 Facets now open and closed at eBay.

Note of course, that many sites rely on the use of an independent control such as a breadbox to communicate the current navigational state (described later in this chapter). If inline breadcrumbs are used instead, then facets must either be shown in their open state by default or use some other method to indicate the presence of existing selections. TravelMatch, for example, displays icons to communicate the presence of selections made within closed facets (Figure 7.5).

DISPLAY FORMATS

As mentioned earlier, facets are independent dimensions by which we can classify an object. Each of these facets is based on an underlying data type. In our book collection, for instance, the values for Author could be stored as text (i.e., character strings), Subjects could be one or more terms from a controlled vocabulary, Dates could be stored as long integers, and so on. Such decisions shape the underlying architecture of faceted search applications. But how should such facets be displayed to the end user, and what kind of interactivity should be provided? In each case, the guiding principle should be to communicate the nature of the underlying data by matching the display format to the semantics of the facet values (Burrell, 2010). In the following section, we examine the main options and discuss the principles for choosing between them.

Hyperlinks

Hyperlinks are probably the most common display format for facets. They represent textual values simply and directly and afford interaction through direct selection (e.g., a single mouse click). When combined with *record counts* (i.e., the number of items matching each facet value), they provide a simple but effective summary of the information space (Yee et al., 2003). This design guides users toward productive navigation choices, helping them understand the relationship between the choices they make and the results they see.

The example from the Food Network shows a typical faceted navigation menu, with ten facets containing textual values that are displayed as hyperlinks (Figure 7.10).

One of the reasons for the popularity of hyperlinks is their simple interaction model: the user selects a value, and the system responds by applying that value as a refinement to the current navigational context. So in the previous, if the user selects *Content Type = Recipe*, the result set is filtered to include only recipes. Likewise, if the user selects *Course = Main Dish*, the results are filtered to include only recipes for main dishes.

This example also illustrates the behavior described earlier in this chapter: single select facets are removed from display after being applied. For example, once a value for Content Type has been applied, the facet disappears. The end result is that the faceted menu shrinks as refinements are applied.

Note that multi-select facets require a different behavior. In this case, the assumption is that more than one value from each facet may be simultaneously applied, so the individual

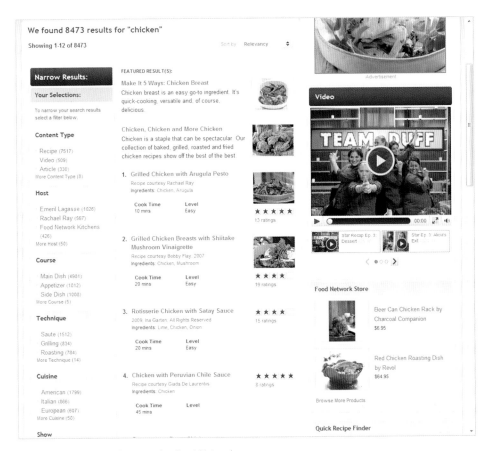

FIGURE 7.10 Hyperlink facets at the Food Network.

facets need to remain visible for further selections to be made by the user. This issue raises an interesting question: if the Food Network did want to make their existing facets multi-selectable (and there is little inherent in their semantics to preclude this), could they maintain the hyperlink format and simply continue to display each facet following a selection? There is no technical reason why this cannot be done—in fact, we see such an example at NCSU libraries (Figure 7.11). In this example, the user can select multiple Subjects, Genres, Formats, and so on, and these are added to the navigational context each time.

But there are two reasons why hyperlinks are not the ideal display format for multi-select facets. First, they are by convention used to display *single-select* facet values, and offer a strong affordance of single-select behavior. Second, there is an alternative display mechanism that is specifically designed to support multiple selections from a number of options: the checkbox.

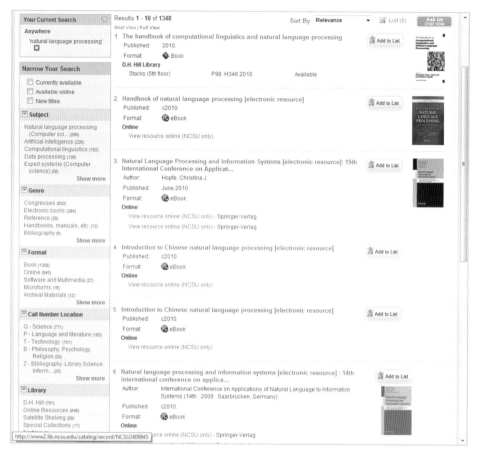

FIGURE 7.11 Hyperlink facets at NCSU Libraries.

Checkboxes

Checkboxes are an ideal format for the display of multi-select facets. An example of their use can be found at many sites, including eBay (Figure 7.12).

Checkboxes support multiple selection and the communication of navigational state (see the upcoming section "Communicating the Navigational State"). In this example, the user can select multiple models (*Golf* OR *Jetta*) and multiple model years (*2009* OR *2008* OR *2007*) and these choices are displayed inline as selected checkboxes.

Using hyperlinks and checkboxes inappropriately can create an inconsistent user experience. It's vital to understand the difference between the facet *semantics* (which, as we discussed earlier, is an inherent property of the data) and the *choice of display mechanism* (which is a design decision). By understanding the constraints presented by the former, we can make more informed choices regarding the latter.

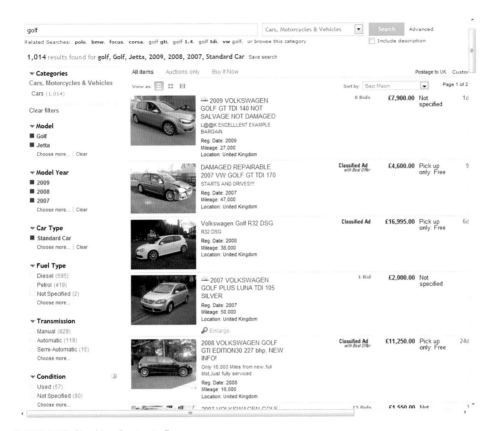

FIGURE 7.12 Checkbox facets at eBay.

Range sliders

In the previous examples, the facet values are *categorical* in nature—qualitative data organized on a *nominal* or *ordinal* scale. But facets often need to display quantitative data, such as price ranges, product sizes, date ranges, and so on. In such cases, a range slider is often a more suitable display mechanism. An example can be found at Molecular's Wine Store (Figure 7.13).

This example shows the use of sliders for quantitative data such as *Price*, *Expert Score*, and *User Rating* and for interval data such as *Vintage*. Note also that this example uses single-ended sliders for the first three but a double-ended slider for the latter. The rationale here is that most users would be interested only in a maximum value for price or a minimum value for *Expert Score* and *User Rating*. However, they might be interested in both a start date and an end date for a particular range of vintages.

This example also illustrates how sliders can be complemented with additional information, such as a histogram showing the distribution of record counts across the

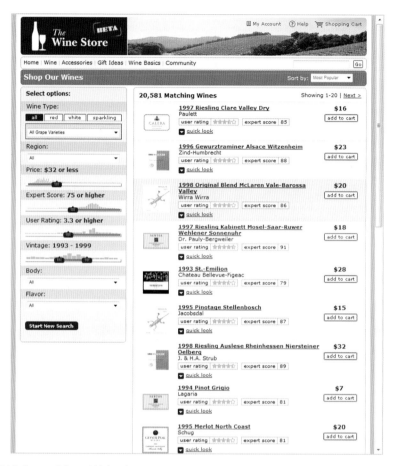

FIGURE 7.13 Range sliders at Molecular.

range. This option helps users understand the information landscape within each facet, guiding them toward more meaningful and productive selections.

Input boxes

One disadvantage of sliders is that they offer a relatively coarse level of control over the values. In the Molecular Wine Store example, it might be relatively easy to specify a precise pair of dates because the entire scale spans just 20 or so values. However, quantitative values can extend over much greater intervals, causing sliders to become cumbersome to use with accuracy. Consequently, sliders are often paired with input boxes, which allow the direct entry of precise values. An example of this can be seen at Glimpse.com, where specifying an exact price range for shoes is much easier using the input boxes than the slider (Figure 7.14).

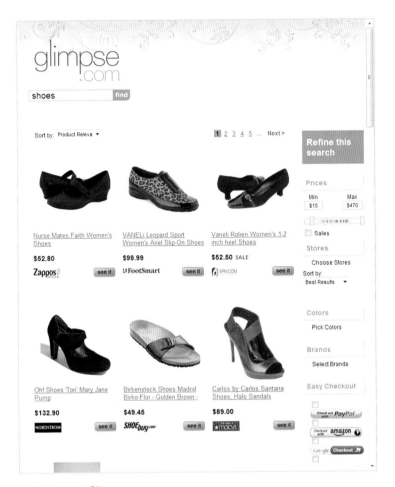

FIGURE 7.14 Input boxes at Glimpse.

Sometimes it is appropriate to transform one data type into another. For example, quantitative data can be transformed into an *interval scale* by subdividing the range into a sequence of smaller ranges and giving each a label. This is the approach taken by Amazon in their treatment of price ranges (Figure 7.15).

Note that the intervals need not be of equal size: in Amazon's case, they divide the overall range into five "bins" of differing size, which spreads the distribution of record counts more evenly across the range.

Color pickers

So far we've discussed how the choice of display format is shaped by the semantics of the underlying data and the intended user experience. In this respect, color pickers

FIGURE 7.15 Interval scales at Amazon.

are perhaps the ultimate custom control: they are designed exclusively to represent the visual dimension of color. However, there are various ways in which this can be executed. Littlewoods, for example, displays a color swatch with corresponding text labels and shows only values that are specific to the current result set (Figure 7.16).

Artist Rising, by contrast, uses a generic color picker, offering a choice across the entire color spectrum (Figure 7.17).

Although the user has great flexibility in selecting a precise color value, the consequence is that it is easy for the user to select a value that is not available (and thus returns zero results).

An alternative to the color picker is simply to use text labels for each value (as often seen on Amazon and eBay). The challenge is, of course, to select textual labels that are meaningful to the end user while faithfully representing the appearance of the item itself.

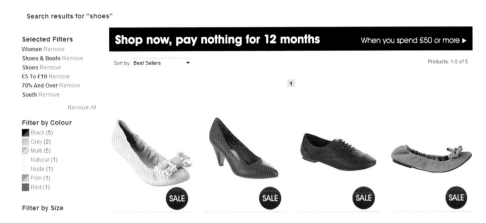

FIGURE 7.16 Color picker at Littlewoods.

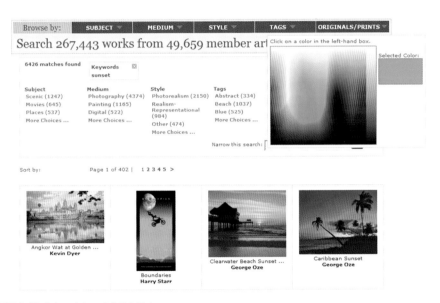

FIGURE 7.17 Color picker at Artist Rising.

Inevitably, once the range extends beyond basic primary and secondary colors, such mappings start to become increasingly tenuous.

Tag clouds

A decade or so ago, there was no such thing as a tag cloud—at least, not outside of a few research labs and data visualization projects. Then along came Flickr, Delicious, and a host of other online community sites with vast repositories of user-generated and user-tagged

FIGURE 7.18 Tag clouds at Artist Rising.

content. Tag clouds, with their ability to visually represent measures such as tag popularity, rapidly became the technique of choice for displaying and exploring such content. Soon, their use was extended to include unstructured content, displaying clouds of terms extracted from text documents.

A decade on, we seem to have come full circle. Perhaps victims of their own popularity, tag clouds are now a much rarer part of the faceted search experience. An example can be found at Artist Rising, which displays a tag cloud as an overlay within a horizontal faceted menu (Figure 7.18).

As tags are selected, they are added to the breadbox alongside other refinements. (Unusually, the tag cloud in this implementation appears to allow only a single value to be applied, which rather compromises its usefulness.)

A somewhat different treatment can be found at PC Authority, which uses tag clouds to present terms extracted from unstructured content (i.e., text documents). These are displayed in a separate container that is disconnected (conceptually and physically) from the left-hand faceted navigation menu. As tags are selected, they are added to the breadbox alongside other refinements (Figure 7.19).

Unlike Artist Rising, the tag cloud in this implementation supports multiple refinements, updating its contents each time.

Data visualizations

In each of the previous examples, the focus of the search experience is on locating and viewing one or more *individual* records. In that context, the role of faceted navigation is to smooth the user's journey from an initial query to a specific record. But as shown in Chapter 3, an increasing number of applications are concerned with understanding higher-level patterns in the collection, where the focus is less on locating individual records and more on understanding patterns of distribution at an *aggregate* level. In these applications, the facets play a fundamental role in the discovery experience, with the focus shifting from findability to broader tasks such as analysis and sensemaking.

Applications such as these are designed to aggregate, organize, and summarize data from numerous quantitative and qualitative sources by using data visualizations to

FIGURE 7.19 Tag clouds at PC Authority.

communicate key metrics, patterns, and overall status. An example of such a visualization could be found at Newssift, in which pie charts were used to communicate the distribution of article sources and associated sentiment (Figure 7.20).

These visualizations provide a simple interaction model: the user selects a value (by clicking on a slice of the pie chart, for instance), and the system responds by applying that value as a refinement to the current navigational context—just like a hyperlink would do. But more important, the facets provide an instant overview of the aggregate distribution for each dimension: we can see at a glance, for example, that the majority of sentiment is positive, and that the majority of articles are sourced from Online News. Of course, such insights could also be facilitated by other display formats, but a well-chosen visualization will do this much more effectively than the more traditional display formats discussed earlier.

Another use of data visualization in faceted search is to communicate patterns in geospatial data. An example of this can be found at WITS (the Worldwide Incidents Tracking System), which uses various forms of visualization to display terrorist incidents overlaid on a map of the world (Figure 7.21).

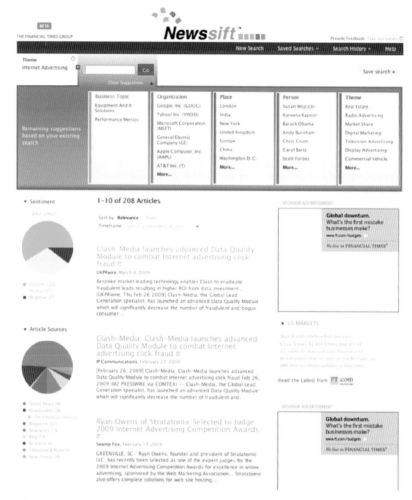

Visualizations such as this allow users to perceive spatial patterns in record distribution and explore relationships between particular facets and aggregate distributions across the map. However, the interaction model in this implementation is different from that of Newssift, in that selecting an item on the map (e.g., a cluster in the rendering in Figure 7.21) centers and zooms the map on that region, rather than applying the selected item as a refinement. In this respect, the visualization is not behaving as a facet in the strict sense, but it nonetheless allows the end user to productively explore patterns at the aggregate level.

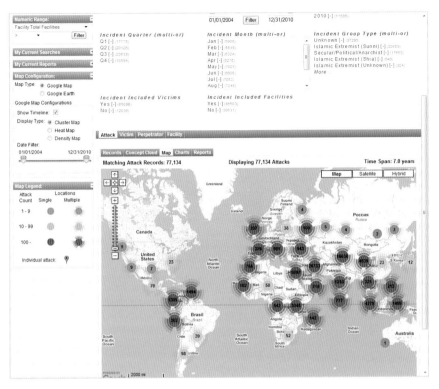

FIGURE 7.21 Data visualization at WITS.

SHOWING ADDITIONAL VALUES

One of the key principles to emerge from our examination of display formats is that it is important for facets to indicate the nature of their content so that users can formulate productive search strategies based on meaningful navigational cues. In practice, this means that facets should be open by default and display a representative sample of facet values (ordered by record count or some other measure of priority). But this design raises the question: if the users do want to see the full list of values, how should the display extend to accommodate them?

There are three main solutions to this problem. The first approach is to display the complete list of facet values by default. The second is to use a flexible container that extends on demand to accommodate the additional values. The third is to use a supplementary container to display the longer list, with an optional transition to communicate the relationship between the two. Let's examine each in turn.

FIGURE 7.22 Scrollable containers for lists of facet values at Carzone.

Displaying all values by default

The most simplistic approach to the problem is to display the complete list of facet values by default. This is possible if a display format is used that can scale to accommodate lists of varying length, such as a scrollable container. However, it also assumes that the lists of values are a manageable size (Kalbach, 2010b). Scroll bars may be infinitely extensible in principle, but in practice few users would wish to deal with lists of more than a hundred items or so (and in many cases significantly fewer).

One such example can be found at Carzone, which by default displays facets in a vertical configuration using scrollable containers for lists of facet values such as Makes & Models (Figure 7.22).

A variation on this approach can be seen at Farnell, which displays facets in a horizontal configuration. This arrangement applies the scalability principle along both axes: the facets themselves are displayed within a horizontal scrollable panel and the values within each of the facets are displayed within vertically scrollable containers (Figure 7.23).

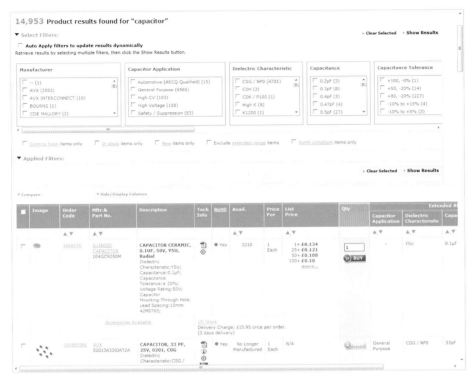

FIGURE 7.23 Scrollable containers for lists of facet values at Farnell.

Extensible containers

For many applications, however, displaying all values by default is not a scalable solution. Instead, an "on demand" approach is needed. One method is to present an option to expand the facet inline, that is, to extend its size to accommodate a larger set of values. An example of this approach can be found at the NCSU Libraries site, which displays the top 5 values by default, but extends this to the top 30 when the "Show More" link is selected (as illustrated by the Subject facet in Figure 7.24).

This approach is conceptually simple; few users would find the transition confusing or intrusive. However, one flaw in this particular execution is that there is no option to show *fewer* values once a facet is expanded except by closing it completely. Consequently, once two or more facets have been expanded, it is very difficult to review the contents of the remaining facets without repeated scrolling.

A second variant can be seen at Hoovers, whose option to see more values results in a vertical scroll bar appearing within each facet (as illustrated by the *Location* and *Employees* facets in Figure 7.25).

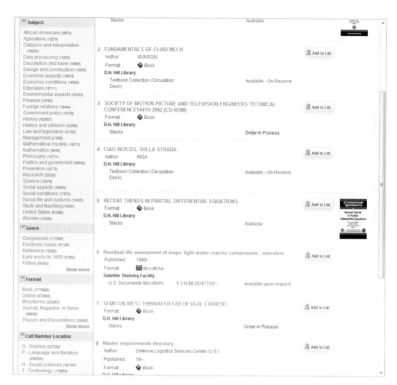

FIGURE 7.24 Extensible containers for showing additional facet values at NCSU Libraries.

FIGURE 7.25 Extensible containers for showing additional facet values at Hoovers.

Separate containers

Although the first two approaches display both the original and extended set of facet values within the same container, a third approach is to display the extended set in a new container.

Perhaps the most lightweight variation on this approach is to use an overlay to display the full set of facet values adjacent to the original set. Artist Rising's "More Choices" link, for instance, displays the remaining facet values as an extended list, preserving the original sort order (Figure 7.26).

A variation on this approach can be seen at the Food Network, which shows a maximum of three values by default, with an option to view more. This approach uses also an overlay, but instead of displaying just the additional values, it displays the entire list sorted alphabetically (Figure 7.27).

Note that in this display the record counts are suppressed, possibly to reduce any confusion that may arise by displaying them in what may seem an unsorted order (or perhaps simply to reduce clutter and allow the alphabetic ordering to be more evident).

A somewhat heavier approach is to use a modal overlay to display the full set of facet values. An example of this design can be seen at eBay, which uses the overlay to present the complete list of values for each facet in its own pane (Figure 7.28). This design allows only one facet to be visible at any given time (an issue we discuss further in an upcoming section).

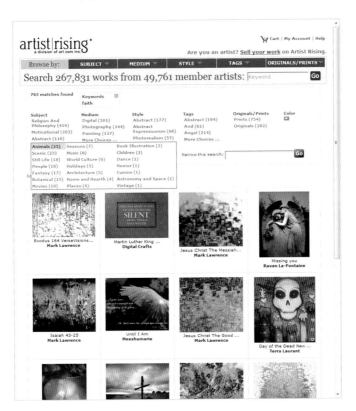

FIGURE 7.26 A separate container for showing additional facet values at Artist Rising.

FIGURE 7.27 A separate container for showing additional facet values at the Food Network.

FIGURE 7.28 A separate container for showing additional facet values at eBay.

Both of these approaches support the principle of minimizing the disruption to the user's mental flow by staying on the page (Scott & Neil, 2009). A more disruptive approach is to present the list of values on a separate page, which is the approach adopted by Amazon on certain sections of their site such as footwear. This shows the use of multi-select facets, with options to "See More" for both *Brand* and *Seller* (Figure 7.29).

Selecting "See More" for *Brands* loads a new page displaying the entire set of values for that facet (Figure 7.30).

Interestingly, this page now presents the options as hyperlinks (rather than checkboxes), which as we saw earlier in this chapter are better suited to single-select facets. And that is exactly how they behave: selecting one value immediately returns the user to the original results page with that value now applied.

Hybrid approaches

So far, we've discussed the primary approaches for showing additional values, from extending the existing container, to displaying a new one, to using a separate page. These approaches allow the user to *browse* a longer list of values to make further selections. However, there is an alternative approach that allows the user to *search* for specific values rather than browse. An example of this design can be seen at LinkedIn in Figure 7.31.

FIGURE 7.29 Options to see additional facet values at Amazon.

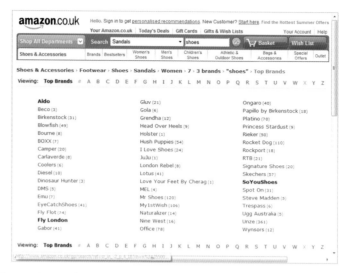

FIGURE 7.30 A separate page for showing additional facet values at Amazon.

FIGURE 7.31 Support for both search and browse of facet values at LinkedIn.

As expected, each of these facets shows a handful of values by default, with an option to "Show More" that extends the list to include the first dozen or so. But what makes this design different is the use of the text field (shown in this example underneath the Location facet). As soon as the user starts to type into this box, an autocomplete dialog appears with up to ten suggested values. This design offers a more complete experience than the others described thus far, supporting both search and browse as independent methods to view and select further facet values.

COMMUNICATING THE NAVIGATIONAL STATE

Throughout this chapter, we've provided examples of the power of faceted search in enabling users to explore complex information spaces by refining their choices in each dimension. But with this power comes a challenge: given the ease with which information spaces can be traversed, what methods should be used to communicate the user's current location and navigation options?

One of the simplest techniques by which navigational state is communicated is through the use of breadcrumbs. Breadcrumbs have a long history in the development of the web (and hypertext systems in general) and have been the subject of many previous research studies (e.g., Blustein, Ahmed, & Instone, 2005). In their simplest form, they are rendered as a trail that indicates the user's current position in an information hierarchy or taxonomy—for example:

Home page>Section page>Subsection page

But the whole point of faceted search is to allow navigation along several independent dimensions rather than just a single hierarchy. So in this case, we need an approach that will scale to accommodate multiple dimensions.

Inline breadcrumbs

Perhaps the simplest example of such a mechanism is the use of multiple *inline breadcrumbs*, as shown on Amazon (Figure 7.32). Looking closely at the faceted navigation menus, we can see that each contains the current selection (e.g., *Format = paperback, language = English*) *and* the means by which the user may remove the current selection for any given facet (e.g., Any Format, Any Language). Note the use of boldface to indicate the currently selected facet value, the use of indentation to indicate hierarchy, and the use of chevrons to imply going "back" to a previous state.

However, there are two shortcomings with this design. First, it doesn't scale well to results that involve a large number of facets whose combined vertical height extends beyond the current screen. In such cases, a portion of the facet menus (and their currently selected values) will be hidden out of view. To a degree, this problem is mitigated by the conventional breadcrumb trail displayed above the search results, but the visibility of this is debatable, and the lack of inherent structure makes it relatively difficult to comprehend at a glance. Second, and more importantly, is the issue of how this approach would scale

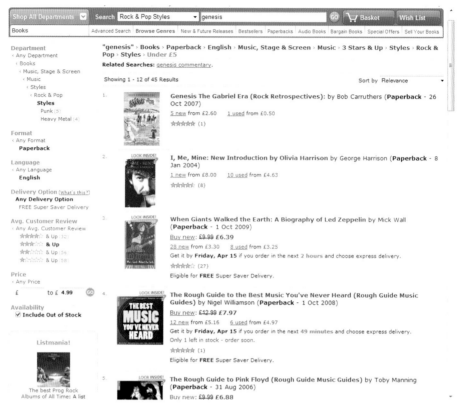

FIGURE 7.32 Inline breadcrumbs at Amazon.

to accommodate multi-select facets. In other words, how would conjunctive (AND) or disjunctive (OR) facet values be rendered and selected?

An extension to the above approach is to maintain the principle of displaying current facet selections inline (i.e., within the facet menu itself), but allow the facet values to be multi-selectable. An example of this can be seen at eBay (Figure 7.33). In this example, we can select multiple models (e.g., *Golf* OR *Jetta*) and multiple model years (*2009* OR *2008* OR *2007*) and these choices are displayed inline as selected checkboxes.

Like Amazon, eBay also includes a conventional breadcrumb trail above the result, with an even less structured treatment: bare facet values delimited by commas. Interestingly, eBay allows users to close individual facets (presumably to optimize vertical screen space) but only if they have no current value selected. So in the previous example, the user can close only the *Fuel Type* facet and the ones immediately below it. This design minimizes the likelihood of the user inadvertently hiding selected refinements from view and ensures that he or she always has visibility of his or her current navigational state.

Despite these useful modifications, the design still suffers from the same fundamental shortcoming as Amazon: when a given result set possesses a large number of facets,

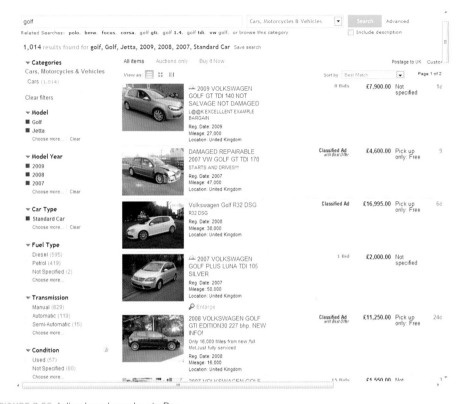

FIGURE 7.33 Inline breadcrumbs at eBay.

their combined height may extend beyond the current screen height, making the overall navigation state difficult to comprehend without vertical scrolling.

For relatively simple applications, such online retail, this may be a suitable compromise to make. However, as mentioned earlier, the applications of faceted search are growing to accommodate a range of information discovery challenges, including more complex applications in business intelligence and analytics. In such cases, the need for a more scalable approach that more effectively communicates navigational state becomes more significant. In the next section, we'll look at other solutions for addressing this problem.

Breadboxes

The fundamental principle of the previous examples is that they display the selected refinements within the facets themselves. An alternative, however, is to display all currently selected facet values in their own dedicated container. In the context of faceted search, this container is often referred to as a *breadbox*. An example of the breadbox can be seen in the box labeled "Your Selections" at the Food Network (Figure 7.34).

FIGURE 7.34 Simple breadbox at the Food Network.

The advantage of this approach is that the currently selected refinements are grouped together in a single place that remains visible no matter how many facets are present. The navigational context is therefore immediately visible without scrolling. However, there is a shortcoming to this approach: the relationship between facets and selected values is now less apparent. For example, to which facet does the selection "recipe" or "main dish" belong? Because these values are no longer displayed in context, the user must either recall which facet was associated with each selected value or attempt to infer that from the labels themselves.

For relatively simple search applications, this may be a minor issue. After all, most users could reasonably interpret the values in the breadbox above, even if the precise facets that gave rise to them are now absent. There are, however, other ways to address this issue. The example from NCSU Libraries illustrates one such approach (Figure 7.35).

In this case, we see that the breadbox contains not just the facet values, but the facet names too, that is, *Format="online"*, *Subject="natural language processing"*, and so on. The word wrapping in this particular example is somewhat unfortunate in that the controls to remove each refinement have wrapped as orphans in two cases, but the principle is clear: each facet value is unambiguously associated with its parent facet. Note also that

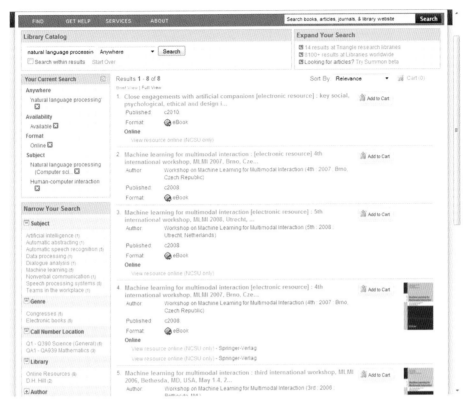

FIGURE 7.35 Vertical breadbox at NCSU Libraries.

this design scales easily to support multi-select facets: the multiple selections for the *Subject* facet are clearly visible and comprehensible in the design.

In both of the previous examples, the breadbox is laid out vertically. But there are variations on this: in the example from University of Toronto Libraries, we see a similar navigational state laid out in a horizontal arrangement (Figure 7.36).

In this example, there are seven separate refinements laid out in sequence, complete with facet labels and removal controls. However, the comparison with the vertical breadbox makes one shortcoming of this approach quite evident: the content of the breadbox is much harder to comprehend, as the structural relationship between the facet:value pairs is now much less apparent.

Note, however, that in all of these examples, we've assumed that the facets themselves are laid out vertically. There are, of course, other configurations: notably *open parametric*,[1] in which the facets are laid out in a consistent horizontal orientation and displayed in their

---

[1] http://patterns.endeca.com/content/library/en/home/patterns/faceted_nav_open_parametric_new.html

FIGURE 7.36 Horizontal breadbox at University of Toronto Libraries.

open state by default. In this configuration, the currently selected facet values are much more immediately visible, to the extent that a separate breadbox may not always be required.

Hybrid techniques

In the previous discussion, we outlined two contrasting approaches to wayfinding in faceted search: breadcrumbs (in particular the inline version) and breadboxes. There are of course other variants, such as the Integrated Faceted Breadcrumb (Nudelman, 2011). At first glance, this design seems quite radical, with the breadcrumb transformed into a flexible container that provides direct support for key navigational functions, such as updating facet values in situ, selecting a "See All" option to remove a refinement, and so on. Nudelman also uses this design to illustrate some key navigational principles such as explicit labeling of the facets (as discussed earlier), retention of the navigational context wherever possible, and so on.

But on closer analysis, it seems that many of these actions and principles are precisely those for which the inline breadcrumb approach has already been shown to work well—particularly the eBay incarnation with its support for complex navigational options such as multi-select AND and OR. So it remains to be seen whether the integrated faceted breadcrumb is the first of a new set of wayfinding techniques in faceted search or essentially a reallocation of navigational functionality from one component to another (i.e., from the facets to the breadcrumbs).

INTERACTION PATTERNS

In this final section, we explore an aspect of faceted search that has received relatively little design attention: the interactive behavior of the facets themselves, that is, how they should respond and update when selected. Surprisingly, the design choices at this level of detail can make a remarkable difference to the overall user experience: the wrong choices can make an application feel disjointed and awkward and can (in some cases) increase the likelihood of returning zero results.

Interaction models

As discussed earlier, one of the fundamental principles of faceted search is to display only currently available facet values. Consequently, it should not normally be possible for a user to select a value that returns zero results. There are of course circumstances under which an empty result set can become unavoidable, such as the use of *search within* (see Chapter 5). However, one of the strengths of faceted search is the support for flexible query modification, which reduces the need for extensive keyword reformulation (English et al., 2002).

In the example from computer manufacturer Dell (Figure 7.37), we can see that there are seven laptop products that match the specification *Screen= "small"* AND

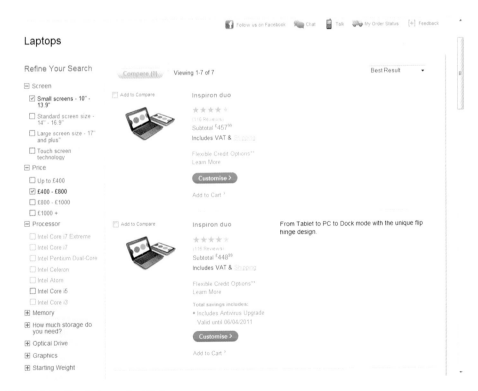

FIGURE 7.37 Faceted search at Dell.

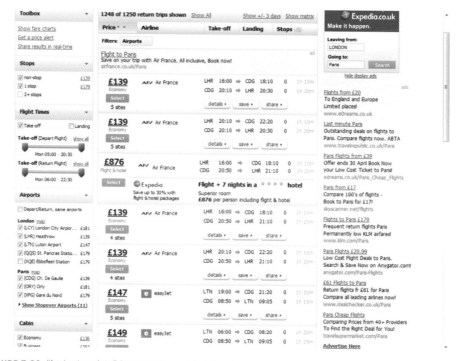

FIGURE 7.38 "Instant update" interaction model at Kayak.

price=£400–800. At this point, users can widen their search to include other screen sizes, such as *Standard*, *Large*, or other price ranges, such as *Up to £400*. Like the earlier Monster.com example, this design uses *smart dead ends* to communicate values that would have been available had the initial selections not been made, that is, the other Processor options (shown here in pale gray).

But the point is that whenever the user makes a selection, the results are updated immediately. As a consequence, the result set and available facet values remain consistent and reflect the products available to the user at any given time.This "instant update" model is very common and forms the basis of many faceted search experiences. Another such example is the travel site Kayak, which combines traditional facet selection options in the form of categorical values (rendered using hyperlinks and check boxes) with quantitative values that are rendered using sliders (Figure 7.38).

It is when we start to examine such nontraditional facet formats that the limitations of the Instant Update model become apparent: in this case, each of the sliders is double-ended, and in many scenarios it will feel more natural for users to adjust both ends as part of a single interaction. But of course doing so is not possible: the user must wait for an update to take place in between each selection. Furthermore, when the sliders provide only a coarse level of selection over the underlying data, it is likely that some degree of iteration with these controls will be required.

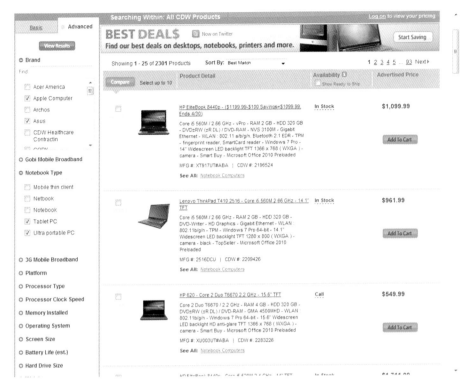

FIGURE 7.39 Two-stage facet selection at CDW.

But there is an alternative approach. In Figure 7.39, computer equipment supplier CDW allows the users to cherry-pick multiple facet values in a single iteration and then submit them en masse via the View Results button.

The advantage is that users can now select as many values as they like without interruption and choose to view the results when they are ready. But the disadvantage is equally apparent—this style of interaction is in effect a type of *parametric search*, and in many instances (including the previous example), this approach can return zero results. In the example shown, there are simply no products available that match the selection of *Brand=(Apple OR Asus)* AND *Type=(Tablet PC OR UltraPortable)*. The user is thus forced to remove the facet selections one by one until a legitimate combination is found or clear them all and start again. Likewise, in the Monster.com example of Figure 7.6, adding the refinements *Category= "R&D/Science"* and *Industry= "Internet Services"* also returns zero results.

From the previous example alone, it would be easy to conclude that the "two-stage" interaction model is fundamentally flawed, as it allows facet selections and result sets to become out of sync. But the shortcoming with this design is not the two-stage model per se; it is the combination of this model with the design decision to allow the end user to arbitrarily open and close facets at will. In the previous example, the range of values

FIGURE 7.40 Two-stage facet selection at Carzone.

revealed when the user opens the Notebook Type facet is not updated to reflect any selections already applied, and thus illegal combinations of facet values can be selected that return zero results.

So how can this problem be avoided? Automotive classified site Carzone provides one such example. In Figure 7.40, we see a similar instance of the two-stage model, with each facet allowing selection of multiple values and an Update button provided to submit them en masse.

But the difference this time is that the user does not have the ability to arbitrarily open and close facets at will: instead, opening one facet will, by default, close any other. This crucial difference means that when a facet is opened, its values can be updated to be consistent with the current navigational state (i.e., any facet values applied thus far). So in the previous example, if the user chooses to apply values from another facet such as Body Type, as soon as the facet is opened, it will be updated to show only values that are consistent with those applied thus far, that is, *Make&Model=(Audi A2* OR *Audi A3* OR *Audi A4).* A dialog overlay is used to remind users to choose whether to commit any values selected thus far (although by default, they will always be applied unless explicitly cancelled).

As seen in the previous examples, both approaches have their strengths and weaknesses. Indeed, it is possible to offer both approaches and let users decide which they prefer.

FIGURE 7.41 User-selectable interaction model at Farnell.

Electronic component distributor Farnell does exactly this, offering a checkbox to "Auto Apply filters to update results dynamically," which applies the instant update model to the facets, and a "Show Results" button to refresh the results pane with the currently selected values (Figure 7.41).

Note that the facet values examined in the two-stage examples above are *disjunctive* (multi-select OR); for example, the selection of a value for a facet such as Make & Model does not preclude the selection of another value from the same facet. In this case, selecting multiple independent facet values has the effect of widening the search. However, if the facet values are *conjunctive* (multi-select AND), then the choice of which interaction model to apply is quite different. An example of a typical conjunctive facet would be "features" (e.g., air con, alloy wheels, sat nav), as these are meaningful only when applied in their totality (i.e., the result should return cars with ALL these features, not just a subset of them). In this case, the facet values are no longer independent, as selecting one value directly affects the number of results for which the other features also apply. In this case, the only meaningful interaction model is the instant update, as this is the only approach that will ensure that facet values and the current result set remain consistent.

Interstitial pages

It is interesting also to compare the various approaches to interstitial pages, that is, the messaging that is provided to indicate that the facets are being updated and results retrieved. Dell, for example, leaves the facets in situ but reloads the entire results pane, which introduces something of a cognitive disconnect between the two result sets. CDW takes this approach further by refreshing the entire page and discarding the open/closed state of the facets, thus introducing an even greater degree of disruption to the user's mental flow. Kayak and Carzone both adopt a more lightweight approach, providing an "Applying your filter choices" overlay but otherwise ensuring that any updates stay on the page (Scott & Neil, 2009).

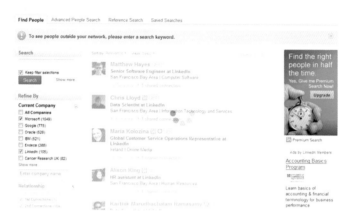

FIGURE 7.42 Interstitial search page at LinkedIn.

But possibly the most sophisticated interstitial treatment is that found at LinkedIn, which provides a semitransparent mask over all the elements that need to be refreshed (e.g., the results pane and any facets other than the one the user just applied) but other than that keeps the disruption to a minimum (Figure 7.42).

SUMMARY AND BEST PRACTICES

Faceted search offers a unique potential to transform the search experience. It provides a flexible framework by which users can satisfy a wide variety of information needs, ranging from simple lookup and fact retrieval to complex exploratory search and discovery. Summarized here are the key principles for designing effective faceted search experiences.

Definitions

- Facets are independent properties or *dimensions* by which we can classify an object.

- Selections are made by applying facet values that determine the set of matching records returned. The set of selections active at any given time is known as the *navigational context*.

- Faceted search should minimize the likelihood of zero results by displaying only currently available facet values.

- Facets can be either *single-select* or *multi-select*. Single-select values are mutually exclusive.

- Multi-select facets can either be multi-select *OR* or multi-select *AND*:
  - Multi-select OR values are combined *disjunctively*.

- Multi-select AND values are combined *conjunctively*.
- Values applied *across* different facets are normally applied conjunctively, whereas values applied *within* a given facet are normally applied disjunctively.

Layout and State

- There are three main choices of layout: vertical, horizontal, and hybrid:
  - Vertical faceted menus are usually placed on the left, and scale well to variations in the number of facets displayed.
  - Horizontal configurations can present a more visible invitation for interaction, but scale less well to variations in the number of facets.
  - Hybrid configurations can use a combination of vertical and horizontal.

- There are three main choices of default state: closed by default, open by default, or a combination of the two:
  - Closed by default minimizes screen space and maximizes the visibility of the full range of facets.
  - Open by default maximizes the information scent of the individual facet values.
  - A combination of open and closed can be used to reflect users' search strategies and mental models.

Display Formats

- The guiding principle should be to match the display format to the semantics of the facet values.

- Hyperlinks provide a simple and direct mechanism for representing textual values.

- Single select facets may be removed from display after being applied, but multi-select facets must remain visible for further selections to be made.

- Checkboxes should be used to display multi-select facets.

- Range sliders are usually the most appropriate format for quantitative data; they can be complemented with additional information to communicate the information landscape within each facet.

- Input boxes allow the entry of precise quantitative values where range sliders would be inappropriate; quantitative data can be transformed into an interval scale by subdividing the range.

- Color pickers can be configured to show only values that are specific to the current result set or to allow selection from a continuous color spectrum.

- Tag clouds can be used to present terms extracted from unstructured content.

- Visualizations are appropriate where the focus is on understanding patterns of distribution at an aggregate level.

Showing Additional Values

- Facets should offer an appropriate information scent—for example, be open by default and display a representative sample of facet values.

- There are three main ways to accommodate long lists of values: display all by default, use an extensible container, or use a supplementary container:
  - Display all by default assumes that the list is bounded in some way to a manageable size.
  - Extensible containers present an option to expand the facet inline.
  - Supplementary containers display the full set of facet values adjacent to the original set. The extended list can be ordered to facilitate visual scanning.

- A text entry box (e.g., one with autocomplete) can be used to locate specific facet values.

Communicating the Navigational State

- Because faceted search allows navigation along several independent dimensions, it is important to communicate the user's current location and navigation options.

- There are three main ways to communicate navigational state: inline breadcrumbs, multi-selectable facets, and breadboxes:
  - Inline breadcrumbs are the simplest way to communicate navigational state, but they do not scale well to accommodate large numbers of facets or multi-select values.
  - Multi-selectable facets use checkboxes to communicate navigational state but do not scale well to accommodate large numbers of facets.
  - Breadboxes communicate navigational state by displaying currently selected facet values in a dedicated container that remains visible no matter how many facets are present.
    - The breadbox should display facet names and values.
    - Vertical breadbox layout makes the structural relationship between the facet:value pairs more apparent.

Interaction Patterns

- Smart dead ends can be used to communicate values that would have been available had the initial selections not been made.

- There are two common interaction models: *instant update* and *two-stage*:
  - In the instant update model, the result set and facet values are updated immediately following selection of a facet value.
  - In the two-stage model, users can select multiple facet values and then submit them as a group. Inappropriate use of the two-stage model can give rise to

inconsistent navigational states that return zero results. To mitigate this problem, the design should ensure that only one facet can be open at any given time.

If the facet values are *conjunctive* (multi-select AND), then the *instant update* model should be applied.

REFERENCES

Anderson, C. (2006). *The long tail: Why the future of business is selling less of more*. New York: Hyperion.

Blustein, J., Ahmed, I., & Instone, K. (2005). An evaluation of menu breadcrumbs for the WWW. *ACM Hypertext Conference*, 202–204.

Burrell, M. (2010). Visualizing facets. Agile Analytics. Retrieved March 9, 2012, from http://facets.endeca.com/2010/08/visualizing-facets/.

English, J., Hearst, M., Sinha, R., Swearingen, K., & Yee, P. (2002). Flexible search and navigation using faceted metadata. Unpublished manuscript.

Hearst, M. (2006a). Design recommendations for hierarchical faceted search interface. ACM SIGIR Workshop on Faceted Search.

Hearst, M. (2006b). Clustering versus faceted categories for information exploration. *Communications of the ACM, 49*(4), 59–61.

Kalbach, J. (2010a). Faceted navigation: Layout and display of facets. Experiencing Information. Retrieved March 9, 2012, from http://experiencinginformation.wordpress.com/2010/06/12/faceted-navigation-layout-and-display-of-facets/.

Kalbach, J. (2010b). Faceted navigation: Showing more values. Experiencing Information. Retrieved March 9, 2012, from http://experiencinginformation.wordpress.com/2010/05/25/facetted-navigation-showing-more-values/.

Nudelman, G. (2011). *Designing search*. Hoboken, NJ: Wiley.

Scott, B., & Neil, T. (2009). *Designing web interfaces*. Sebastopol, CA: O'Reilly Media.

Tunkelang, D. (2009). *Faceted search*. San Rafael: Morgan Claypool.

Yee, P., Swearingen, K., Li, K., & Hearst, M. (2003). *Faceted metadata for image search and browsing. Proceedings of ACM CHI*. New York, NY, USA.

Navigating the Long Tail: Challenges for UI Design

The *long tail* is a popular term used to describe power laws such as Zipf's law or Pareto distributions, more commonly known as the 80/20 rule. On a graph, there is a tall "head" to the left and a long "tail" extending to the right (Figure 7.43), which reflects situations in which there are a few items that are very common and a large number of items that are very rare. For example, the most popular albums represent only a tiny fraction of all music recorded, yet they account for the bulk of the sales.

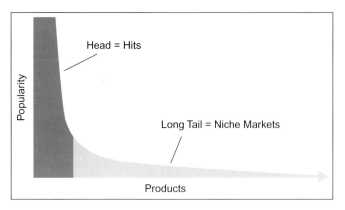

FIGURE 7.43 A diagram of the long tail.

The long tail has significant economic implications. Offline businesses are constrained by physical limitations: there's only so much shelf space in a store, for example. Owners are financially motivated to focus on the most popular products.

Online, however, there is essentially no limit to what can be offered. With digital goods, there is infinite shelf space that is *virtually free* to the provider: you just add more to the database. What's more, online providers are finding that the more items they add, the more people buy.

In his renowned book *The Long Tail* (2006), Chris Anderson outlines the impact the long tail has on business: instead of focusing on the most popular items, there's now an increasing expansion of products in the tail. He writes, "The *hits* now compete with an infinite number of *niche markets*, of any size.... Increasingly, the mass market is turning into a mass of niches" (p. 5).

The Navigation Layer

For long tail economics to work, however, there needs to be a good "navigation layer," as Anderson calls it. The navigation layer is the sum of all the metadata, categories, and filters necessary to make items discoverable.

As it turns out, simply adding more information isn't "virtually free." It comes with a cost: the long tail is a really *noisy* place. As we add more information to accommodate these markets, and consequently more metadata, the navigation layer becomes critical.

This, in turn, places challenges on interface design. Making the long tail clear and simple for everyday consumers is not easy. Sensemaking, information interaction, and information architecture will become increasingly important.

UI Design Challenges

There are two primary types of challenges in the design of user interfaces (UIs) for search systems with long tail dynamics:

1. The *representation*, or display, of information. The challenge here is: how do you display large amounts of information and metadata so that people can better understand and comprehend it intuitively?
2. The *interaction* with information also presents challenges: how can people, including novice users, interact with information to satisfy their information seeking goals?

For designers of search UIs, it's imperative to have a firm grasp of these two dimensions. Each discussed briefly next.

Representation

A typical computer screen has limited space. Even large monitors with high resolutions have their limitations: there's only so much information you can display legibly. This is a major constraint when designing systems with large bodies of information.

The field of information visualization has been dealing with this problem for many years, investigating ways to visualize information in a way that increases understanding. For example, Figure 7.44 is a visualization of my personal LinkedIn network. Each dot is a connection in my network. Selecting one of them shows shared links to other people, as well as a brief profile on the left of the person represented by the dot (in this case, the author of this book, Tony Russell-Rose). The dots are clustered together by layout and color, indicating groups of related connections.

Complex information visualizations like these, despite being fun and engaging to look at, aren't necessarily helpful. They reveal patterns in the data, but there's a considerable level of abstraction. At first glance, the everyday web user may not recognize their meaning.

An alternative that may be more useful is that of text-based visualizations. Instead of abstracting information into dots or colors, as in the previous example, these displays use text itself as a key part of the visualization.

Newsmap relies on this type of visualization (Figure 7.45). This example shows top news stories for any given day, with the most popular stories in larger text—similar to a tag cloud. But it

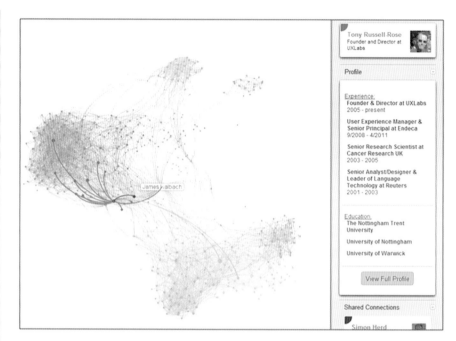

FIGURE 7.44 Visualization of the LinkedIn network for James Kalbach.

FIGURE 7.45 Newsmap visualizes news stories using text size to show relative priority.

also groups and color codes stories with similar topics. This design projects an immediate sense of what people are reading and writing about, with the headlines directly visible as part of the display.

Displays even simpler than this example may be used to increase understanding. For instance, the use of a table rather than a list for the results for a flight search on the Lufthansa website (Figure 7.46) provides valuable insight. Through this design, the passenger can easily see how changing the day of departure or return affects the ticket price.

Or consider an even simpler example: so-called *sparklines*, a term coined by information design guru Edward Tufte. These compact lines show relative trends or variation along a single dimension. We can think of this as "micro visualization," as opposed to the macro visualization of a LinkedIn network shown earlier, for instance.

Figure 7.47 shows sparklines that indicate the performance of key financial markets over a one-year period (left column) and a five-year period (right column). This example comes from www.Finianz.de, a German financial portal. Together with color-coded figures for the high point

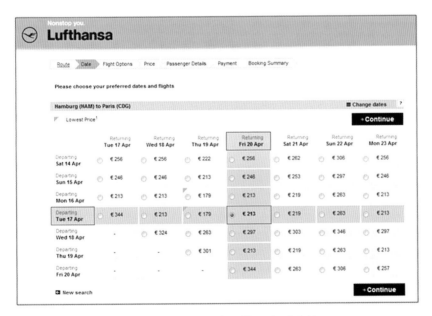

FIGURE 7.46 Search results on Lufthansa.com displayed in a simple table.

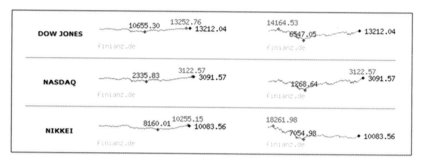

FIGURE 7.47 Sparklines showing stock markets performance over one year (left) and five years (right).

(green), low point (red), and current market value (blue), readers get a rapid summary of the market variation.

The point is to not overlook the use of simple visualization techniques to increase understanding. Complex and elaborate visualizations—although perhaps novel, colorful, and superficially pleasing—often have limited effectiveness in real world contexts. These are best reserved for specialist users, such as subject matter experts who engage with such displays on a regular basis. In the long tail, any and all types of information displays may be appropriate, at a macro or at a micro level.

Interaction

Not only is space on a computer screen is limited, so too is user attention and expertise. In casual seeking situations, such as shopping online or finding a suitable vacation spot, many users have a low threshold for learning how a system works. They give up easily and go elsewhere.

You can't assume people will take the time to learn your system. When dealing with systems that require a high degree of interaction, this behavior presents a challenge.

Take Grokker, for example, a now defunct search service. This search UI represents an attempt to visualize results with a novel interaction: zoomable clusters. In Figure 7.48, a search for "interaction design" yields topic circles, each with web pages inside. Clicking one of the topic regions zooms into that area with a smooth animation. There is a sense of physically moving in a topic with Grokker.

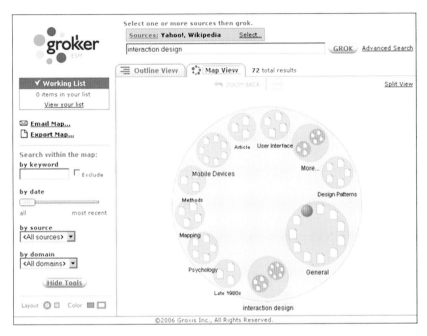

FIGURE 7.48 Grokker search results (circa 2006).

For the most part, this type of interaction wasn't successful. For the average web user, it was unfamiliar. And simulating a physical zoom didn't seem to help find information in any way.

An alternative way to zoom, metaphorically speaking, is faceted navigation. This approach has become popular in recent years and can be found on many ecommerce websites. Search filters, often on the left side of a results list, allow users to narrow and broaden a set of items successively; that is, they can zoom in and out of topics, similar to Grokker, but with a much different interaction.

Figure 7.49 shows my list of contacts from LinkedIn. These can be filtered by various facets on the left. In this image, I've selected to "zoom in" on my contacts from the UK only. The interaction here is a simple click. And with a bit of dynamic page loading, the pane with the list of contacts updates within seconds.

Conclusion

The navigation layer drives long tail economics. Without meaningful information representation and interaction, customers won't be able to find the niche markets and the products they are

FIGURE 7.49 Filtering contacts on LinkedIn—a type of "zooming."

looking for. This precipitates many challenges in UI design. Limited screen space makes the display of large sets of information problematic, and limited user attention and expertise require the interaction to be as simple as possible. As designers attempt to address these challenges, we'll likely see innovation in search UIs. The success of long tail economics depends on it.

James Kalbach is a Principal UX Strategist with USEEDS°, a leading design and innovation agency in Germany, and is the author of Designing Web Navigation *(O'Reilly Media, 2007). He blogs at http://www.experienceinformation.com and can be found on Twitter under @jameskalbach.*

Reference

Anderson, C. (2006). *The long tail: Why the future of business is selling less of more.* New York: Hyperion.

Mobile Search

Mobile devices, networked resources, and real-time information systems are
making our interactions with information constant and ubiquitous.

—Andrea Resmini and Luca Rosati (2011)

Morgan Stanley predicts that by 2014 there will be more mobile Internet users around the
world than there are desktop Internet users (Meeker, Devitt, & Wu, 2010). Not only are
more people connecting with mobile devices, but they're also consuming more and more
data—mobile data usage more than doubled every year between 2008 and 2011 and is
predicted to grow from 0.6 exabytes (EB) per month in 2011 to 6.3 EB/month by 2015
(Cisco, 2011). The numbers are impressive, but all it really takes is a quick glance at the
people around you to recognize that mobile Internet is pervasive.

In this chapter, we'll examine the driving forces behind mobile information seeking,
consider design principles for mobile search, and conclude by surveying design solutions
for entering the query, viewing results, and refining the query on mobile devices.

MOBILE INFORMATION SEEKING

Although the concepts of information seeking we investigated in Part 1 are just as
applicable on mobile devices, it's worth considering what differentiates mobile information
seeking from that conducted on the desktop. By first examining the characteristics of
mobile users, their unique mix of information needs, and the role of context, we'll then be
prepared to consider the design guidance later in the chapter.

Mobile users

Desktop interfaces are designed with a set of assumptions: a screen width of at least
1024 pixels, a full-size keyboard, and a fully attentive user, to name but a few. These go

out the window on mobile devices. Twinkling from the sidewalk of a busy street, hidden beneath the conference room table, and gripped amidst chasing a toddler though the house—mobile devices are often used under conditions of mental and physical scarcity. (I'm actually typing this very sentence into a tablet while traversing London's Waterloo train station.) In *Mobile First*, Luke Wroblewski (2011) caricatures this condition as "one eyeball and one thumb":

When reflecting on a lot of mobile usage patterns, I like to imagine people as "one eyeball and one thumb." One thumb because they are likely to be holding their mobile in one hand and using a single thumb to control it; one eyeball because in many locations where mobile devices are used we only have people's partial attention. (p. 37)

Although this maxim isn't universal—there are plenty of occasions when users do use their mobile device with undivided attention—it is common enough to warrant our scrutiny. In fact, such mental and physical limitations point to a single guiding principle for mobile applications: *simplicity*. Features must be prioritized, navigation consolidation, and fluff eliminated so that mobile users can satisfy their information needs with as little friction as possible, even when using just one eyeball and one thumb. Southwest Airlines, as Wroblewski has pointed out, epitomizes the opposing assumptions driving desktop and mobile design: their desktop website is filled with competing calls to action, while their mobile application is concise and to the point (see Figures 8.1 and 8.2). As this illustration demonstrates, the inherent constraints of mobile can actually become virtues.

In addition to mobile users sometimes facing greater mental and physical constraints than their desktop peers, there are also behavioral differences—and some surprising similarities—between them. Researchers from Google and Stanford University (Kamvar et al., 2009) collected more than 100,000 Google queries during a 35-day period from three segments—desktop users, iPhone users, and conventional mobile phone users. They uncovered two particularly interesting metrics: the average length of queries and number of queries per search session.

Of the three groups, one might expect desktop users to enter the longest queries, with those of smartphone and conventional mobile users becoming progressively shorter. Yet the Google study found that iPhone users enter queries of virtually the same length as desktop users: an average of 2.93 words (Table 8.1). This finding suggests that users are unencumbered by the input methods of smartphones (or, at least, of the iPhone) and that they exhibit similar search behavior to those using a computer. The users of conventional mobile phones (often described as "feature phones" to distinguish them from smartphones), on the other hand, enter just 2.44 words per query. Perhaps they struggle with data entry on non-QWERTY keyboards or simply have low expectations and thus put forth only a half-hearted effort.

In addition to query length, the Google study also investigated the average number of queries per search session—a session being defined as a set of queries occurring with less than a five-minute gap between them. They found that iPhone users reformulate their queries less often than desktop users—1.82 and 1.94 queries per session,

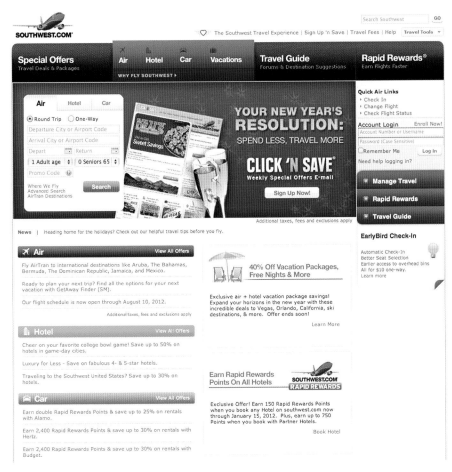

FIGURE 8.1 Southwest Airlines' website.

FIGURE 8.2 Southwest Airlines' iPhone application clearly presents the most important actions—and nothing else.

Table 8.1   The average length of Google queries performed on desktop computers, iPhones, and conventional mobile phones, as reported by Kamvar et al. (2009).

	Desktop	**iPhone**	**Feature Phone**
Words	2.93	2.93	2.44
Characters	18.72	18.25	15.89

Table 8.2   The average number of queries per Google search session (Kamvar et al., 2009).

Desktop	**iPhone**	**Feature Phone**
1.94	1.82	1.7

respectively—with conventional mobile users even less at 1.7 (Table 8.2). There are two potential explanations for the disparity between desktop and mobile search sessions. The most obvious theory is that mobile users have less time available to devote to searching and therefore reformulate their queries less often. A second explanation, however, could be that iPhone and conventional mobile users may be more likely to have straightforward information needs that require simple, easy-to-find answers.

Information needs

Analytic data shines at reporting behavior but leaves us in the dark as to the user's intent. To understand what sets mobile users apart, we must look at both quantitative and qualitative indicators. In particular, identifying the spectrum of information needs that mobile users encounter will help us to put ourselves in their shoes.

But before delving into the specific needs of mobile users, let us first identify two dimensions by which an information need (mobile or otherwise) may be classified: search motive and search type (Tate & Russell-Rose, 2012).

The *search motive* dimension describes the sophistication of the information need, including the degree of thinking it involves, and the time commitment required to satisfy it (Figure 8.3). The *lookup*, *learn*, and *investigate* elements of motive are derived from Gary Marchionini's work on exploratory search (2006); the *casual* element has been more recently studied by David Elsweiler and colleagues (2011):

- **Casual:** Undirected activities with the goal of having fun or killing time rather than completing a task.

- **Lookup:** Retrieving a simple fact. It is a short-term motive, with few queries and little time needed to resolve the information need.

- **Learn:** Information gathering to gain literacy on a given topic. It is medium term in nature, requiring a greater number of queries and a greater amount of time than the lookup motive.

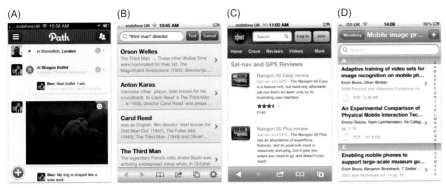

FIGURE 8.3 A, B, C, AND D Examples of search motive. **(A)** The notification screen of Path (a social network) can facilitate the casual motive. **(B)** Textual search results on Wikibot—a Wikipedia app for iPhone—represent the lookup motive. **(C)** Product reviews on CNET help satisfy the learn motive. **(D)** Mendeley's personalized library of academic papers represents the investigate motive.

FIGURE 8.4 Examples of search type. **(A)** Google excels at meeting informational type needs. **(B)** Yelp helps users satisfy their geographic type needs. **(C)** Greplin enables users to search their own personal information. **(D)** Groupon demonstrates transactional type needs.

- **Investigate:** Long-term research and planning geared toward becoming a semi-expert in a given topic. It is a long-term commitment that demands a significant investment of time and effort.

The *search type* dimension, on the other hand, is concerned with the genre of the information being sought (Figure 8.4). Broder (2002) is often cited for recognizing the *informational* and *transactional* nature of many needs;[1] the *geographic* and *personal information management* goals have been identified by Church and Smyth (2009):

- **Informational:** Textual information about a topic.

- **Geographic:** Points of interest or directions between locations.

---

[1] Broder also treated *navigational* queries as a distinct element. However, though users may enter search *queries* that are navigational in nature (the subject of Broder's study), such queries are simply the means by which to satisfy the real goal but are not the information need itself. For this reason, *navigational* does not appear in our classification.

	Casual	Lookup	Learn	Investigate
Informational	**Window Shopping** I don't know what I want. Show me stuff.	**Trivia** "What did Bob Marley die of, and when?"	**Information Gathering** "How to tie correct knots in rope?"	**Research** What is Keynesian economics and is it sustainable?
Geographic	**Friend Check-ins** "Where are Sam and Trevor?"	**Directions** "Directions to Sammy's Pizza."	**Local Points of Interest** "Where is the nearest library or bookstore?"	**Travel Planning** Flights, accommodations, and sights for my trip to Italy.
Personal Information Management	**Checking Notifications** "Email update for work."	**Checking Calendar** "Is there an open date on my family calendar?"	**Situation Analysis** "What is my insurance coverage for CAT scans?"	**Lifestyle Planning** What should my New Year's resolutions be this year?
Transactional	**Acting on Notifications** Mark as read, delete, respond to, etc.	**Price Comparison** "How much does the Pantech phone cost on AT&T.com?"	**Online Shopping** I want to buy a watch as a gift. But which one?	**Product Monitoring** I know the type of used car I want. Alert me when new ones are listed.

FIGURE 8.5 A matrix of mobile information needs.

- **Personal information management:** Private information not publicly available.

- **Transactional:** Action-oriented rather than informational goals.

Although *search motive* and *search type* provide us with two dimensions of the information need spectrum, they don't actually tell us about the many specific information needs that occur within that spectrum. Fortunately, Sohn and colleagues (2008) and Church and Smyth (2009) have each conducted diary studies in which smartphone-equipped adults were instructed to record every information need that arose over a period of weeks. This research—along with the *motive* and *type* dimensions—enables us to populate a matrix of mobile information needs (Figure 8.5).

Although there is certainly significant overlap between the information needs of mobile users and desktop users (and, as mentioned before, the *motive* and *type* dimensions apply equally well to both), the information needs represented in this matrix are the result of first-hand observation of mobile users.

Following are examples of each information need. The statements in quotation marks were recorded in the original diary studies; those without quotation marks have been added by the authors.

Informational

- **Window shopping.** "I don't know what I want. Show me stuff."

- **Trivia.** "What did Bob Marley die of, and when?"

- **Information gathering.** "How to tie correct knots in rope?"

- **Research.** "What is Keynesian economics and is it sustainable?"

Geographic

- **Friend check-ins.** "Where are Sam and Trevor?"

- **Directions.** "I need directions to Sammy's Pizza."

- **Local points of interest.** "Where is the nearest library or bookstore?"

- **Travel planning.** "I need flights, accommodations, and sights for my trip to Italy."

Personal Information Management

- **Checking notifications.** "Email update for work."

- **Checking calendar.** "Is there an open date on my family calendar?"

- **Situation analysis.** "What is my insurance coverage for CAT scans?"

- **Lifestyle planning.** "What should my New Year's resolutions be this year?"

Transactional

- **Act on notifications.** Mark as read, delete, respond to, etc.

- **Price comparison.** "How much does the Pantech phone cost on AT&T.com?"

- **Online shopping.** "I want to buy a watch as a gift. But which one?"

- **Product monitoring.** "I know the make and model of used car I want. Alert me when new ones are listed."

The occurrence of an information need does not, of course, guarantee its fulfillment. Sohn and colleagues (2008) found that only 45 percent of mobile information needs such as the ones above were fulfilled at the time that they arose. Twenty-five percent, they found, were addressed later, though a significant 30 percent of information needs were never satisfied. Reasons for this low success rate could include poor (or nonexistent) Internet access, being busy with other tasks such as driving a car, or simply running out of time to carry the task through to completion. The 25 percent of information needs with delayed gratification, however, highlight the importance of helping users capture and revisit unmet information needs at a later time, such as when they've returned to their desktop computer.

Context

Sohn and colleagues (2008) also found that the majority of mobile information needs— 72 percent in his study—are prompted by *context*. We already introduced four components of context in Chapter 3—task, physical, social, and environmental—but they are worth revisiting through the lens of mobile search. Chua, Balkunke and Goh (2011) observed that the *task*, *physical*, and *social* components were the most common triggers of information needs: *environmental* context, on the other hand, tends to inhibit information needs from being investigated.

Task

We've already discussed (in Chapter 3) how the work task—itself driven by an organizational or personal goal—is the primary source of many information needs. This argument still holds true for mobile users, but with a crucial twist; rather than being driven by an intrinsic task, mobile information needs are more likely to emerge from the context of the user's present activity. Cooking, for instance, is likely to produce a need for recipes or measurement conversions, while repairing a bicycle might trigger a need for how-to information.

Physical

The two subcomponents of physical context—time and space—are central to the mobile experience. The available time, for instance, dictates whether an information need can be fulfilled immediately or whether it must be postponed. Though time is often a limitation, it can also provide opportunities: "in between" times, as brief as waiting at a crosswalk for the pedestrian signal to change, can prompt users to engage in micro sessions of casual information seeking such as checking notifications.

Though we typically associate mobile device usage with being on the move—typified by a business worker catching up on correspondence during his or her commute—mobile usage often takes place in stationary spatial contexts as well (Figure 8.6). A significant level of usage occurs in the home, for instance, from multitasking while watching television to browsing from bed (Cui & Roto, 2008). Whether out and about or stationary, location prompts a greater number of mobile information needs than any other contextual factor (Sohn et al., 2008).

Social

Mobile devices are often used in the presence of other people. Though sometimes used inappropriately—checking messages at the dinner table, for instance—mobile devices are many times used as *conversation enhancers* (Cui & Roto, 2008). This usage often precipitates the "trivia" category of information need identified earlier. Although social situations can discourage the use of mobile devices, especially for substantial periods of time, they nevertheless commonly spark new information needs.

Environmental

We focused on the "information landscape" subcomponent in Chapter 3, but Internet connectivity is probably the most significant aspect of environmental context facing mobile users. "Dead zones" lacking connectivity such as elevators or metro trains disrupt users' activities; slow connection speeds force a trade-off between inefficient task completion at present, or more efficient completion later; limited or pay-as-you-go bandwidth incentivizes users to respond only to vital information needs that can be accomplished with limited data transfer. In other words, connectivity is a factor that often prohibits information needs from being satisfied when they arise.

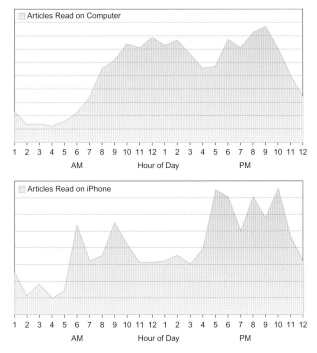

FIGURE 8.6 The distribution of reading activity throughout the day by computer users (top) and iPhone users (bottom) of the Read It Later service, a platform that enables people to retrieve web content they've previously saved. The chart shows iPhone usage peaking at around 6:00 a.m., 9:00 a.m., 5:00–6:00 p.m., and 8:00–10:00 p.m. (Read It Later, 2011).

Context is significant for all types of users, but it plays a particularly acute role for mobile users—prompting new information needs and influencing whether they can be satisfied in the available time and under potential conditions of mental and physical scarcity. We've seen that smartphone users tend to enter queries just as lengthy as desktop users but reformulate their queries less often. And we've explored the gamut of information needs encountered by mobile users. This survey of how mobile users engage in information seeking underpins the design guidance that we'll explore for the remainder of the chapter.

Exploring the Social Side to Mobile Search
Karen Church

When was the last time you used a mobile search engine? Can you remember what you searched for, where you were located and who you were with?

The last time I performed a mobile search was yesterday evening. I was at home with friends. We were sitting on the sofa watching a movie—*The Talented Mr. Ripley*, to be precise—and my friends and I were trying to guess what year the movie was released. A competition started, a friendly bet was made, and after a quick search on my mobile phone, we found the answer. I lost the bet.

Such casual, social mobile search behavior has been underappreciated in the past. In the following text, I will outline three key shifts in mobile web behaviors that are leading to more casual, social mobile search trends. I will highlight key differences in social mobile search behavior compared to general mobile search behavior and discuss what these differences mean for designers of mobile search experiences.

Shift 1: Mobile Is Not Always on the Move

More and more people are accessing the mobile Web in everyday settings like at home or at work. Nylander, Lundquist, and Brännström (2009) show that mobile Internet access occurs at home more than any other setting (31 percent). A more recent study by Church and Oliver (2011) shows that more than 70 percent of mobile Web access occurs when users are in familiar, stationary settings like at home and at work. Cui and Roto (2008) discovered a similar trend in a series of studies they carried out between 2004 and 2007: mobile Web access is becoming a more stationary activity. These studies indicate that location isn't the only contextual factor to consider in mobile search. With more and more mobile users connecting to online content while engaging in their everyday lives, designers of mobile search services will need to focus on how we can build innovative services that integrate seamlessly into their world.

Shift 2: Mobile Web Access Is Not Always Motivated by Awareness

Although research has shown that mobile Web access is motivated mainly by awareness—that is, the desire to stay informed (Taylor et al., 2008)—curiosity and diversion also account for a significant proportion of mobile Internet motivations (Church & Smyth, 2011). These motivations relate to the user's desire to kill time, alleviate boredom, or learn about an unfamiliar topic. Search has traditionally been viewed as driven by a specific information need, with success defined as finding the desired information in a minimal amount of time. In casual search scenarios, however, quickly finding the right information may not be the main goal (Wilson & Elsweiler, 2010). The measure of success for the casual search process is typically based on the level of user enjoyment during the search activity and/or for how long the user has been entertained. Given that recent research highlights that more and more users access content to kill time, eliminate boredom, and satisfy their curiosity, we should support such casual search scenarios in mobile settings.

Mobile Search Is Not a Solitary Act

We often think of search as a personal, private act, conducted in isolation. However, mobile search in particular is often a social act, sparked by conversations and carried out among groups of people. For example, Church and Oliver (2011) have shown that in more than 65 percent of cases, mobile search was conducted in the presence of other people. Likewise, a recent study of local mobile search has shown that in 63 percent of cases, mobile searches took place within a social context and were discussed with someone else in the group (Teevan et al., 2011). Given the social side to mobile search, we should try to understand how we can develop engaging mobile search experiences targeted not only for individuals but also for groups.

This shift in mobile web behaviors indicates that using mobile search in a casual, social manner among groups of friends represents a potentially fruitful area of research that has been largely ignored to date. And although past research has shed key insights into mobile web behaviors and lead to a number of advances in mobile web services, little research has focused on understanding social mobile search behaviors.

Our recent work at Telefonica Research takes a first step toward this goal. By conducting two field studies—a survey involving almost 200 users and a two-week diary and follow-up interview study of 20 users—we explored the motivations, circumstances, and experiences of using mobile search in social settings to satisfy group information needs. Key findings from this research include:

- Social mobile search behaviors tend to occur in more unfamiliar and mobile-specific locations than general mobile search (approximately 50 percent compared to greater than 70 percent).
- Social mobile search tends to happen among tightly knit social groups (i.e., friends and family) of mixed sizes.
- Curiosity and alleviating boredom are the primary motivations (almost 50 percent of responses).
- The most popular information needs relate to trivia and pop culture (almost 40 percent).
- Social mobile search is primarily sparked from conversations and is used primarily to engage or enrich those conversations.

Results from this study also highlight that sharing the mobile search experience is a difficult task. Mobile users often stumble upon interesting search results that they would like to share with their friends. And existing mobile search engines provide limited support for sharing mobile search results with one another, which means that mobile users currently share their experiences by speaking aloud or showing their phone. There is scope to support richer, more collaborative mobile search experiences among groups of mobile users; however, developing such experiences is not a trivial task. As well as designing for dynamically changing contexts and the inherent limitations of mobile devices, designers of mobile search experiences now need to consider how to connect groups of mobile users, how to engage these users through collaboration and sharing, and how to do so in an easy, fun, and intuitive manner.

Our aim in this short piece was to highlight the changing pace of mobile search, to describe some initial research efforts aimed at understanding why and how people use mobile search in social settings, and to highlight the challenges that these social behaviors bring to designers. Social mobile search behavior is gaining momentum, but we have a lot more work to do if we are to unleash the full potential of this uniquely mobile experience.

Karen Church is a Researcher within the User and Media Intelligence group in Telefonica Research, Barcelona, Spain. She received her PhD in Computer Science from University College Dublin, Ireland in 2008. Her PhD thesis was entitled, "A Study of Mobile Internet Usage and Implications for Mobile Search Interfaces." Karen's research interests include the mobile Web and mobile search space, mobile HCI, social mobile services, mobile user experience, and mobile interfaces. Karen was awarded a Marie Curie Fellowship in 2010. The fellowship involves investigating future mobile information access behaviors and trends. Her current research focus is on social mobile search services.

References

Church, K., & Oliver, N. (2011). Understanding mobile web and mobile search use in today's dynamic mobile landscape. MobileHCI '11, August 30–September 2, 2011, Stockholm, Sweden.

Church, K., & Smyth, B. (2009). Understanding the intent behind mobile information needs. IUI '09, February 8–11, 2009, Sanibel Island, FL.

Cui, Y., & Roto, V. (2008). How people use the Web on mobile devices. WWW 2008, April 21–25, 2008, Beijing, China.

Nylander, S., Lundquist, T., & Brännström, A. (2009). At home and with computer access. CHI '09, April 4–9, 2009, Boston, MA.

Taylor, C. A., Anicello, O., Somohano, S., Samuels, N., Whitaker, L., & Ramey, J. A. (2008). A framework for understanding mobile internet motivations and behaviors. CHI'08, April 5–10, 2008, Florence, Italy.

Teevan, J., Karlson, A., Amini, S., Brush, A. J. B., & Krumm, J. (2011). Understanding the importance of location, time, and people in mobile local search behavior. MobileHCI '11, August 30–September 2, 2011, Stockholm, Sweden.

Wilson, M. L., & Elsweiler, D. (2010). Casual-leisure searching: The exploratory search scenarios that break our current models. HCIR'10, August 18–22, 2010, New Brunswick, NJ.

MOBILE DESIGN PRINCIPLES

We've already established that simplicity is vital to the design of mobile applications in general. But there are a number of design principles that can help us achieve effective mobile *search* experiences in particular. Namely, most mobile search applications should prioritize content over controls, provide answers over results, and ensure cross-channel continuity.

Content trumps controls

Search, as the previous few chapters have shown, is usually accompanied by a number of knobs and dials: filters, breadcrumbs, sort controls, pagination—the list goes on. When moving from the design of desktop to mobile search interfaces, the temptation is to replicate all of these controls on the main search results screen. Yielding to this temptation, however, leads to cluttered, frustrating interfaces that add stumbling blocks to the user's path.

The primary search screen of a mobile application should be focused on the clarity of search results; bells and whistles must take a back seat (Figure 8.7). Mobile users, after all, often use their devices for short bursts of time, enter fewer queries per search session than do desktop users, and often seek answers to simple, lookup-based information needs. These realities suggest that navigation bars should be kept to a minimum, filtering and sorting displaced off-screen, and pagination controls omitted so that the search results receive as much screen space as possible.

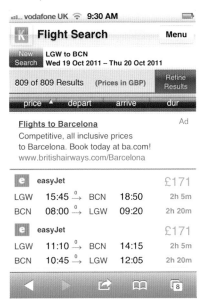

FIGURE 8.7 Kayak.com's mobile website—with four rows of controls and a large advertisement—clearly fails to adequately prioritize its search results.

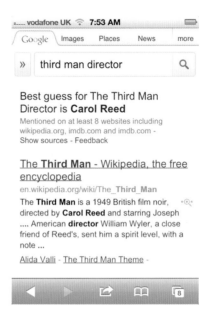

FIGURE 8.8　Google sometimes provides direct answers to the user's query.

Answers over results

In addition to minimizing search controls and emphasizing content, focusing on *precision* over recall can make search more efficient for mobile users with lookup information needs. Precision, as you will remember, describes the accuracy of the top results. Because mobile users reformulate their queries less often than desktop users—and are more likely to use their devices for short bursts of time—prioritizing the relevance of the top few results is generally more useful than delivering high recall.

Providing direct answers to users' lookup queries can make the mobile search experience more efficient still. Rather than force users to click on a search result to discover straightforward facts, such as "director of third man movie" (Figure 8.8), a more desirable approach is to provide a computed answer directly on the search page, eliminating the need for further action.

However, both of these approaches—emphasizing precision over recall and answers over results—are optimized for short-term, lookup-based information needs, and will have diminishing returns for learning and investigative motives when users are willing to invest greater amounts of attention. In other words, it depends on the user's context.

Cross-channel continuity

Every business recognizes the value of consistency across channels: customers benefit from a coherent, holistic experience in which the learning from one channel can be applied to all

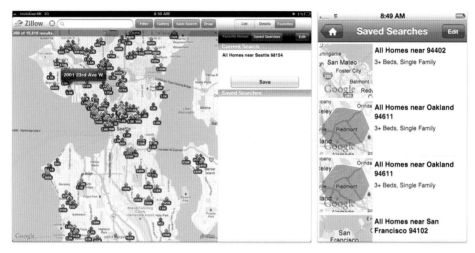

FIGURE 8.9 Zillow allows users to save searches but fails to synchronize them across devices.

the rest. A user familiar with Amazon on the desktop will instantly recognize the similarity of Amazon's mobile application, for instance. But although *consistency* ensures the learnability of each channel, *continuity* makes it personal. Continuity is adding an item to the shopping cart via a desktop computer and having it appear in the shopping cart on your phone; it's saving a search on your phone and returning to it later on your tablet. In other words, continuity ensures that your actions aren't performed in isolation but propagate from the source channel to each of the others.

As shown earlier, mobile users satisfy only 45 percent of their information needs at the time they arise, with 25 percent being completed later and 30 percent not at all. Continuity between channels can enhance the figure-it-out-later approach often taken by users, as well as reduce the number of information needs that fall through the cracks. For starters, search history should be synchronized across devices so that inconclusive information seeking can be easily completed later. What's more, facilitating saved searches that can be accessed from every channel enables users to organize and return to important, ongoing information needs (Figure 8.9).

MOBILE DESIGN SOLUTIONS

Although understanding mobile searchers and following high-level principles when designing for them are prerequisites to any successful mobile search experience, the rubber meets the road with pixels on the screen. In this section, we'll apply our understanding of mobile information seeking to the design of the search box, nontextual input methods, displaying search results, and refining the query. In each case, the design solutions are

FIGURE 8.10 Anatomy of a mobile layout.

meant to be as cross-platform as possible and apply equally to both native (i.e., software built specifically for a mobile operating system) and web-based applications.

But before getting started, it's helpful to agree on a vocabulary for describing the common layout components of a mobile application.[2] Figure 8.10 illustrates the following three regions:

- **Status bar.** The thin top-most bar indicating signal, time, battery life, and other information.

- **Navigation bar.** The dominant bar often containing a title and back button.

- **Toolbar.** An optional bar for additional controls, located at either the top or bottom of the screen.

The search box

Mobile devices offer a number of alternative input options often not practical on desktop computers; however, keyword queries are still the mainstay of mobile searching. There are at least three common approaches to displaying the search box, each with advantages and disadvantages (Figure 8.11):

- **Within the navigation bar.** Maximizes space efficiency and places strong emphasis on search. Use when search is the dominant action of the application.

- **In a secondary toolbar.** Retains emphasis on search, but leaves less room for content. Consider this approach when search is a dominant action and when placing the search box within the navigation bar is not an option.

- **Via a pull-to-reveal gesture.** Because the search box is hidden by default, this approach maximizes the available screen space but makes search more difficult to discover. This method is a good choice when search isn't the primary action.

Even when the search box is in a secondary toolbar—as in the Pinterest iPhone app (Figure 8.12)—it's common practice to hide other navigation bars once the user taps the

---

[2] For the sake of simplicity, we have used the same terms defined by Apple in the iPhone and iPad Human Interface Guidelines.

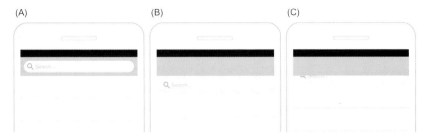

FIGURE 8.11 Three approaches to displaying the search box: **(A)** within the navigation bar, **(B)** in a secondary toolbar, or **(C)** via a pull-to-reveal gesture.

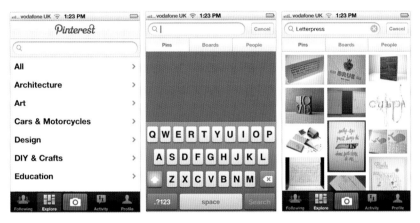

FIGURE 8.12 Pinterest, an online pinboard, hides their iPhone application's navigation bar and adds a segmented control when the user focuses on the search box.

search box. This both provides greater focus on the search task, and allows more space for presenting as-you-type suggestions.

Users have come to expect as-you-type suggestions as an integral part of the mobile search experience. Small mobile devices typically devote all of the screen space not consumed by the top bars and onscreen keyboard to presenting search suggestions (Figure 8.13), and tablet devices often use a popover for this same purpose (Figure 8.14). All three types of as-you-type suggestions outlined in Chapter 5—autocomplete, autosuggest, and instant results—apply equally well to the mobile environment.

Nontextual input methods

Although typing into the search box is the most common means by which to initiate a search, the integration of cameras, microphones, sensors, and touchscreens present in mobile devices opens the door to many new types of input. From location-awareness to voice search, image-based queries to finger-drawn shapes, these emergent forms of input have the potential to change the way people search on their mobile devices.

FIGURE 8.13 Three types of as-you-type suggestions. **(A)** DB Navigator provides autocomplete on train station names. **(B)** Google Search provides autosuggest. **(C)** Nutshell delivers instant results.

FIGURE 8.14 Tablet applications, such as Thomson Reuter Marketplace app, often present as-you-type suggestions in a popover.

Location is the most obvious form of nontextual input enabled by mobile devices (though it's not exclusive to mobile—most desktop browsers now support location lookup as well). Offering an option for the user to select his or her current location is useful whenever the expected input is geographical. This usefulness applies when the user is searching for a location alone—such as in the Zillow and Rightmove real estate examples

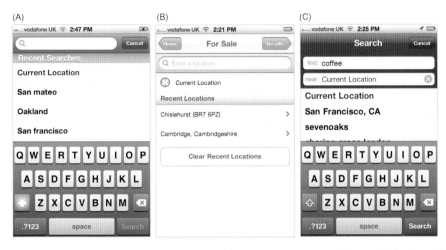

FIGURE 8.15 Example of location input at **(A)** Zillow, **(B)** Rightmove.co.uk, and **(C)** Yelp, which all provide a "Current Location" link within the as-you-type suggestions.

FIGURE 8.16 **(A)** Siri on the iPhone and **(B)** Voice Search on Android both allow users to speak their queries; **(C)** SoundHound retrieves song information on the music playing in the background.

in Figure 8.15—as well as when a keyword search is being geographically scoped, as in the case of Yelp.

Voice interaction with machines is far from a new idea, yet only recently has its execution reached a threshold of maturity. Apple, Google, and Microsoft all provide mobile voice-activated searching in one form or another (Figure 8.16). In addition to spoken input, applications such as SoundHound can listen to music playing in the surrounding environment and retrieve information about the song.

In addition to location and audio input, connected cameras mean that visual information can also be harnessed for searching (Figure 8.17). Common uses include scanning product barcodes—such as with Amazon's native Android and iPhone

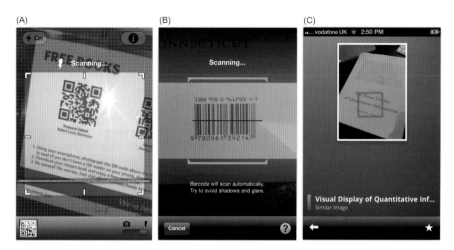

FIGURE 8.17 **(A)** QRReader turns QR codes into URLs; **(B)** Amazon scans barcodes to pull up exact matches; and **(C)** Google turns images into textual queries.

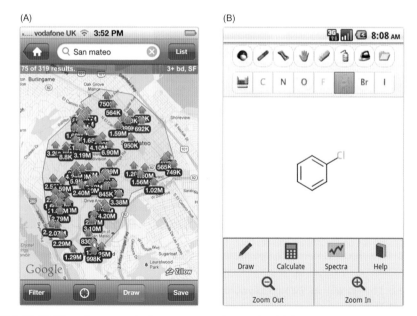

FIGURE 8.18 **(A)** Zillow allows users to draw an area on the map in which to constrain their search, while **(B)** ChemDoodle enables users to visually compose molecular compounds that serve as the query.

applications—and QR codes—two-dimensional barcodes typically used to encode URLs. Google also provides visual searching that can read text from an image and run a keyword search using the detected words.

Drawn shapes, made possible by the advent of touchscreens, provide a final form of non-textual input. The most common use of finger-drawn figures is to add a bounding box

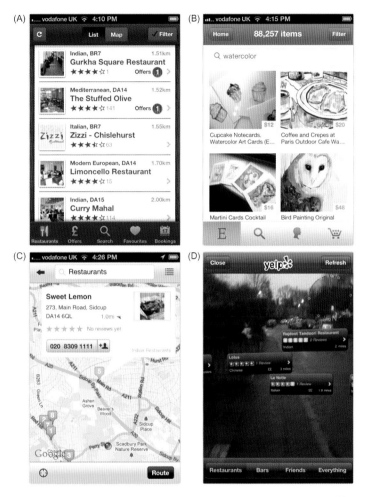

FIGURE 8.19 Search results presented as **(A)** a list on Toptable, **(B)** thumbnails on Etsy, **(C)** map pinpoints on Yell, and **(D)** augmented reality on Yelp.

around a region on a map, illustrated by Zillow in Figure 8.18. ChemDoodle, also shown in Figure 8.18, allows users to construct molecular diagrams that can then be used as a query, demonstrating the potential of shape input in scientific settings.

Viewing search results

Regardless of how the query was originally constructed, the results for that query must be presented in one of several formats (Figure 8.19). The most common display methods are:

- **List.** Lists provide the most space for titles, descriptions and metadata, but deemphasize the visual and geographical dimensions of the results. Lists are effective at helping users quickly peruse the textual information of numerous results.

- **Grid.** Image grids provide a strong visual emphasis but lack the space to accommodate much textual information. They're efficient when the content is predominantly visual.

- **Map.** Maps are ideal when location is the most important characteristic of the search results, though they're more difficult to systematically review than are lists or grids.

- **Augmented Reality.** Still an immature medium, augmented reality (AR) uses the mobile device's camera and screen to superimpose information onto a representation of the surrounding environment. AR is especially useful for providing directions.

- **Voice.** The other four formats are visual, but it's not always possible to look at a screen. Activities such as driving, as well as disabilities such as visual impairment, call for a purely verbal rendition of search results.

Although each display format is better suited to some types of content over others—image grids for photographs, maps for locations, and so on—users often desire to switch between display modes depending on their task. When choosing a restaurant, for instance, a hungry user might prefer a map if his or her goal is to minimize travel, but a textual list sorted by rating if the priority is the quality of the restaurant. As such, it's often necessary to provide controls for toggling between display formats (Figure 8.20). Four common solutions to toggling the display format include:

- **A full-width segmented control in a toolbar.** This approach allows for the greatest number of labels (three or four) but eats into space that could otherwise be used for content.

- **A compressed segmented control centered in the navigation bar.** With room for two or three labels, this method avoids the need for an additional toolbar but demands that the search box be hidden off-screen.

- **A single button in the navigation bar.** Though it can only toggle between two display formats, it's the most concise control of the three.

- **Tabs.** Though a ubiquitous pattern on the Web, traditional tabs are rarely seen in native mobile applications (excluding, of course, the bottom "tab bar" convention in iOS). However, it's still a valid approach, especially for web-based apps that don't attempt native resemblance.

Refining the query

Inputting the query and viewing the returned search results is often only the beginning of the information journey. We saw earlier in the chapter that mobile users are slightly less likely to reformulate their query than are desktop users, yet this finding does not preclude the need for refinement. In particular, information needs falling into the "learn" and "investigate" motives of the mobile information need matrix rely heavily on the ability to iteratively refine the query. However, refinement tools must not detract from the content

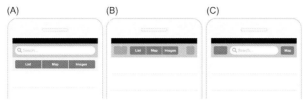

FIGURE 8.20 Common approaches to toggling between display methods: **(A)** a full-width segmented control in a toolbar, **(B)** a compressed segmented control centered in the navigation bar, and **(C)** a single button in the navigation bar.

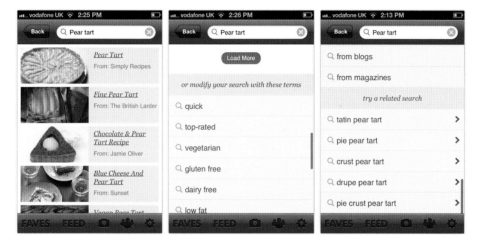

FIGURE 8.21 Foodily provides two forms of query suggestions below the list of search results: modifier terms and related searches.

itself. Related searches, faceted navigation, sorting, and breadcrumbs should be discretely designed to offer adequate control without getting in the way.

Providing related searches at the bottom of the page effectively matches query assistance with the moment of need: if users don't find what they were looking for in the first batch of results, they're likely to consider a query modification. Foodily, as shown in Figure 8.21, actually provides two different types of query suggestions: first suggesting modifier terms to add to the existing query (words like "quick" and "gluten free"), followed by related searches that alter the query more drastically. This method lives up to the criteria of providing support without detracting from content.

Faceted navigation and sorting are more sought-after query refinement tools than related searches, but are a bit more difficult to achieve unobtrusively. The first decision that must be made is whether faceted navigation or sorting should be provided on the primary search screen or whether they should have a dedicated view of their own. Adding them to the main screen would typically involve adding a toolbar containing either a

FIGURE 8.22 (A) A segmented control for sorting, **(B)** a segmented control for top-level categories, and **(C)** scrollable capsules representing a facet.

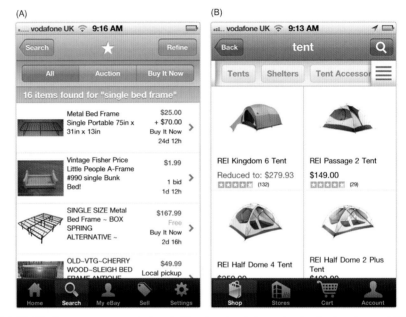

FIGURE 8.23 (A) eBay uses a segmented control for choosing between top-level categories, and **(B)** REI uses scrollable capsules to display filters.

segmented control (for either sorting or top-level categories) or horizontally scrollable capsules representing a facet (Figures 8.22 and 8.23).

Presenting refinement options in a toolbar on the main search screen provides quick, easy access for users, yet the approach has substantial drawbacks: not only does it occupy space otherwise reserved for content, but it is limited to presenting only a handful of items. A less crowded approach is to dedicate an entire screen to sorting and faceted navigation (Figure 8.24).

Designing faceted search for mobile interfaces follows the same principles discussed in Chapter 7. In fact, matching the display format of a given facet to the semantics of its data is even more essential on mobile devices than elsewhere. The eBay example shown in Figure 8.25, for instance, treats all facets the same: as simple, plain text options. This method provides little visibility into the contents of each facet and requires at least two taps to apply any one filter. The Yelp and Airbnb examples in Figure 8.25, on the

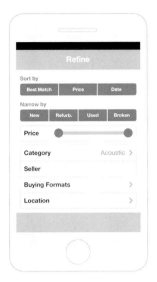

FIGURE 8.24 A dedicated refinement screen for sorting and filtering.

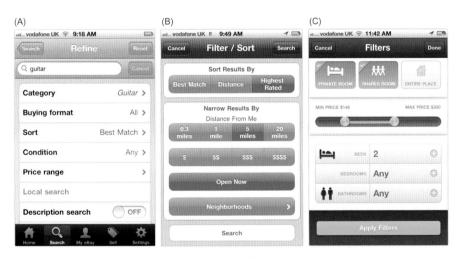

FIGURE 8.25 Faceted search on (A) eBay, (B) Yelp, and (C) Airbnb.

other hand, are more proactive about providing suitable display methods for each facet; they use plain text, segmented controls, and sliders where each is most appropriate. This approach enables more information to be presented in less space and makes many controls actionable with just a single tap.

Reserving an entire screen for faceted navigation can accommodate numerous controls without compromising the search results screen. Such dedicated panels are usually

(A)   (B)   (C)

FIGURE 8.26   Filter/Refine buttons on **(A)** eBay, **(B)** Yelp, and **(C)** Airbnb.

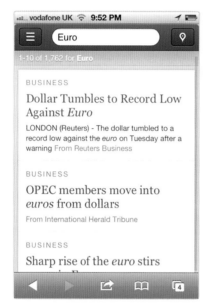
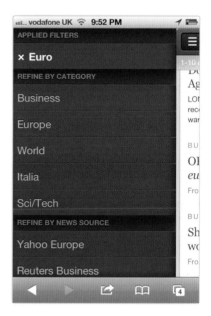

FIGURE 8.27   TwigKit's faceted navigation sidebar can be accessed with either a button or through a swipe gesture.

activated by a button on the main screen containing the word "Filter," "Refine," or an equivalent icon (Figure 8.26), though gestures can also be used to reveal and hide the controls. TwigKit's web-based search user interface shown in Figure 8.27, for example, reveals faceted controls in a side panel that can be opened and closed both by tapping a button, as well as through left/right swipe gestures.

Although dedicated control panels are often ideal on smartphones, presenting a full screen of knobs and dials on much larger tablet devices would likely be overwhelming. Instead, tablets often take advantage of popovers (Figure 8.28) to display refinement options (in fact, the popover often contains the very same view presented on phone-sized devices).

Last of all, breadcrumbs help users keep track of their query and applied filters, as usual. Unlike on the desktop, however, mobile breadcrumbs need not be clickable; devoting finger-size touch targets to breadcrumbs could drown out the content. Instead, mobile breadcrumbs should be small, but legible (Figure 8.29). Users can always interact with the refinement panel to remove or alter any unwanted filters.

FIGURE 8.28 Toptable's iPad app uses a popover present refinement options.

FIGURE 8.29 Mobile breadcrumbs should be legible but don't have to be clickable.

SUMMARY

Much more could be said about designing the mobile search experience: from interaction and visual design, to tablet and smartphone differences, to native versus web-based implementation strategies—we've only scratched the surface! Yet by beginning with an investigation of what makes mobile users tick, formulating principles of design, and surveying design solutions for the basic components of mobile search, we hope we've at least whetted your appetite for this exciting frontier.

REFERENCES

Broder, A. (2002). A taxonomy of web search. *SIGIR Forum*, *36*(2), 3–10.

Chua, A., Balkunje, R., & Goh, D. (2011). Fulfilling mobile information needs: A study on the use of mobile phones. *ICUIMC'11*, February 21–23, 2011, Seoul, Korea. ACM.

Church, K., & Smyth, B. (2009). Understanding the intent behind mobile information needs. *IUI'09*, February 8–11, 2009, Sanibel Island, FL.

Cisco (2011). *Cisco visual networking index: Global mobile data traffic forecast update, 2010–2015.* Retrieved June 9, 2012, from: http://www.cisco.com/en/US/solutions/collateral/ns341/ns525/ns537/ns705/ns827/white_paper_c11-520862.pdf.

Cui, Y., & Roto, V. (2008). How people use the web on mobile devices. *WWW 2008*, April 21–25, 2008, Beijing, China.

Elsweiler, D., Wilson, M. L., & Kirkegaard-Lunn, B. (2011). Understanding casual-leisure information behaviour. In A. Spink, & J. Heinstrom (Eds.), *New Directions in Information Behaviour*: Bingley, UK: Emerald Group Publishing Limited, 211–241.

Marchionini, G. (2006). Exploratory search: from finding to understanding. *Communications of the ACM, 49*(4), 41–46.

Meeker, M., Devitt, S., & Wu, L. (2010). *Internet trends.* Morgan Stanley. Retrieved June 9, 2012 from http://www.scribd.com/doc/29850507/Internet-Trends-Mary-Meeker-04-12-2010.

Kamvar, M., Kellar, M., Patel, R., & Xu, Y. (2009). Computers and iPhones and mobile phones, oh my! A logs-based comparison of search users on different devices. *WWW 2009*, April 20–24, 2009, Madrid, Spain.

Read It Later. (2011). Is mobile affecting when we read? Readitlater.com. Retrieved June 9, 2012, from http://readitlaterlist.com/blog/2011/01/is-mobile-affecting-when-we-read/.

Resmini, A., & Rosati, L. (2011). Pervasive information architecture: Designing cross-channel user experiences: *xvi*. Burlington, Massachusetts: Morgan Kaufmann.

Sohn, T., Li, K., Griswold, W., & Hollan, J. (2008). A diary study of mobile information needs. *CHI 2008*, April 5–10, 2008, Florence, Italy.

Tate, T., & Russell-Rose, T. (2012). The information needs of mobile searchers: A framework. Searching4Fun workshop at *ECIR 2012*.

Wroblewski, L. (2011). *Mobile first.* New York: A Book Apart 37.

More Like This: A Tablet Design Pattern
Greg Nudelman

More like this is a simple yet powerful search and browse design pattern that is greatly underused on touch devices. It is particularly effective for larger touch devices such as tablets, where it can be used to transform a variety of search tasks into a pleasurable, visual browsing experience.

How It Works

The "more like this" design pattern itself is quite simple: search results are placed in a gallery format across several rows, with each row representing a particular subdivision of the result set. Rows can be created from any division that makes sense, such as subcategory, brand, date or prices ranges, and so on. On larger touch devices, it makes sense to equip each row with

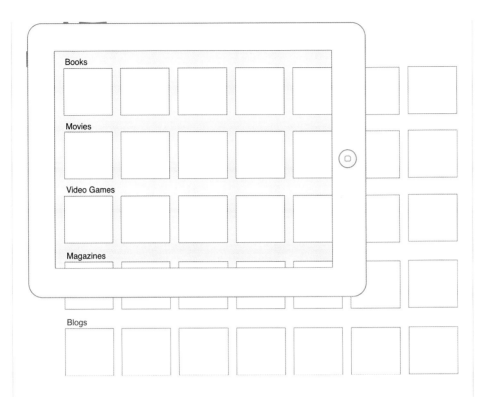

FIGURE 8.30 How the "more like this" pattern works on tablets.

a carousel control: that is, in addition to a few thumbnails that can be displayed to the user, each row also extends two or three screen-widths to the right, enabling the customer to view additional elements in each row by swiping right to left, as shown in Figure 8.30.

In addition to scrolling to the right, the page can also be scrolled down to see more rows, resulting in a two-dimensional scrollable matrix of thumbnails organized by topic. It is important to note that each row should also be equipped with a "more like this" link, which is essential to the success of this pattern. The link should be placed somewhere in the row so that no scrolling is required to select it. On touch screens, this can typically be accomplished by making the row title clickable. For best results, the "more like this" link could also be placed as the last spot in the scrollable carousel, as shown in Figure 8.31. That way, if the customers do not find what they are looking for in the carousel, they can tap the link to see more search results that match both their query and the topic of that particular row.

FIGURE 8.31 Placement of "more like this" links.

FIGURE 8.32 The "more like this" pattern in NPR's iPad app.

Example

Although this pattern is at present greatly underused, there are a few good implementations. Among them is NPR's iPad app, pictured in Figure 8.32.

NPR's iPad app uses the "more like this" pattern on its home screen. The home screen divides NPR's content into individual rows by topic, allowing people to easily browse over topics in an attractive visual page design.

When and Where to Use It

The "more like this" pattern can be used for a wide variety of search tasks:

- Organizing content on the home screen
- Browsing landing pages
- Query disambiguation
- Anytime you have a more general query that invites browsing exploration

This pattern works well on larger touch devices such as tablets whenever the result set exceeds what can be shown comfortably on the screen of the device. It works best for result sets that are primarily visual but may include additional captions or even text snippets.

Why Use It

Tablets such as the iPad lend themselves to "contemplative consumption" of important information accessed using large, sweeping gestures, appropriate to the larger size of the device, with minimal typing. There are few search design patterns better suited to taking advantage of this than "more like this."

People typically use pages designed using the "more like this" pattern by scrolling the page down and up through large, sweeping gestures and looking for the row most appropriate to the task (or simply the row that looks like it would be most interesting to browse). Upon finding the row, people scroll the row to the right and left checking out other items on the row. The page lends itself to larger gestures (up-down and left-right) while also boasting large targets of individual item thumbnails to enable simple, foolproof drill-down. Well-designed "more like this" pages take full advantage of the available surface area of the device, work well in both landscape and portrait, and provide excellent ergonomics. Overall, this pattern contributes to the feeling of flow: immersive, elegant, strain-free flight through visual information.

Caution

Although this pattern is difficult to misinterpret, people always try their best. Here are a few common pitfalls to avoid:

1. **Don't get stuck with the same dimension for each row on the page.** Though this is a common application of this pattern, it is by no means the only one available. "More like this" is not just for displaying the subcategories of a single parent category. Instead, use subdivisions that make sense for your audience: one row can be subdivided by category, the second by brand, the third by price range, and so on. My research shows that people find this approach very useful and practical and do not get lost in trying to figure out the information architecture of individual rows. Instead, they dive straight in and begin using the information by exploring the rows that make most sense to them.

FIGURE 8.33 Truncating with ellipsis versus the "fading text" pattern used in individual "more like this" items.

2. **Don't forget the teasers.** If you do use carousels in each row (which I highly recommend on touch devices), remember that this extra content is not entirely intuitive or discoverable. The best way to showcase that more information can be obtained by scrolling is by showing a *teaser*—a partial view of the next item. Teasers can be used on the right to show that there are more items in each row, as well as on the bottom of the page, to show that more rows can be accessed by scrolling down. Don't forget that teasers need to work well in portrait and landscape orientations. The best way to ensure that is to increase the number of rows and items across the row, respectively, based on the particular device orientation.

3. **Use real items.** Although it's possible to use this pattern with all kinds of visuals, the best implementations of "more like this" use real item thumbnails in each row, not icons or drawings.

4. **Use the accelerators.** Some implementations of this pattern use the alternative "one page at a time" scroll behavior in scrolling horizontally across a row. I recommend against this. In order to maintain the feeling of flow, each row's carousel needs to have the same smooth acceleration as the rest of the page, ideally adjusting the scroll speed of the row in response to the speed of the horizontal swipe gesture.

Related Patterns

Because "more like this" is primarily visual, one of the best patterns to use it with is the *fading text* pattern, which allows the page to display as much text as possible. Using this pattern, the text under the image gently fades as it reaches the end of the row to indicate that more text is available upon drill-down. This design allows the most efficient use of limited display space while removing the need for premature truncation and annoying, repetitive ellipses. One example is shown in Figure 8.33.

For more than 12 years, Greg has been designing experiences that work for Fortune 500 companies. Greg is the author of Designing Search: UX Strategies for eCommerce Success (Wiley, 2011). Greg's second Wiley book on mobile and tablet design is due out later this year. He writes about mobile and tablet UX design on designcaffeine.com.

Social Search

9

The opinion of this little circle... outweighs that of a thousand outsiders.

— *C. S. Lewis*

Search often appears personal, introspective, and private—an activity of the individual in isolation. Yet a 2008 survey found that 97.1 percent of respondents had engaged in at least one form of collaborative search (Morris, 2008). The survey established that users frequently work together on the process of search, which could be as simple as watching over someone's shoulder and making suggestions for other query terms to try, as well as share the products of their efforts—emailing links to newly discovered web pages, for instance.

Such collaborative behavior often flies under the banner of "social search." Yet the term seems to mean different things to different people. Brynn Evans and Ed Chi (2009) broadly define social search as:

An umbrella term used to describe search acts that make use of social interactions with others. These interactions may be explicit or implicit, co-located or remote, synchronous or asynchronous. (p. 485)

In this chapter, we present our own take on social search. We begin by establishing a framework of collaboration composed of three concentric circles. Once that foundation is in place, we'll then take a closer look at how to design for the unique forms of collaboration that take place in each of the three circles.

THREE CIRCLES OF COLLABORATION

Social search encompasses many different activities, including explicit cooperation with others during information seeking, enlisting help from one's social groups, and implicit

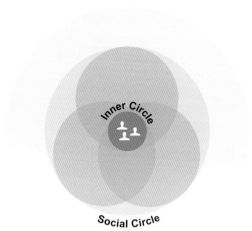

FIGURE 9.1 Three circles of collaborative search: the inner circle, the social circle, and the outer circle.

collaboration with strangers. In order to effectively design collaborative search experiences, we must first attain a holistic view of social search itself. We see collaborative search as three circles: the inner circle, the social circle, and the outer circle (Figure 9.1).

The inner circle

The *inner circle* forms the nucleus of collaboration. It is made up of one or more active participants with a shared work task—that is, a shared personal or organizational goal (Järvelin and Ingwersen, 2004). This shared goal provides the underlying motivation for inner circle collaboration: working together requires less effort from each participant than if he or she were approaching the task alone. Here are three examples of inner circles formed around a common goal:

- Angela Baer has agreed to go on a trip to Mexico with two of her friends. They need to plan the excursion: book flights, choose accommodation, and arrange activities.
- Fane Tomescu and his wife are looking to buy a car. They need to screen potential candidates and agree on which vehicles to pursue.
- Simon Carter and three other patent analysts must determine whether their corporation's new technique for manufacturing solar cells can be patented.

The inner circle is characterized by a shared work task, but the information needs of each participant need not be identical. Collaborators may adopt a *divide-and-conquer* strategy in which each participant is assigned a subtask and must report his or her findings back to the group (Morris, 2008). For example, Angela Baer might decide to research flights herself but ask her friends to investigate hotels and activities.

Alternatively, some inner circles may take a *brute force* approach, with each participant doing his or her own, uncoordinated research and then comparing notes later (Morris, 2008). Simon Carter and his team of analysts, for example, might begin by individually familiarizing themselves with existing solar cell patents. Though this approach gives each participant free reign and helps everyone gain literacy on the topic as a whole, it can also lead to duplicated efforts.

Last, collaborators may choose a *backseat driver* method when physically gathered around a single display (Morris, 2008). For instance, Fane Tomescu might be controlling the mouse and keyboard while his wife reads the screen over his shoulder, making suggestions about which cars to view. This method can often cause frustration, however, as the collaborators must constantly compromise on the pace and direction of the search.

The social circle

Each collaborator within the inner circle is likely also connected with a number of wider social groups. Often organized around a shared interest (e.g., scuba diving), job role (e.g., UX design), or place (e.g., the London office), these social circles can be pictured as layers surrounding the inner circle. From time to time, inner circle collaborators may reach out to one or more of their social circles for help. For example:

- Angela Baer and her friends hadn't yet decided exactly where to visit in Mexico, so Angela posted a status update on Facebook, saying: "Hmm, wonder what places I should visit on my Mexico trip?"

- Fane Tomescu's brother had recently bought a car, so Fane called him on the phone to see if he had any recommendations for websites to use or dealerships to visit.

- Simon Carter searched for internal documents from their solar cell division and, noticing that a single engineer authored many of them, emailed the engineer with a few questions of his own.

Morris, Teevan, and Panovich (2010) surveyed 624 users of social networking services to investigate why people use status update messages to pose questions to their social circles, as Angela Baer did in the earlier example. The respondents felt that for matters of opinion, people were more reliable than search engines. What's more, they identified trust as the greatest driver for posing questions to their social circles, with one respondent saying, "I trust my friends more than I trust strangers."

The incentive for responding to such publicly posed questions is a bit more nuanced, however. Many of Morris' survey respondents indicated *altruism* and *expertise* as two motivations for volunteering answers to questions. But other respondents were more honest and descriptive about their motives: the desire to maintain relationships with others, establish themselves as experts in certain areas, or to increase the likelihood of their own questions being answered in the future.

Motives aside, there are a number of benefits that occur when inner circle collaborators reach out to other individuals in their social circles. Cross and Sproull (2004), surveying

40 managers at a major accounting firm, identified five common outcomes: answers to questions, referrals to other information sources, reformulations of the problem, validation of plans, and legitimization (i.e., a "stamp of approval" from a respected person). Fane Tomescu's brother, for instance, probably didn't tell Fane exactly which car to buy (i.e., the "solution"), but he may have referred Fane to a reliable website or dealership.

The outer circle

Both the inner and social circles reflect an *explicit*, intentional form of collaboration between individuals who share some degree of social connectedness. The outer circle, on the other hand, is the realm of *implicit*, unintentional collaboration, predominantly amongst strangers. Here, search engines and recommendation systems use large quantities of user-generated data to drive personalization. For example:

- Angela Baer accessed a travel website she'd used in the past and was presented with recommended holiday packages under the heading: "Travelers similar to you enjoyed these resorts."
- Fane Tomescu entered the query "Opel Corsa reviews" into a web search engine. The results that came back were partially based upon the number of times other users had clicked on each item.
- Simon Carter visited an online bookstore and searched for a book on the physics of solar cells. He was then presented with a list of similar books described as: "Customers who bought this item also bought ...."

One form of implicit collaboration involves using *clickthrough data*—the number of times a given search result has been clicked—to influence the ranking of search results, as Fane Tomescu experienced. The approach taken by Agichtein, Brill, and Dumais (2006), for instance, is to infer that a click on the third result implies that results one and two must be less relevant than result three. Other behavioral cues such as query reformulations, bookmarks, and ratings can also be used to alter ranking.

Indeed, recommender systems also rely on behavioral cues. One technique they often employ is *collaborative filtering* (Goldberg et al., 1992), which most often works by grouping together similar users based on the content they've viewed, purchased, or rated and then providing a set of recommendations to all the users within that group. This approach could be used to power the "Travelers similar to you enjoyed these resorts" recommendations seen by Angela Baer and is notably also used to power Netflix's movie recommendations (Koren, Bell, & Volinsky, 2009).

User-based similarity, on the other hand, relies on having a critical mass of usage data for a given person, data that may not exist for a new user. A way around this "cold start" problem is to use *item-to-item collaborative filtering* (Linden, Smith, & York, 2003). Rather than profile users, this approach concerns itself only with finding similar items. When Simon Carter viewed a book about the physics of solar cells, for example, the online store recalled all the users who had purchased that title in the past, then queried other items those users had also purchased, and arrived at a list of recommendations (e.g., "Customers who bought this item also bought"). Amazon has used this approach quite successfully.

Stepping back

Having begun at the inner circle—the focal point of explicit collaboration—then zoomed out to the social circle, and continued to the outer circle of implicit collaboration, we can now consider collaboration from a higher vantage point. In particular, we should compare this three-circle model with the dimensions of collaboration that have been enumerated by others, namely:

1. **Intent:** explicit versus implicit (Morris & Teevan, 2008)

2. **Concurrency:** synchronous versus asynchronous (Rodden, 1991)

3. **Location:** co-located versus remote (Rodden, 1991)

4. **Means of interaction:** human-centric versus document-centric (Hansen & Järvelin, 2005)

The three-circle model is certainly compatible with these dimensions: explicit versus implicit differentiates the outer circle from the other two; synchronous versus asynchronous (whether collaboration occurs in near real-time or intermittently) and colocated versus remote affects both inner circle and social circle collaboration.

Finally, it's worth considering two common permutations to the three-circle model that we haven't yet explored. First, the inner circle often contains only a single individual. In such cases, no one shares the user's work task or information need, but explicit collaboration may still occur between the user and his or her social circles. A second permutation is when search engines take the techniques typically associated with outer circle collaboration (clickthrough data, collaborative filtering, item-to-item filtering, etc.) and apply them specifically to one's social circles to provide personalized search results. Bing, for instance, integrates with Facebook, and Google incorporates Google+ social data to influence results. Each of these alters the nature of collaboration but is accommodated by the three-circle model.

Next, we'll consider how to design for collaboration in each of the circles, starting from the inside out.

DESIGNING FOR INNER CIRCLE COLLABORATION

J. R. R. Tolkien and C. S. Lewis—creators of *The Lord of the Rings* and *The Chronicles of Narnia*, respectively—are famously known for forming an informal literary group called the Inklings. Every Thursday evening they would gather with a handful of peers at the Eagle and Child pub in Oxford, where they would read and discuss one another's works in progress. This close-knit group of writers exemplifies several key ingredients of collaboration, such as a communal space, shared artifacts (draft manuscripts, in their case), and group conversation—elements modern collaboration tools would do well to emulate.

In this section, we look at five components of effective inner circle collaboration tools: a shared workspace, social objects, quick add, instant communication, and persistence.

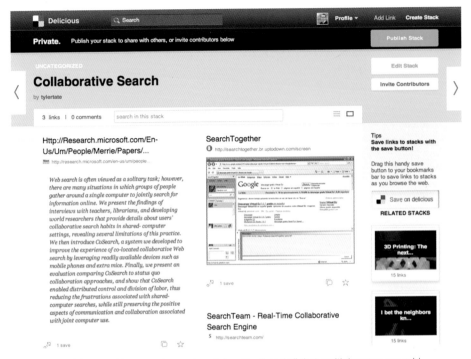

FIGURE 9.2 Delicious enables users to create collaborative "stacks" that multiple users can add bookmarks to and post comments on.

Shared workspace

Collaboration needs space in which to occur, a single destination where the inner circle gathers. A shared workspace provides the environment where web pages, documents, photos, videos, and other items can be shared, where conversation between collaborators can occur, and where conclusions can be documented.

Social bookmarking tools such as Delicious—popular in the 2000s before being spun off by Yahoo in 2011 and subsequently rebuilt—demonstrate a traditional approach to collaborative information seeking (Figure 9.2). Users can create "stacks," add bookmarks to those stacks, and invite others to add their own contributions.

Another take on curated content is Pinterest, which bills itself as an online pinboard (Figure 9.3). Rather than bookmarking websites, its members "pin" images that they find around the Web onto one of their "boards," resulting in a themed collage. Although most of Pinterest's boards are curated by a single individual, ownership can also be shared, enabling an inner circle to collectively gather images.

Delicious and Pinterest each cater to a specific medium—web pages and images, respectively; others such as Zootool (Figure 9.4) make virtue of organizing everything in one place, regardless of the media type. Zootool allows users to create a "stack," add virtually any type of file to the stack, and then filter by type for quick retrieval. But surprisingly, Zootool's stacks cannot be shared with others.

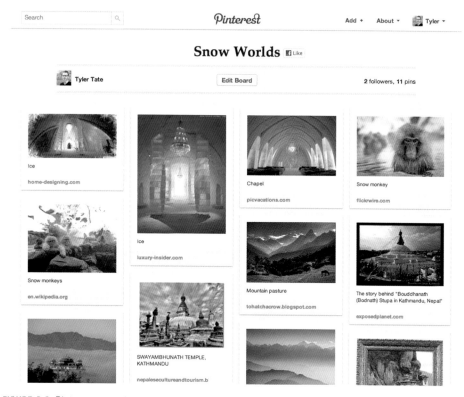

FIGURE 9.3 Pinterest, an online pinboard.

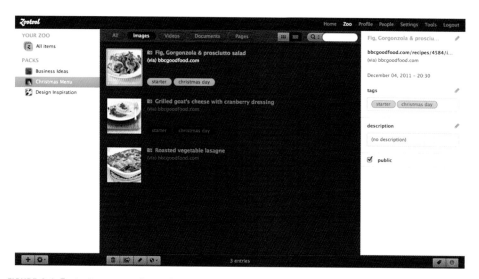

FIGURE 9.4 Zootool, a personal organization tool.

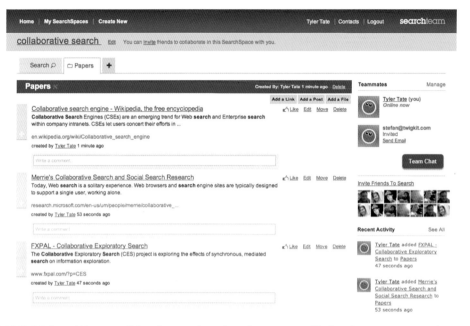

FIGURE 9.5 SearchTeam, a collaborative search engine, allows users to "like" and comment on saved items.

Social objects

A fundamental purpose of the shared workspace is to host collected items meaningful to the inner circle. Transforming these saved web pages, documents, photos, and videos into *social objects*—by facilitating such interactions as ratings and annotations, for instance—provides an important channel for inner circle collaboration.

The collaborative search engine SearchTeam (Figure 9.5), for example, allows users to create "SearchSpaces" to which they and their teammates can add links, posts, and files. These social objects can then be annotated and "liked" by teammates, providing the means to both save and discuss items of interest to the group.

But collaborative search need not be limited to the realm of standalone tools; many existing applications would also be wise to incorporate collaborative elements. Property search site Globrix (Figure 9.6), for instance, allows users to save, rate, and annotate properties.

Quick add

Of course, in order for a social object to appear in the inner circle's shared workspace, someone must put it there. Saving an item to the workspace is the most critical action of collaborative search and the greatest barrier to entry. It must be as painless a process as possible, lest users decide it's not worth their effort. Forms should be kept short; fields should be prepopulated; the previously selected workspace should remain selected by default; and users should be able to create new workspaces without navigating away.

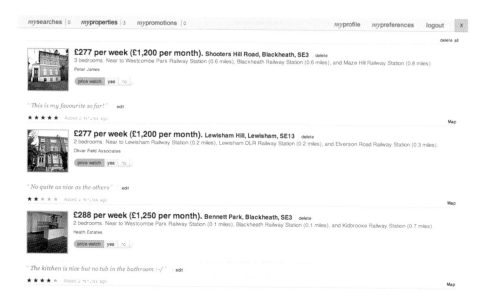

FIGURE 9.6 Globrix allows individual users to save, rate, and annotate properties but doesn't enable sharing with others.

FIGURE 9.7 TwigKit Collective, an enterprise collaborative search tool, displays a star icon beside each search result.

When the shared workspace and the website or application in use reside in the same ecosystem—for instance, a user searching Globrix and adding houses to his or her "my saved properties" list—the action to save an item can be invoked from within the website or application itself. For instance, TwigKit Collective (Figure 9.7)—an enterprise collaborative search tool—displays a star icon as the user hovers over a given result, inviting the user to bookmark a result with no more than two clicks.

FIGURE 9.8 Amazon provides a special bookmark that allows users to add items from any web page to their Amazon wish list.

In other situations, the user may wish to save an item from an external source. Amazon, for instance, provides a small snippet of code that users can save as a bookmark in their browsers that can add an item from any web page to the users' Amazon wishlists (Figure 9.8). The widget is usually intelligent enough to prepopulate the title and price, includes a comment field, and lets users choose which of their wish lists the item should be added to.

Instant communication

In addition to collaborating around social objects—the *output* of search—collaborators also strive to work together during the *process* of search. Because inner circle collaborators share a common work task, facilitating *real-time communication* is vital. This allows collaborators to help shape one another's information needs and share search strategies. Morris (2008) found that remote users reported using email, instant messaging, and phone calls to collaborate on search tasks. Integrating such real-time communication channels into search tools would make remote collaboration much more accessible.

Although communication flows freely between colocated individuals, the "backseat driver" strategy mentioned earlier isn't the only approach to colocated collaboration. When each participant has his or her own device, collaborators may choose to adopt unique roles. For instance, Cerchiamo (Figure 9.9)—a tool for searching through video clips—provides different interfaces for the "prospector," whose job is to sift through large quantities of video clips, and the "miner," responsible for investigating selected clips more closely (Golovchinsky et al., 2008).

Facilitating remote real-time communication however, is a bit more challenging. Morris and Horvitz (2007) devised SearchTogether—a desktop application that incorporates instant messaging, search results, and a browser window—to coordinate communication during multiperson search activities (Figure 9.10). The application displays each user's query history in the sidebar to increase awareness of others' search tactics; pages visited by other collaborators are flagged accordingly, and results can be annotated, rated, and recommended to others.

FIGURE 9.9 Cerchiamo—a tool for colocated, collaborative search in which one participant takes on the role of prospector and the other operates as miner.

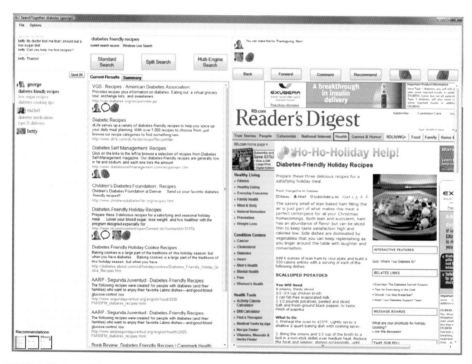

FIGURE 9.10 SearchTogether—a tool for remote collaborative search.

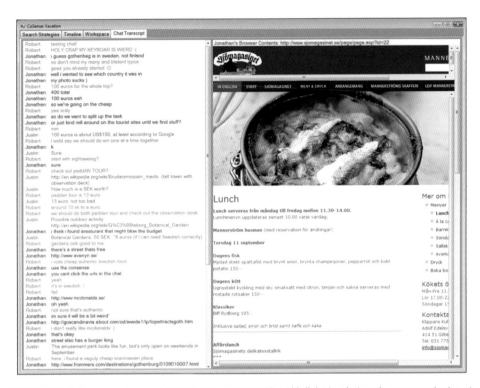

FIGURE 9.11 CoSense combines an instant message transcript with links to what each user was viewing at the time of writing each message.

In an attempt to support division of labor among the participants, SearchTogether also incorporated an optional "split view" method for delegating search results. In this mode, a single user would enter a query and the results would be split evenly between the collaborators. Although the principle is appealing, this tightly coupled approach risks causing participants to grow weary of constantly needing to agree on what queries to run and having to match one another's pace. Indeed, Morris and Horvitz (2007) reported that this division of labor tool was seldom used.

CoSense, a research prototype meant to extend SearchTogether, also incorporated instant messaging (Paul & Morris, 2009). When viewing the chat transcript, however, CoSense transforms each instant message into a link to the page the user was viewing when he or she composed that message, making it easier to reconstruct the original thought process (Figure 9.11).

Persistence

Although instant communication is certainly valuable, collaboration isn't always instantaneous. Often, inner circle collaborators participate at different times, asynchronously searching, communicating, and sharing objects. Collaborative search tools

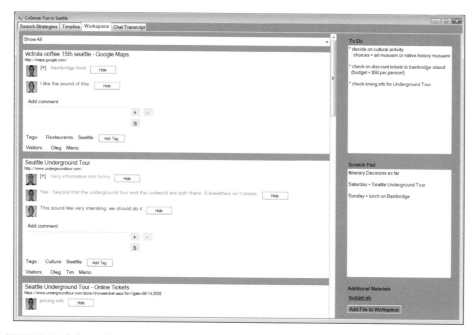

FIGURE 9.12 CoSense features a to-do area and a scratch pad to help collaborators document their progress.

should support this common occurrence by *persisting* the shared workspace over time. What's more, the workspace should make it easy to quickly catch up on what's changed since the last viewing and to record any conclusions arrived at by the inner circle.

Paul and Morris (2009)—the researchers behind CoSense—studied groups of SearchTogether users and found a common thread among those who were absent during the initial collaboration process but signed on later to review the progress made: they wished the initial collaborators had left notes about what they were thinking. In other words, just reviewing an activity feed, chat history, and list of bookmarks still left unanswered questions in the latecomers' minds. To remedy this, Paul and Morris added a to-do area and a free-form "scratch pad" to their CoSense prototype (Figure 9.12), which they envisioned collaborators using to plan their efforts and record decisions made, respectively. In their follow-up study, they found that roughly half of users made use of the to-do and ScratchPad to understand the current search state, and the other half of users relied on the original method of closely reviewing the project's history.

Rather than offer two predetermined text areas, a second approach is to enable users to add as many notes as they see fit. Wunderkit, a collaborative (but not search-focused) organization tool, allows users to create notes for shared projects that can be commented upon, tagged, and "liked" by users (Figure 9.13).

Together, these five elements—shared workspace, social objects, quick add, instant communication, and persistence—are the catalysts that empower inner circle collaborative search.

FIGURE 9.13 Wunderkit, a personal organization tool, allows users to create multiple notes that can be commented upon, tagged, and "liked."

DESIGNING FOR SOCIAL CIRCLE COLLABORATION

While a small handful of individuals form the inner circle, hundreds of people make up the surrounding social circles. Yet there are several manifestations of social circle collaboration: direct, one-on-one communication; social networks; and even wider communities of practice. Because these three types of collaboration have their own challenges and incentives, it's worth taking a closer look at each.

Direct communication

The inner circle's information needs drive them to seek information through the quickest, most reliable sources possible. Often this process involves using a search engine and skimming websites. From time to time, however, it entails eliciting the advice of a friend, colleague, or subject matter expert. Though the barrier is lowest with people we know, sometimes—especially in large organizations—we must also approach strangers. But identifying precisely the right person to contact leads us back to a classic search application: the staff directory (Figure 9.14).

The best staff directories support not only lookup—finding the contact details for someone we already know, for instance—but are also conducive to *exploration*. The ability to pivot on people by such criteria as expertise, department, and location significantly increases the usefulness of such applications.

Social networks

Direct communication facilitates explicit collaboration between two or more individuals; social networking tools are convenient for more open-ended collaboration.

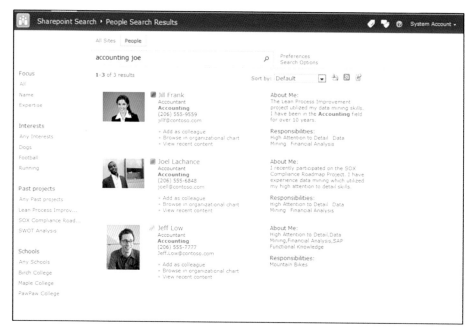

FIGURE 9.14 People search in Microsoft SharePoint.

We're accustomed to using tools such as Facebook and Twitter to keep up with our friends, post status updates, and occasionally ask for advice. But social networking tools are also becoming commonplace in the workplace. Aside from providing yet another method for circulating cat videos around the office, enterprise social networks provide a nonconfrontational channel conducive to informal collaboration. Key to their success, however, is the ability to *thread*—that is, to facilitate multiple groups, each with its own timeline (Figure 9.15). Such threading allows users to efficiently allocate their attention by, for example, vigilantly following the groups most meaningful to them, yet not fretting if they miss a few posts from peripheral threads.

Communities of practice

Beyond both one-to-one dialogue and broadcasts to our social networks lies a third degree of social circle collaboration: communities of practice. These groups are bound together by enthusiasm for a shared discipline. Whereas our social networking acquaintances may number in the hundreds, communities of practice often encompass thousands. Here the incentive is not just to maintain friendships (though that may be one driver) but to establish one's own expertise. The most effective communities of practice are the ones that best harness this underlying motive.

For example, LinkedIn, the social networking site for professionals, allows its users to set up forum-like groups that others can join (Figure 9.16). Group members can post

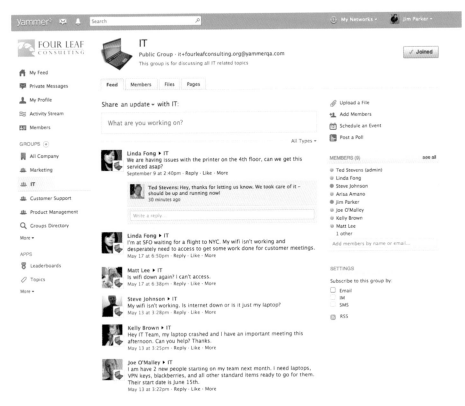

FIGURE 9.15 A group thread in Yammer, an enterprise social networking tool.

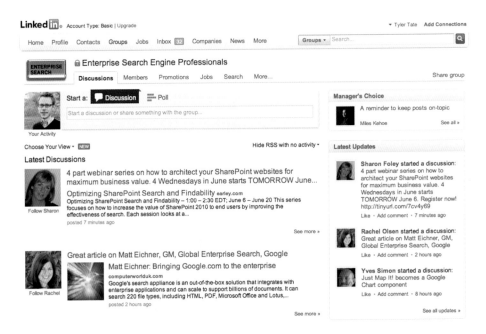

FIGURE 9.16 The Enterprise Search Engine Professionals Group on LinkedIn.

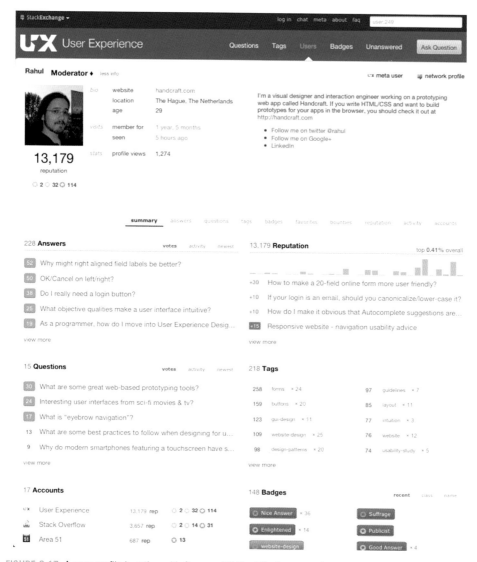

FIGURE 9.17 A user profile bursting with flare on UX StackExchange, a sister site of Stack Overflow.

messages to the group and respond to other people's posts. With no other constraints or incentives in place, some LinkedIn groups function primarily as venues for self-promotion.

LinkedIn's *laissez faire* approach is in stark contrast with that of Stack Overflow, a question and answer site for programmers. Stack Overflow (and its network of sister websites covering a range of other topics) has put in place an extensive framework of guidelines and incentives for users. To begin with, every user's reputation score—a measure of community trust that increases with participation—is displayed next to his or her name alongside the number of badges he or she has collected (Figure 9.17).

What's more, users unlock a range of "privileges" when their reputation score hits certain thresholds, giving them increased authority in the meritocracy. These elements of *gamification*—a term that describes making nongame applications feel game-like—can help make communities of practice more engaging and objective while still providing a healthy incentive for participation.

These three degrees within the social circle—ranging from one-to-one to one-to-many collaboration—are distinct from the inner circle because they lack a shared work task, yet both the inner and social circles share the trait of explicit, intentional collaboration. Next, we conclude the chapter by switching to the implicit, unintentional collaboration that occurs in the outer circle.

DESIGNING FOR OUTER CIRCLE COLLABORATION

The implicit use of social data driving the personalized recommendations and search results found in the outer circle is distinctly different from the other two circles of collaboration. Rather than engage in intentional collaboration with another person, in the outer circle we interact only with the remembrances of other people, the ripples left in their wake.

Using the past behavior of others to provide more meaningful results is a sound principle—even Google's PageRank algorithm, which heavily relies on the social signal of inbound links, is based on this principle. Traditionally, such social cues have been anonymized and aggregated *en masse*. But more recently, search engines have begun using the behavior of our social circles—as well as our own individual behavior—to provide highly personalized search results. Indeed, such socially aware personalization has the potential to deliver more pertinent search results.

Yet the execution of such personalization is fraught with concerns over both privacy and objectivity; in particular, does personalization threaten to turn the Internet into a self-reinforcing echo chamber in which the world is bent to match one's impression of it? To succeed at outer circle collaboration, companies must earn the trust of users by observing two vital principles: be *transparent*, and give users *control*.

Transparency

When departing from objectivity in favor of personalization, search applications should signal the change to users. Better still, they should explain *why* the users see the results that they do. This simple step of transparency can help communicate the value of personalization, while providing the users with peace of mind that they aren't being somehow misled. Personalizing beneath a facade of objectivity, on the other hand, smacks of deception and can erode the users' trust.

Bing takes the straightforward approach of placing social results—using information from Facebook, in this case—in a separate list, clearly distinguishing the personalized recommendations from the objective result list (Figure 9.18). Although this approach ensures a sharp distinction between the two types of content, it limits the efficacy that a blended result list can offer.

FIGURE 9.18 Bing inserts Facebook-influenced results under a clearly labeled heading.

FIGURE 9.19 Social news site Digg displays numerous social indicators: votes, likes, tweets, and comments.

Rather than rely on a secondary list, another approach is to incorporate social indicators into the display of the search results themselves. Digg (a social news site), for instance, displays the number of votes each article has received, as well as the number of Facebook likes, Twitter mentions, and comments associated with the article (Figure 9.19). Using similar indicators to signal when and why personalized search results appear would give users a clearer understanding of how the search engine performs its magic.

Control

In addition to being transparent about personalization, search applications should also give users *control* over it. The ability to enable or disable personalization, to control the parameters driving it, and to repair or remove poor recommendations makes personalization all the more useful, while minimizing the frustration when things go wrong.

Google's proclaimed "search, plus your world" features, which use data from the Google+ social network, espouse giving users more control over personalization. The concept is to both add a small icon to indicate which results are personal, as well as to allow users to easily toggle personalization on and off (Figure 9.20). However, this approach doesn't go nearly far enough. In reality, Google personalizes search results for virtually everyone—Google+ users or otherwise—and offers scarcely little transparency or control over the process.

Amazon, famous for its personalized recommendations, does a more effective job of putting users in control by offering a "Fix this recommendation" link beneath each item that it recommends (Figure 9.21). Upon clicking the link, Amazon explains the past purchasing decisions that led to the current recommendation. They allow users to not only

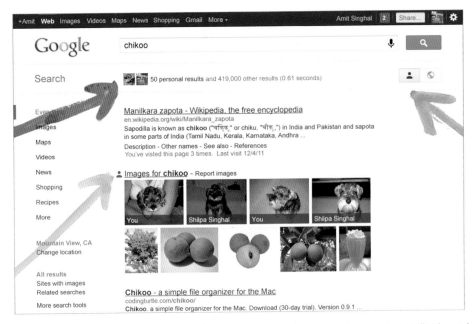

FIGURE 9.20 Google's "search, plus your world" features add greater user control over personalized search results, but don't go far enough.

FIGURE 9.21 Amazon allows users to fix inaccurate recommendations.

dismiss the current recommendation but also exclude any past purchase from being used to derive recommendations.

Characterized by implicit collaboration with the past behavior of others, outer circle collaboration is growing both more valuable and more invasive as it taps into our social circles to deliver a personalized search experience. To succeed in the new era of personalization, however, search applications must provide both transparency and control in order to earn the trust of users.

SUMMARY

Social search is a broad topic. It ranges from the explicit collaboration of a few committed individuals in the inner circle, to looser, more casual collaboration within the social circle, and to the implicit collaboration of the outer circle. Though collaboration plays a significant role in information seeking, most current search applications either do not support collaboration or support it very poorly. In the future, search will surely become much more social.

REFERENCES

Agichtein, E., Brill, E., & Dumais, S. (2006). Improving web search ranking by incorporating user behavior information. *SIGIR'06*, August 6–11, 2006, Seattle, WA.

Cross, R., & Sproull, L. (2004). More than an answer: Information relationships for actionable knowledge. *Organization Science*, *15*(4), 446–462.

Evans, B. M., & Chi, E. H. (2009). Towards a model of understanding social search. In Proc. of Computer-Supported Cooperative Work (CSCW'08), pp. 485–494. ACM Press.

Goldberg, D., Nichols, D., Oki, B. M., & Terry, D. (1992). Using collaborative filtering to weave an information tapestry. *Communications of the ACM - Special issue on information filtering*, *35*(12), 61–70.

Golovchinsky, G., Adcock, J., Pickens, J., Qvarfordt, P., & Back, M. (2008). Cerchiamo: A collaborative exploratory search tool. *CSCW'08*, November 8–12, 2008, San Diego, CA.

Hansen, P., & Järvelin, K. (2005). Collaborative information retrieval in an information-intensive domain. *Information Processing and Management*, *41*(5), 1101–1119.

Järvelin, K., & Ingwersen, P. (2004). Information seeking research needs extension towards tasks and technology. *Information Research*, 10(1), paper 212.

Koren, Y., Bell, R., & Volinsky, C. (2009). Matrix factorization techniques for recommender systems. *IEEE Computer Society* 0018-9162/09.

Linden, G., Smith, B., & York, J. (2003). Amazon.com recommendations: Item-to-item collaborative filtering. *IEEE Internet Computing*, *7*(1), 76–80.

Morris, M. R. (2008). A survey of collaborative web search practices. *CHI 2008*, April 5–10, 2008, Florence, Italy.

Morris, M. R., & Horvitz, E. (2007). SearchTogether: An interface for collaborative web search. *UIST'07*, October 7–10, 2007, Newport, RI.

Morris, M. R., & Teevan, J. (2008). Understanding groups' properties as a means of improving collaborative search systems. *Proceedings of the Workshop on Collaborative Information Retrieval*, June 20, 2008, Pittsburgh, PA.

Morris, M. R., Teevan, J., & Panovich, K. (2010). What do people ask their social networks, and why? A survey study of status message Q&A behavior. *CHI 2010*, April 10–15, 2010, Atlanta, GA.

Paul, S., & Morris, M. R. (2009). Enhancing sensemaking for collaborative web search. *CHI 2009*, April 4–9, 2009, Boston, MA.

Rodden, T. (1991). A survey of CSCW systems. *Interacting with Computers*, 3(3), 319–354.

The Uncanny Valley of Personalization
Rory Hamilton

Through mimicking the tone and personal touch of the real world, online services set themselves up for a fall.

The "uncanny valley" is the space in a human's relationship with a nonliving object where the object's human-like appearance or behavior causes revulsion or, at the least, a creepy feeling. Industrial robots are fine; C3PO is mostly fine; automatons, animated corpses, and Tom Hanks in Polar Express … not fine.

Most prevalent in robotics, games, and films, the uncanny valley also crops up in online and real-world services. Users' expectations are built up by friendly language or seemingly personal service, yet they then discover the service to be inflexible and definitely not "powered by people." Or worse, when speaking to a human representative, the user discovers that the representative is powerless to help—gagged by protocol and simply reading a script from a screen. They are the Zombie Call Center, the human equivalents of Microsoft's Clippy.

In search, the likes of Amazon and Google bombard us with recommendations and personalized (sometimes sponsored) search results. Of course the "smartness" of these recommendations can be useful (though we all realize they are usually trying to sell us more stuff), but when this smartness becomes too invasive and shows itself for what it is, it can be disturbing. It's then that we fall into the uncanny valley of personalization.

At the moment, my Amazon account is recommending vampire novels, the films of Maggie Smith, postwar brutalist architecture, the *Green Lantern* DVD, descant recorders, and Woly shoe polish.

I may have searched for all of these things at some point, but seeing them displayed on one page is the equivalent of those scenes in diet programs where they show the horrified subject a table containing all of the pies, crisps, Mars bars, and takeaways they have eaten in a week. Our recommendations lay out our flighty, faddy, mundane sins before us. We feel judged.

These recommendations are treading the fine line of C3PO: useful, unthreatening (mostly), but quite easily getting on our nerves.

In the future, we might just expect to have everything personalized for us and never think anything of it. Or we might choose to reject automated recommendation for serendipity, peer-selected results, or just hard graft.

How Google, Amazon, and others can convince us that the usefulness of their services outweighs the increasing lack of privacy is still to be seen. Making recommendations feel like they are part of *your* style, *your* personality—rather than being thrust on you by an unseen, controlling/ condemning presence—should be their goal. Perhaps they can avoid the uncanny valley by being clear it is we who have made the mess we're in—and giving us the power to tidy things up, rather than them thrusting their marketing on us.

We will have to see if we can avoid falling further into the uncanny valley.

Rory has worked in service design and innovation for ten years, recently with live|work and Orange (France Telecom). He helps clients make service design part of their culture through ethnographic activities, co-creation, ideation workshops, and service blueprinting. He is interested in breaking through the "siloed" structure of organizations to help stakeholders see the transversal nature of the products and services they offer the customer, and help them to see this through the customer's eyes. Rory taught Interaction design at the Royal College of Art and the Bartlett School of Architecture for 12 years. He blogs at everythingiknow.co.uk.

It's a Saturday morning in September. Groggy-eyed Amir draws the blinds, squinting as sunshine pours into his 61st-floor apartment. Putting on his BlinkIt-equipped eyeglasses, Amir looks out over the crisp London landscape for a few moments before moving into the kitchen to start the coffee. He hears the morning post fall through the door and is pleased to see the outdoor clothing catalog he had requested from EveryWare among the contents. With his camping trip to the Lake District with Simon and Shannon coming up the following weekend, Amir really needed to find a lightweight, windproof, water-resistant jacket that wouldn't cost a fortune. He'd spent well over an hour searching online during the week—and had shortlisted a few—but he just wasn't sure about any of them yet.

Amir flipped through the catalog as he nursed his coffee and bowl of porridge. Coming across a jacket that piqued his interests, Amir focused his sight on a tiny two-dimensional barcode next to the jacket's title and rapidly blinked twice, activating the BlinkIt technology in his glasses. BlinkIt superimposed a menu on top of the paper catalog with options such as "View item details," "Buy now," "Add to favorites," or "Send to a friend." Amir focused on the "Add to favorites" option and blinked twice to select it.

After breakfast, Amir sat down in front of his computer and reviewed the list of jackets he'd favorited so far. He read a couple of reviews of the jacket he'd found in the catalog, added short notes to a few of the items to help him remember which was which, and sorted the list in approximate order of preference. But still, Amir wasn't completely sure which jacket was best. He decided to just go over to the EveryWare store in the West End, try a few on, and buy one there.

Just before noon he emerged from the Oxford Circus tube station and set off down Oxford Street toward the EveryWare store. While musing to himself how much he disliked fighting through the crowds, he spotted a man crossing the street wearing a jacket that he really liked. Amir blinked twice. This time BlinkIt captured a still frame of the man crossing the street and presented a menu option to "Look up this item," which Amir selected. Sure enough, BlinkIt was able to identify the jacket, after which he selected the "Add to favorites" option. He then pulled out his mobile phone (which instantly updated his favorites list to include the new item) and quickly reviewed the jacket's features, price, and customer rating before sending a quick message to his friend, Simon, saying, "Hey, what do you think of this one?"

Amir slipped the phone back into his pocket as he stepped through the EveryWare entrance. The store was massive: 20 floors covering hundreds of thousands of square meters and stocking everything from clothes and electronics to gardening tools. Detecting that he'd entered the store, BlinkIt superimposed the items from his favorites list onto their physical locations within the store. As he approached the atrium, Amir noticed a cluster of BlinkIt indicators appearing on the third floor and looked around for the nearest escalator.

Cross-Channel Information Interaction

10

In Part 1 we established a conceptual framework of search by considering the user, information seeking, context, and search modes. In Part 2, we then applied those principles to the practical design of search user interfaces. In this third and final act of the book, we return to higher ground and cast our gaze toward the future.

But predicting the future isn't what it used to be. History is brimming with predictions that never came to pass and filled with inventions that no one anticipated. So instead of speculating about the gadgets and behaviors that *might* arise—which may or may not be anything like BlinkIt eyeglasses (Figure 10.1)—we're putting our money on a much more reliable prediction: that the future *will* hold new gadgets and behaviors of one sort or another.

More specifically, our concern isn't with any single medium on its own, but rather how information seeking can occur across multiple channels that form a coherent ecosystem. We want to understand the fabric that binds ecologies together; we want to equip ourselves to design information interactions that flow seamlessly from one channel to the next.

In this chapter, we discuss the implications of living in a postdesktop era, outline three principles for designing across channels, and consider two methods for planning cross-channel ecosystems.

THE POSTDESKTOP ERA

Mark Weiser coined the term "ubiquitous computing" in 1991. He envisaged a future not in which people are forced to enter the computer's world through screen, mouse, and keyboard, but one in which computing pervades the natural human environment (Weiser, 1991). He, and later Adam Greenfield, saw the personal computer and its desktop metaphor being

FIGURE 10.1 Google has created a prototype (called Project Glass) that is not too dissimilar to the BlinkIt eyeglasses in our story. Although such a device is itself a novel (but completely unproven) idea, the future is bound to hold disruptive technologies that we haven't even thought of yet.

replaced by myriad inexpensive, networked devices embedded in everything from clothing and furniture to walls and doorways. (Greenfield described these devices as "everyware"—a name we borrowed in our story.) In Greenfield's own words (Greenfield, 2006):

Most of the functionality we now associate with these boxes on our desks, these slabs that warm our laps, will be dispersed into both the built environment and the wide variety of everyday objects we typically use there. (p. 18)

We are a long way from fully realizing the vision of ubiquitous computing, yet we've made significant strides since Weiser (Figure 10.2) gave birth to the idea. Cloud computing has transferred much computational and storage responsibility from the local device to the remote server; smartphones, tablets, and ebook readers occupy an increasing amount of our attention, not to mention satellite navigation systems, personal music players, clever wristwatches for athletes, and other digital paraphernalia.

Although we haven't reached the device saturation level foreseen by Weiser, nor migrated from plastic and LCD to wool and plaster as envisioned by Greenfield, this much is certain: we have entered the postdesktop era, and we're not going back. No longer confined to the single channel of the PC, personal computing is now dispersed across multiple computers and mobile devices, kept in sync by the cloud. As a result, effective design is becoming less about creating the end-all-be-all website, and more about fostering a cohesive ecosystem where the digital—such as web and mobile—works in harmony with the physical—from print media to the natural environment.

This transition from single-channel to multi-channel is mirrored by a shift in focus from human–*computer* interaction (HCI), to that of human–*information* interaction (HII). As technology becomes increasingly distributed and transparent, *information* is freed to permeate the foreground, with *information seeking* becoming the dominant means

FIGURE 10.2 A photo of the late Dr. Mark Weiser.

of interaction. Gary Marchionini (2004) describes how this embodiment of information seeking extends far beyond any single channel:

Imagine information seeking as a core life process where people are constantly connected to information sources just as our bodies are connected to the environment through filters and selectors that are highly tuned to the environment. In such a paradigm, the crucial system design challenges become the control mechanisms for interacting with representations in agile and engaging ways. (p. 4)

Fortunately, our roots in information seeking from Part 1 will serve us well in the postdesktop era of information interaction. The principle of information foraging, for instance, is manifest in this new order—guiding users to maximize information gain while minimizing cost. Sensemaking is central to how users internalize the information they find. The stages of information seeking identified by Kuhlthau—initiation, selection, exploration, formulation, collection, and action—gain an even greater significance. And of course context, in all its forms, is more important than ever.

Amir's story demonstrates how an information seeking task—such as finding a new jacket—can take place across multiple channels (Figure 10.3). From searching the Web on his desktop to browsing a print catalog, and from asking for advice from a friend via his phone to trying on jackets in the Oxford Street store, Amir's journey flowed coherently from one channel to the next. The channels were *optimized*, with each channel playing to its own strengths; they were *consistent*, following similar organization patterns; and they were *continuous*, propagating actions from one channel to all the rest (Morville, 2011). Let's investigate each of these cross-channel design principles in more detail.

FIGURE 10.3 While probably a bit shy of the fictional 20-story EveryWare store, outdoor retail REI demonstrates the various channels already being used by retailers, including brick-and-mortar stores (often with in-store kiosks), print catalogs, a website, and a mobile application.

OPTIMIZATION

In the opening pages of *The Wealth of Nations*, Adam Smith demonstrates the power of the division of labor through the example of a pin factory. At that time, the process for manufacturing sewing pins consisted of about 18 operations, such as drawing out the wire, straightening it, cutting it, pointing it, sanding it, and so on. Each task was sufficiently involved, Smith maintained, that a single individual could perhaps "make one pin in a day, and certainly could not make twenty." Yet when each operation was distributed to one of ten tradesman specialized in that task, the team "could make amongst them upwards of 48,000 pins in a day".

Steve Jobs made a similar, though less profound realization around the turn of the millennium: he saw the computer acting as the central hub for digital devices. This strategy would allow both the computer and the device to play to their respective strengths, just as the specialized tradesmen at the pin factory were able to do. Rather than expect each device to deliver the entire experience—the equivalent of a generalist cranking out one pin a day—dividing the labor appropriately between computer and device would allow each

FIGURE 10.4 The first iPod embodied a division of labor between the iPod, computer, and iTunes software.

to specialize and, as a result, deliver a better experience on the whole. Biographer Walter Isaacson summarizes Jobs' thoughts on the matter (Isaacson, 2011):

A lot of the functions that the devices tried to do, such as editing the video or the pictures, they did poorly because they had small screens and could not easily accommodate menus filled with lots of functions. Computers could handle that more easily. (p. 354)

This insight most notably led to Apple's introduction of the iPod (Figure 10.4). Rather than designing the portable music player to be self-sufficient, as their competitors had done, the iPod was designed as part of a symbiotic ecosystem. The iPod was freed to do what it did best—play music—while the computer handled the more complex task of managing the music collection and the iTunes Store enabled users to acquire new songs.

The division of labor between the iPod, iTunes, and the Mac enabled the three to collectively achieve more than they could have on their own. This is the principle of *optimization* at work. Each channel within the ecosystem should focus on what it does best. Put another way, each component should be optimized for its forte. A small handheld device, for instance, lends itself to being used on the go and for short bursts of time; a keyboard-equipped desktop computer, on the other hand, affords more focused attention and a greater amount of data entry. By optimizing each element of the ecosystem, we can achieve cross-channel experiences that empower users.

CONSISTENCY

The principle of optimization is focused on each component playing to its strengths; yet we must also ensure that the ecosystem *as a whole* provides the user with the best possible experience across its many parts. To accomplish this goal, local optimization must be paired with global *consistency*.

The Merriam-Webster Dictionary defines consistency as the "agreement or harmony of parts or features to one another or a whole." Although consistency seems like an intuitive concept, beneath the surface it is rife with tension and competing forces. Distilling consistency into its component parts promises to bring clarity to this important concept.

The realm of consistency

The elements of consistency are often enumerated as internal, external, functional, and aesthetic (Butler, Holden, & Lidwell, 2007). "Internal" and "external" refer to the scope at which consistency occurs—what we could term the *realm* of consistency (we'll return to the functional and aesthetic components in a few moments). A kitchen fork, for instance, has internal consistency if its handle and prongs fit together agreeably and is externally consistent if it is harmonious with the spoon and knife from the same set of cutlery.

Although the internal and external realms offer an excellent starting point, cross-channel design typically involves a third: the local realm. This realm considers not whether the internal components of the kitchen fork are agreeable, nor whether the fork is harmonious with the spoon and knife from the same set, but rather how this particular fork relates to its own class—other kitchen forks.

At this point, it's probably worth leaving the kitchen and applying the realms of consistency directly to a cross-channel scenario. Let's consider the EveryWare mobile phone application in Amir's story. It could be evaluated *internally* (are the elements within the application consistent with one another?); *locally* (is the EveryWare application consistent with other applications built for the same mobile operating system?); and *externally* (is the mobile application consistent with the other channels within the EveryWare ecosystem, such as their catalog, website, and store?).

In fact, since we've already been using the term "ecosystem" when referring to external consistency, we could extend the same analogy to describe the local realm as the "habitat" and, for completeness, the internal realm as the "creature" (Figure 10.5).

To summarize, the three realms of consistency we've looked at are:

- **Internal consistency.** Do the constituent parts of the *creature* itself (a mobile application, for instance) work together harmoniously?

- **Local consistency.** Does the creature live agreeably with its neighbors in the immediate *habitat* (such as other mobile applications built for the same platform)?

- **External consistency.** Does the creature work harmoniously with its allies in the *ecosystem* (for example, other channels such as the website and store)?

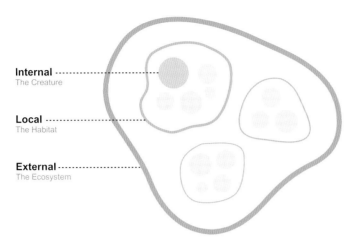

Internal
The Creature

Local
The Habitat

External
The Ecosystem

FIGURE 10.5 The three realms of consistency are analogous to creature, habitat, and ecosystem.

The nature of consistency

In addition to the realm of consistency, there is a second aspect that must be considered. Let us return to the functional and aesthetic components of consistency that we mentioned a few moments earlier. These components describe the attribute for which the "agreement or harmony" exists—what we could call the *nature* of consistency. For example, the fork, spoon and knife—each optimized for its own specialty such as stabbing, scooping, and cutting—are by definition functionally inconsistent; that is, they each serve different purposes. However, they may be aesthetically consistent if the stem and terminal of their respective handles share like dimensions, curves, weighting, and so on. Within the ecosystem of a cutlery set, in other words, the aesthetic nature of consistency is highly prized, and functional consistency is unwanted.

When it comes to cross-channel design, however, the nature of consistency could be extended to a number of additional attributes. For instance, the function of an object could be differentiated from its behavior, or how it "feels" to use. The EveryWare mobile application, for example, should follow the conventions of the operating system for which it's built in order to feel similar to other mobile applications.

In addition, ensuring that the information architecture or *organization* of an application is consistent with that of the other channels is crucial to creating a coherent experience. A simple example of organizational consistency could be to use the same set of product categories across a retailer's website, catalog, and physical store.

To recap, the four natures of consistency that we've considered are:

- **Function.** The purpose of the object. (The function of a retailer's Android mobile application, for instance, might be to enable users to shop when they're away from their computers.)

- **Behavior.** How it feels. (The retail app feels like a native Android app rather than a website or iPhone app.)

- **Organization.** How it's organized. (The mobile app's information architecture.)
- **Aesthetics.** How it looks. (The visual style of the application.)

Designing with consistency in mind

This deconstructionist exercise allows us to bolster our common sense understanding of consistency with a more rigorous, systematic approach. To put theory into practice, however, we must ask the obvious question: which realms and natures of consistency should take precedence over the others?

It's a difficult challenge to be sure—the internal, local, and external realms are each in competition for a bigger slice of the functional, behavioral, organizational, and aesthetic pies. Yet coherent cross-channel experiences are contingent on finding the right balance. Although the ideal mix is unique to each situation, there are a few general guidelines:

- The *function* of a channel should be optimized for its own comparative advantage; in other words, what it has the potential of doing better than any other channel in the ecosystem. In this way, its function need not be externally consistent, as much as it should be complimentary to the rest of the ecosystem.

- There is a *behavioral* tension between the local habitat—be it website conventions or operating system patterns—and the process flows of the ecosystem. Great effort should be exerted to reconcile these differences. Where perfect integration isn't possible, erring on the side of local consistency is often the more conciliatory approach.

- *Organizational* consistency should almost always favor the external ecosystem over the local or internal. Using a consistent organizational scheme across all channels of the ecosystem is one of the most important factors in delivering a coherent cross-channel experience.

- *Aesthetics* has major implications across all three realms. It should certainly maintain internal consistency. Yet there is again a tension between the local habitat and external ecosystem that must be carefully negotiated. Although the visual aspects that involve branding (such as color) should be consistent with the ecosystem, the overriding style of the user interface should match its local habitat.

Together, optimization and consistency ensure that a given channel is effective both on its own right, and in the context of the wider collective. But there is a third element needed in order for an ecosystem to achieve a coherent cross-channel experience: continuity.

CONTINUITY

Good writers and filmmakers have the ability to so engage their audiences in the human drama of their stories that even when dealing with the fantastic, they are able to induce

FIGURE 10.6 Amazon's Kindle ecosystem—consisting of both their own devices, as well as software that runs on third-party devices—puts continuity into practice by delivering the user's entire library to any device and even synchronizes their current page.

a willing suspension of disbelief in their readers and viewers. Yet this suspension can be shattered by errors in continuity.

In Homer's *Iliad*, for example, Menelaus—the husband of Helen of Troy—kills a man named Pylaimenes in battle. Yet later in the story, Pylaimenes somehow reappears to witness the death of his son. Although such an error could be attributed to the oral heritage of the *Iliad*, it didn't stop the Roman poet Horace from moaning, "Yet I also become annoyed whenever the great Homer nods off."

In the same way that a good novel or film can pull us into the story and suspend our disbelief, so digital experiences also have the potential to engage us so fully that we suspend our awareness of the outside world. This condition of "being in the zone" has been described by psychologist Mihály Csíkszentmihályi as an *optimal experience* or a state of *flow* (Csíkszentmihályi & Csíkszentmihályi, 1988).

Yet the state of flow is also put at risk by "Homeric nods." If we leave our desk to make a quick cup of tea, we expect our computer to be in an unaltered state when we return. If we send an email from our phone, we expect it to appear in the sent folder on our computer. When we add an item to our favorites list using our tablet, we expect it to show up in the favorites list on our phone.

Continuity—the principle of propagating the user's state across all channels of the ecosystem—is an expectation (Figure 10.6). When it's absent, it nags us, nudging us out of our state of flow and back into the nitty-gritty of reality. Although it's true that limited quantities of bandwidth, storage, and processing power deter us from realizing complete continuity, we must make continuous experiences an utmost priority.

THE CROSS-CHANNEL BLUEPRINT

In order to design optimal, consistent, and continuous cross-channel experiences, we need to equip ourselves with the right tools for the task. In particular, we need to view the ecosystem as a cohesive whole, as well as understand how users traverse its many parts. Two tools can assist us in these pursuits: the cross-channel blueprint and the experience map.

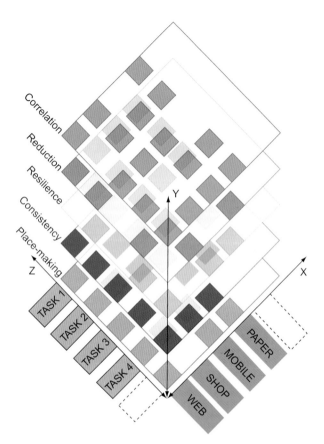

FIGURE 10.7 Andrea Resmini and Luca Rosati's CHU cube diagram.

The cross-channel blueprint provides an overview of the ecosystem's two most fundamental attributes: the channels of which it's composed, and the user actions it must facilitate. But before we dive in, a bit of history.

The juxtaposition of channels and actions isn't a new idea. G. Lynn Shostack, a visionary in the field of *service design*, devised "service blueprints" in the 1980s to coordinate customer touchpoints across multiple channels (Shostack, 1982). Although it is an ideal tool for orchestrating the front stage (the portions of a service with which customers interact), back stage (the internal parts of a service hidden from the customer's view), and support processes needed to successfully deliver a service to customers, it's not as well suited to the design of cross-channel experiences.

In *Pervasive Information Architecture*, Andrea Resmini and Luca Rosati (2011) present what they call the CHU cube—an acronym for channels, heuristics, and users (Figure 10.7). Not only does their diagram capture channels and tasks, but it also introduces a third dimension where heuristics are documented for each intersection of channel and task.

PHOTOGRAPHY / CONNECTING THE DOTS

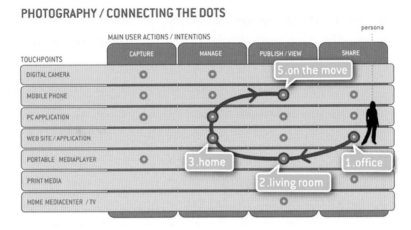

FIGURE 10.8 Gianluca Brugnoli's touchpoints matrix.

Although the diagram is comprehensive, its three-dimensional nature makes it a bit tedious to work with.

Similarly, Gianluca Brugnoli (2009) combines touchpoints and user intentions in what he calls a touchpoints matrix (Figure 10.8). Central to the matrix is the ability to trace the user's journey through the ecosystem by connecting the dots—a topic we will return to shortly.

Building upon these foundations, the cross-channel blueprint is meant to be an exercise as well as an artifact (Figure 10.9). It is detailed enough to facilitate brainstorming in front of a whiteboard, yet simple enough to document a concise overview. Follow these four steps to create your own cross-channel blueprint:

1. **Identify user actions.** What are the actions that users desire to perform throughout the ecosystem as a whole? The zoom level can vary: high-level user goals offer a succinct overview, and low-level tasks provide completeness.

2. **List the channels.** What channels compose (or will compose) the ecosystem? Think both digital and physical.

3. **Prioritize and describe each channel-action.** Once the user actions and channels have been identified and placed on the two axes of the blueprint, determine the priority that each action should receive for a given channel. At the same time as setting priorities, also briefly describe how each action would be achieved.

4. **Identify shared components.** As a last step, think about the behind-the-scenes components that will be necessary to empower each user action. Stacking these shared components in the final row of the matrix will help tie the user experience vision to the reality of the underlying technology.

	Lookup	Explore	Compare	Organize	Purchase
Print Catalog	Low priority Table of contents Index	High priority Immersive photography	Low priority Flip pages back/forth	N/A Flip pages back/forth	High priority Order by phone Order by mail Order online
Website	High priority Search box	High priority Browse by category	High priority Table view of selected items	High priority Favorites Wish list / gift registry	High priority Standard checkout Expedited checkout Order by phone
Tablet App	High priority Search box Voice input	High priority Catalog-like browsing experience	Medium priority Table view of selected items	Medium priority Favorites Wish lists	High priority Expedited checkout Standard checkout
Mobile App	High priority Search box Voice input Barcode scanner	Medium priority Browse by category	N/A Impractical due to screen size	Low priority Add items to favorites and wish list, but limited ability to edit	High priority Expedited checkout
Physical Store	High priority Clear signage Store map Helpful staff	High priority Wander the aisles	Medium priority Compare side by side Ask staff	Low priority Gift registry / wish list	High priority Attendant-assisted Self-checkout Scan-as-you-go
Shared Assets	Product taxonomy All channels powered by a single set of categories		Compare engine Web & tablet powered by one component	Universal Favs Favorites list shared by web, tablet, mobile	Checkout workflow Universal checkout process for web, tablet, and mobile

FIGURE 10.9 A cross-channel blueprint.

The cross-channel blueprint provides several benefits once it has been developed:

• A global view of important user actions

• The possible channels through which users might attempt those actions

• A set of action priorities for each channel

• A set of channel priorities for each action

• An overview of which components need to be shared across channels

Although the cross-channel blueprint provides a concise overview of the ecosystem at large, this system-based approach should also be paired with a user-centered perspective.

EXPERIENCE MAPS

Experience maps are the ideal companion to the cross-channel blueprint. The latter is a canonical representation of the system and its parts; the former provide experiential stories of how users interact with the system's components to accomplish their goals.

Sometimes called a *customer journey map*—a reflection of the tool's origin in service design—the experience map helps us put ourselves in the *user's* shoes, customer or otherwise. Experience maps visually represent not only a user's interactions with the system but are also concerned with the emotional state of the user throughout the entire process (Figure 10.10). And unlike cross-channel blueprints, which can be brainstormed in front of a whiteboard, experience maps depend upon user research. Both quantitative measures— such as log data and survey results—and qualitative techniques such as field studies should be used to shape an accurate depiction of the user's experience.

Experience maps come in many different forms. For one, they can focus either on a group of users—portraying their behavior and attitudes in aggregate—or on a single user. But beyond this question of scope, experience maps can be created with any number of elements—from pain points to "moments of truth" (crucial junctures in the user's journey)—and presented in many different formats—from a linear list to a complex workflow.

There are, however, a handful of elements that are included on most every experience map. Follow these three steps to create a map of your own:

1. **Outline the user's journey.** Start by creating a list of all the occurrences that constitute the user's experience—not just within the ecosystem, but throughout the entire journey from beginning to end. These occurrences can then be arranged horizontally to form a timeline.

2. **List the channel and goal** for each step of the user's journey. "Channel" refers to the medium through which the action is performed. "Goal" describes the underlying motivation for performing the action. These components should be consistent with the channel and actions dimensions of the cross-channel blueprint.

3. **Describe the user's emotion** and rate his or her satisfaction for every step of the process. In order to be useful, however, such reporting should be based on first-hand observation of the user.

Ideally, creating the cross-channel blueprint and experience map can be performed as an iterative process, with each tool influencing the development of the other. The experience map, for instance, should feed into the actions contained in the blueprint, and both should refer to the same set of channels.

These two tools offer complimentary perspectives on the ecosystem. Together, they can help us design the optimal, consistent, and continuous cross-channel experiences of both today and tomorrow.

SUMMARY

Just as a user's journey of information seeking takes him or her across many channels of the ecosystem, so search is itself in motion. From the birth of the computer to the arrival of the World Wide Web, search has grown to become an indispensable part of negotiating the information landscape. And as our journey leads us out of the desktop era and into the information-centric future, search promises to be more vital to us than ever before. *Bon voyage.*

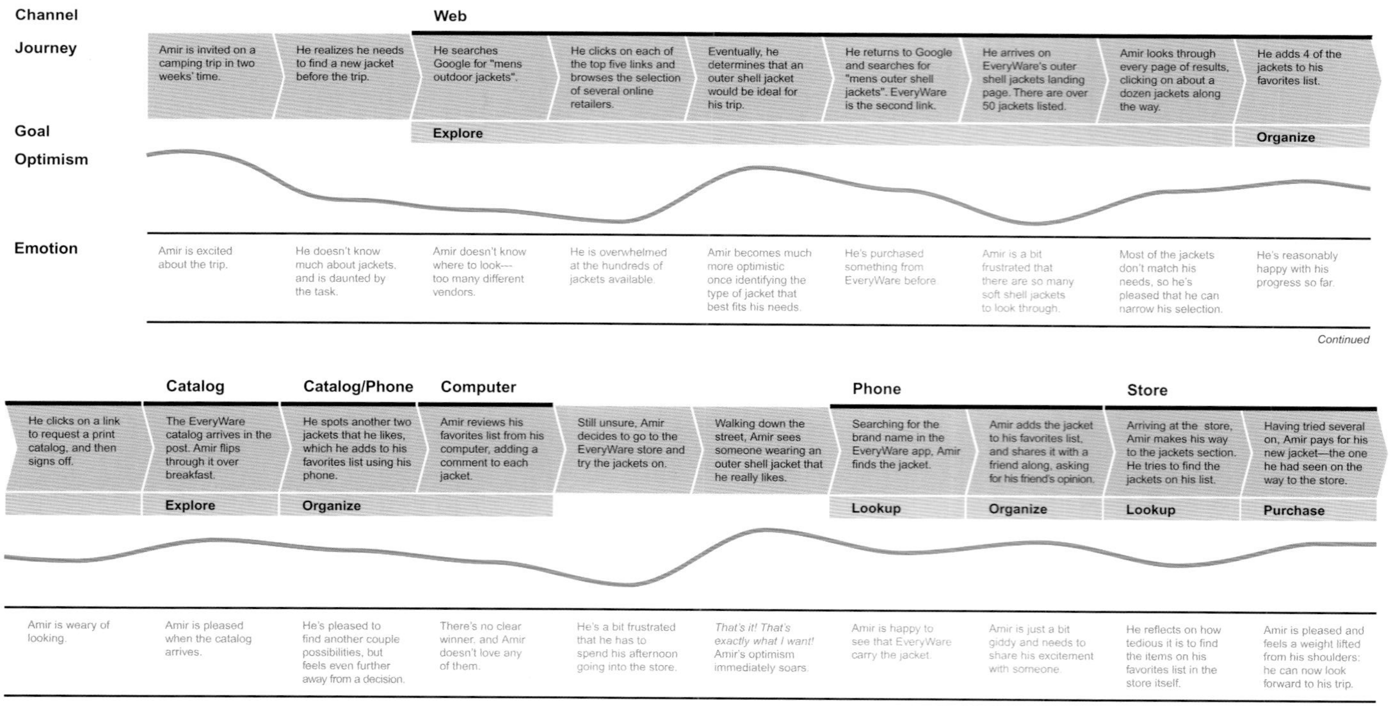

Web

Channel: Web

Journey:
- Amir is invited on a camping trip in two weeks' time.
- He realizes he needs to find a new jacket before the trip.
- He searches Google for "mens outdoor jackets".
- He clicks on each of the top five links and browses the selection of several online retailers.
- Eventually, he determines that an outer shell jacket would be ideal for his trip.
- He returns to Google and searches for "mens outer shell jackets". EveryWare is the second link.
- He arrives on EveryWare's outer shell jackets landing page. There are over 50 jackets listed.
- Amir looks through every page of results, clicking on about a dozen jackets along the way.
- He adds 4 of the jackets to his favorites list.

Goal: Explore → Organize

Optimism (curve)

Emotion:
- Amir is excited about the trip.
- Amir doesn't know where to look—too many different vendors.
- He is overwhelmed at the hundreds of jackets available.
- Amir becomes much more optimistic once identifying the type of jacket that best fits his needs.
- He's purchased something from EveryWare before.
- Amir is a bit frustrated that there are so many soft shell jackets to look through.
- Most of the jackets don't match his needs, so he's pleased that he can narrow his selection.
- He's reasonably happy with his progress so far.

Continued

Channel: Catalog | Catalog/Phone | Computer | | Phone | | Store

Journey:
- He clicks on a link to request a print catalog, and then signs off.
- The EveryWare catalog arrives in the post. Amir flips through it over breakfast.
- He spots another two jackets that he likes, which he adds to his favorites list using his phone.
- Amir reviews his favorites list from his computer, adding a comment to each jacket.
- Still unsure, Amir decides to go to the EveryWare store and try the jackets on.
- Walking down the street, Amir sees someone wearing an outer shell jacket that he really likes.
- Searching for the brand name in the EveryWare app, Amir finds the jacket.
- Amir adds the jacket to his favorites list and shares it with a friend along, asking for his friend's opinion.
- Arriving at the store, Amir makes his way to the jackets section.
- He tries to find the items on his list.
- Having tried several on, Amir pays for his new jacket—the one he had seen on the way to the store.

Goal: Explore | Organize | | Lookup | Organize | Lookup | Purchase

Optimism (curve)

Emotion:
- Amir is weary of looking.
- Amir is pleased when the catalog arrives.
- He's pleased to find another couple possibilities, but feels even further away from a decision.
- There's no clear winner, and Amir doesn't love any of them.
- He's a bit frustrated that he has to spend his afternoon going into the store.
- That's it! That's exactly what I want! Amir's optimism immediately soars.
- Amir is happy to see that EveryWare carry the jacket.
- Amir is just a bit giddy and needs to share his excitement with someone.
- He reflects on how tedious it is to find the items on his favorites list in the store itself.
- Amir is pleased and feels a weight lifted from his shoulders: he can now look forward to his trip.

FIGURE 10.10 An experience map.

REFERENCES

Brugnoli, G. (2009). Connecting the dots of user experience. *Journal of Information Architecture*, *1*(1), 6–15.

Butler, J., Holden, K., & Lidwell, W. (2007). *Universal principles of design: 100 ways to enhance usability, influence perception, increase appeal, make better design decisions, and teach through design.* Minneapolis, MN: Rockport Publishers. 46.

Csíkszentmihályi, M., & Csíkszentmihályi, I. S. (1988). *Optimal experience: Psychological studies of flow in consciousness.* Cambridge, UK: Cambridge University Press. 3–15.

Greenfield, A. (2006). *EveryWare: The dawning age of ubiquitous computing.* Berkeley, CA: New Riders. 18.

Isaacson, W. (2011). *Steve Jobs: The exclusive biography.* New York: Simon & Schuster. 354.

Marchionini, G. (2004). From information retrieval to information interaction. Proceeding of the 26th European Conference on Information Retrieval research. *ECIR 2004*, Sunderland, UK. 1–11.

Morville, P. (2011). Cross-channel strategy. Findability.org. Retrieved June 8, 2012, from http://findability.org/archives/000652.php.

Resmini, A., & Rosati, L. (2011). *Pervasive information architecture: Designing cross-channel user experiences.* Burlington, MA: Morgan Kaufmann. 201–203.

Shostack, G. L. (1982). How to design a service. *European Journal of Marketing*, *16*(1), 49–63.

Weiser, M. (1991, September). The computer for the 21st century. *Scientific American*, 94–104.

Index

Note: Page number followed by "*f*" and "*b*" are refer to figures and boxes respectively.

Navigational context, 168
Navigational state, communicating, 197–203
  breadboxes, 199–202
  hybrid techniques, 202
  inline breadcrumbs, 197–199
Navigation bar, 234
Navigation layer, 212–213
NCSU Libraries
  open and closed facets at, 176
  showing additional facet values at, 192*f*
  vertical breadbox at, 200, 201*f*
Netflix, 77, 78*f*
Network of search modes, 85, 86*f*
Newssift, 61*f*, 62–63, 84, 84*f*
Nontext queries, 107–108
Nontextual input methods, 235–239
Norman's cognitive model, 25*f*
Novices and experts, 3–14
  big-picture visionaries, 10
  brick-by-brick craftsmen, 10
  domain expertise versus technical expertise,
    4, 8–9
  double experts teleport, 5–7
  double novices orienteer, 4–5
  in-betweeners, 7–9
  learnability, designing search user interfaces
    for, 11–13
  performance gap, 11
  rod-and-frame test, 9–10, 9*f*, 10*f*
  serial and holistic thinkers, 9, 15*f*
NPR's iPad app, 248*f*

O
Object, 59
"Olympics", 49
Ontology, 36
Open by default, 174–175
Open/closed hybrid, 175–178, 175*f*
Optimal foraging theory, 27
Optimization, 282–284
Orienteering, 4–5
Outer circle collaboration, designing for, 256,
    270–273
  control, 271–273
  transparency, 270–271

P
Pagination, in search result manipulation,
    150–151
  benefits of, 150

Parametric search inhibits exploration,
    80*f*, 81
Partial matches, 118–120
  at Amazon, 119, 119*f*
  at eBay, 120*f*
PC Authority
  tag clouds at, 187*f*
Performance gap, 11
Personalization, uncanny valley of,
    274*b*–275*b*
Physical context, 226
Pinterest, 258, 259*f*
Pipl search box, 101, 101*f*
Planning Managers, 90, 95
Pogosticking, 129
Preattentive attributes of visual perception,
    62–64, 63*f*
Preattentive processing, example of, 63*f*
Precision, 50
Previews
  in Bing, 134
  in Google, 134
  of search result, 132–134
Programmable Web, 151*f*
Pushed versus pulled information, 57–58

Q
QR codes, 237–238
Query, formulating, 99
  advanced search, 105–106
  best practices, 123
  beyond keywords
    natural language, 106–107
    nontext queries, 107–108
  keeping on track, 115–123
    autocorrect, 117–118
    "did you mean" suggestion, 115
    partial matches, 118–120
    related searches, 120–123
  refining, 108–115
    autocomplete, 109
    autosuggest, 109–111
    instant results, 111–114
  scoped search, 102–103
  search box, 99–101
  search within, 103–104
Query, refining, 240–244
Query by example, 108
Query clarification, in search result manipulation,
    154–158
Quorum-level ranking, 119–120